"This wonderful volume orients readers to relevant themes and literary techniques and enriches our understanding of these notable wisdom and poetic books as Christian Scripture. Ansberry engages with important theological themes that have relevance for living out our faith in humility, faithfulness, and honesty before the Lord. The beautiful illustrations are invaluable and contribute to an enhanced reading experience."

—**May Young**, Taylor University

"I wish that this book had been available when I was a student! Ansberry is a sage guide—technically astute and theologically engaged—regarding Wisdom and the Psalms. These pages are full of compelling images, informative sidebars, and elegant prose—all pointing to the God-given richness of biblical truth."

—**Daniel Treier**, Wheaton College

"*Reading Wisdom and Psalms as Christian Scripture* has made me fall in love with these formative books more than ever before! With attention to poetics, historical context, and intertextuality, Ansberry shows how each book offers a unique vantage point of 'faith seeking understanding.' He introduces readers to key interpretive and theological issues, both historical and contemporary, inviting them into an ancient and global conversation with those who desire to know and fear the Lord."

—**Elizabeth H. P. Backfish**, Jessup University

"Ansberry has produced an aesthetically satisfying and powerfully illuminating introduction from a Christian perspective for a typical poetry and wisdom literature course for advanced undergraduates and seminarians. Not only is it written in easily understandable yet beautiful prose, but its numerous sidebars have gorgeous, apropos illustrations and helpful diagrams. Ansberry's great breadth is reflected in his use of philosophy and historical theology as lenses for synthesizing and interpreting this important biblical corpus."

—**Mark Sneed**, Lubbock Christian University

"Ansberry is an excellent guide to the main themes and interpretive issues surrounding the wisdom books, the Psalms, and the Song of Songs. The book is well written, engaging, and well informed, and it always keeps in focus how these works of Christian Scripture relate to the life of faith. Ansberry has an excellent theological sense and is particularly attentive to questions of philosophy, virtue ethics, and New Testament connections. Highly recommended!"

—**Scott C. Jones**, Covenant College

READING
WISDOM
and PSALMS
as CHRISTIAN
SCRIPTURE

• READING •
CHRISTIAN
SCRIPTURE

VOLUMES AVAILABLE

——

Reading the New Testament as Christian Scripture
Constantine R. Campbell and Jonathan T. Pennington

——

Reading Wisdom and Psalms as Christian Scripture
Christopher B. Ansberry

——

Reading the Prophets as Christian Scripture
Eric J. Tully

——

Reading the Gospels as Christian Scripture
Joshua W. Jipp

——

Reading Paul as Christian Scripture
Constantine R. Campbell

——

READING
WISDOM
and PSALMS
as CHRISTIAN
SCRIPTURE

A LITERARY, CANONICAL, AND THEOLOGICAL INTRODUCTION

CHRISTOPHER B. ANSBERRY

Baker Academic
a division of Baker Publishing Group
Grand Rapids, Michigan

© 2024 by Christopher B. Ansberry

Published by Baker Academic
a division of Baker Publishing Group
Grand Rapids, Michigan
BakerAcademic.com

Printed in the United States of America

Library of Congress Cataloging-in-Publication Data
Names: Ansberry, Christopher B., author.
Title: Reading wisdom and Psalms as Christian scripture : a literary, canonical, and theological introduction / Christopher B. Ansberry.
Description: Grand Rapids, Michigan : Baker Academic, a division of Baker Publishing Group, 2024. | Series: Reading Christian scripture | Includes bibliographical references and index.
Identifiers: LCCN 2023040908 | ISBN 9781540961914 (cloth) | ISBN 9781493445813 (ebook) | ISBN 9781493445820 (pdf)
Subjects: LCSH: Wisdom literature—Criticism, interpretation, etc. | Bible. Proverbs—Criticism, interpretation, etc. | Bible. Job—Criticism, interpretation, etc. | Bible. Ecclesiastes—Criticism, interpretation, etc. | Bible. Song of Songs—Criticism, interpretation, etc. | Bible. Psalms—Criticism, interpretation, etc.
Classification: LCC BS1455 .A665 2024 | DDC 223—dc23/eng/20231109
LC record available at https://lccn.loc.gov/2023040908

Unless otherwise noted, Scripture quotations are the author's own translation.

Italics in Scripture quotations have been added by the author for emphasis.

Cover image of King David, drawing for the rose window of the Cathedral of Leon, 14th century, from PRISMA ARCHIVO / Alamy Stock Photo

Baker Publishing Group publications use paper produced from sustainable forestry practices and postconsumer waste whenever possible.

24 25 26 27 28 29 30   7 6 5 4 3 2 1

Contents

Acknowledgments

In his *Homilies on Ecclesiastes*, Gregory of Nyssa describes his encounter with Ecclesiastes in terms of a wrestling match. Proverbs served as the warm-up, making him supple for his struggle with Ecclesiastes. The book you are now reading is the product of years of struggle with Proverbs, Job, Ecclesiastes, the Song of Songs, and Psalms. In other words, the struggle continues. But I have not struggled alone. Countless students across continents and over the course of more than a decade have provided much-needed help through my classes on the Old Testament in general and wisdom literature in particular. Though their names are not mentioned in this book, these students have sharpened my thinking and enriched my life. The names of many authors from the early church to today are found in the endnotes. Like my students, these writers have served as companions and training partners in my struggle with the wisdom books and the Psalter. I am indebted to their wisdom, which has directed me in my pilgrimage of faith seeking understanding.

Special thanks are due to specific people. I am honored that Jim Kinney invited me to contribute to this series. Both Brandy Scritchfield and James Korsmo were invaluable sources of support and incisive sounding boards across the development of the book. My teaching assistant, Nicholas Zannis, read every chapter and offered constructive feedback. Cheers, Nick! And both colleagues and administrators at Grove City College have provided encouragement along the way. Among others, I would like to thank Peter Frank, Paul Kemeny, and Seulgi Byun.

My wife, Carolyn, and our four children ensure that life and work remain in proper perspective. I am so grateful for each of you. To channel Augustine, you are divine gifts, perpetual sources of love and joy that help me in my journey toward home.

Abbreviations

Old Testament

Gen.	Genesis	Eccles.	Ecclesiastes
Exod.	Exodus	Song	Song of Songs
Lev.	Leviticus	Isa.	Isaiah
Num.	Numbers	Jer.	Jeremiah
Deut.	Deuteronomy	Lam.	Lamentations
Josh.	Joshua	Ezek.	Ezekiel
Judg.	Judges	Dan.	Daniel
Ruth	Ruth	Hosea	Hosea
1 Sam.	1 Samuel	Joel	Joel
2 Sam.	2 Samuel	Amos	Amos
1 Kings	1 Kings	Obad.	Obadiah
2 Kings	2 Kings	Jon.	Jonah
1 Chron.	1 Chronicles	Mic.	Micah
2 Chron.	2 Chronicles	Nah.	Nahum
Ezra	Ezra	Hab.	Habakkuk
Neh.	Nehemiah	Zeph.	Zephaniah
Esther	Esther	Hag.	Haggai
Job	Job	Zech.	Zechariah
Ps(s).	Psalm(s)	Mal.	Malachi
Prov.	Proverbs		

New Testament

Matt.	Matthew	1 Cor.	1 Corinthians
Mark	Mark	2 Cor.	2 Corinthians
Luke	Luke	Gal.	Galatians
John	John	Eph.	Ephesians
Acts	Acts	Phil.	Philippians
Rom.	Romans	Col.	Colossians

1 Thess.	1 Thessalonians		1 Pet.	1 Peter
2 Thess.	2 Thessalonians		2 Pet.	2 Peter
1 Tim.	1 Timothy		1 John	1 John
2 Tim.	2 Timothy		2 John	2 John
Titus	Titus		3 John	3 John
Philem.	Philemon		Jude	Jude
Heb.	Hebrews		Rev.	Revelation
James	James			

Deuterocanonical Works

Wis.	Wisdom of Solomon		Sir.	Sirach

Bible Versions

NIV	New International Version (2011)	NRSV	New Revised Standard Version

General

b.	Babylonian Talmud		e.g.	*exempli gratia*, for example
ca.	circa		esp.	especially
cf.	*confer*, compare		i.e.	*id est*, that is

CHAPTER ONE

Introduction to Wisdom Literature and Psalms

Faith Seeking Understanding

> For I do not seek to understand so that I may believe; but I believe so that I may understand.
>
> Anselm of Canterbury[1]

The Christian act of biblical interpretation is an exercise in faith seeking understanding (*fides quaerens intellectum*). Far from hindering human understanding, faith serves as the volitional precondition for discerning and receiving the voice of the triune God across the canon of Scripture. Faith, put simply, frames the performance of Christian biblical interpretation; it provides an appropriate theological account of God, Scripture, the reader, and the interrelationship among them.[2] Within this theological frame of reference, God is author of canonical Scripture; Scripture is the unique means of the triune God's self-presentation, an authoritative collection of diverse texts, by which God establishes and maintains covenant relationship with his people;[3] and the reader is a historically situated and conditioned creature, who attends to the way that the words of the biblical text go, what these words mean, and the reality to which they refer.

This theological sketch of Christian biblical interpretation will inform a reading of the wisdom books and the Psalms in this work. These biblical texts are

THEOLOGICAL ISSUES

"Faith Seeking Understanding"

The motto "faith seeking understanding" was formulated by Saint Anselm and expressed in his *Proslogion*. Like Augustine's *Confessions*, the *Proslogion* reads like an extended prayer, where faith seeks to know God and, in so doing, strengthen the assurance of faith. While Anselm coined the motto, the posture of faith seeking understanding marked many before Anselm in the history of the church; it serves as a crisp summary of the Christian pursuit of knowledge.

Figure 1.1. Praise seeking understanding. *King David* by Adamo Tadolini (1856).

Christian Scripture. They are part of the two-Testament witness to the one triune God—that is, discrete witnesses to the self-same God in a historically distinct economy of salvation.[4] As Christian Scripture, these texts make distinct contributions to the Christian pursuit of faith seeking understanding. When they are heard within the world out of which they speak and received in the contemporary church, each raises a basic, perennial question. Proverbs asks, What is the good life? The book of Job explores how one lives in the absence of God and the absence of answers to life's atrocities. Ecclesiastes considers what it means to be human. The Song of Songs awakens desire and contemplates the question, What is love? And Psalms probes the nature of the life of faith as well as how one maintains covenant relationship with God.

These basic questions and perennial issues are foregrounded in the wisdom books and Psalms. The questions raised and the issues addressed by these texts, however, are neither asked nor answered in a vacuum. They are asked and answered within the broader context of the canon and from the posture of faith seeking understanding. This context and posture explain the contribution of each text to the project of faith seeking understanding. Proverbs inculcates fear seeking understanding. Job stages a performance of suffering seeking understanding. Ecclesiastes exemplifies finitude seeking understanding. The Song depicts desire seeking understanding. The Psalter attunes the life of faith in accord with praise seeking understanding.

Pursuing Understanding through Poetry

Faith's pursuit of understanding across these biblical texts takes different forms. On the whole, understanding is mediated through the poetic forms within these books.[5] Poetry is a powerful form of discourse. In the words of Jill Peláez Baumgaertner, "It does what no other art form can do. It compresses experience; it intensifies language; it uses words to say the unsayable. . . . Poetry cracks open our everyday lives, the mundane worlds

Figure 1.2. Finitude seeking understanding. *Saint Jerome* by Caravaggio (1605–6).

in which we spend so much unconscious time, and it releases the extraordinary, bringing us to a different level of attentiveness."[6]

This description indicates that poetry is a form of art, and it moves beyond what poetry is to capture what poetry does. It is a medium that awakens the senses, arouses the emotions, stimulates the mind, and inspires the imagination.[7] As a form of art that illuminates the extraordinary nature of the ordinary, poetry is an instrument of action or, better, an instrument of *responsible action*.[8] Through the imaginative use of language, the poet conveys certain actions and intentions; by receiving these actions and intentions, the reader is challenged to think about and act within the world in particular ways.[9] Far from inviting the reader into a Kantian world of disinterested contemplation, poetry prepares a person for concrete action within the world.[10] It accomplishes what simple, straightforward commands cannot: it moves one to virtuous action.[11] In this respect, it is a literary form uniquely qualified to fuel and fund the pursuit of faith seeking understanding. ⚖

Among the ways the poet conveys and performs actions, "world-projection"

PHILOSOPHICAL ISSUES ⚖

Kant and Disinterested Contemplation

Kant's reflections on the aesthetics of poetry bear witness to a "disinterested interest"—that is, to a disinterest in a person's own desire and an interest in the interest of reason in a person. This is the ground of Kant's moral motive: what a person ought to do, not what a person wants to do. Kant argues that poetry may evoke aesthetic ideas that are inexpressible as literal truths. These aesthetic ideas may allude to ideas of reason. Poetry and poetic language, however, do not move a person to virtuous action. According to Kant, poetry presents ideas for rational reflection.[a]

Asymmetry in Proverbs

The asymmetrical relationship between corresponding elements in parallel lines invites a fuller reading in which the reader supplies additional elements to create symmetry. Proverbs 10:16 and 27:6 are clear examples of asymmetrical or disjointed parallelism. According to Proverbs 10:16,

The wages of the righteous, for life;
the produce of the wicked, for sin.

The asymmetry between "life" and "sin" invites the reader to extend the lines:

The wages of the righteous, for virtue and life;
the produce of the wicked, for sin and death.

The parallel lines in Proverbs 27:6 are also asymmetrical:

Faithful, the wounds of a friend,
but profuse, the kisses of an enemy.

The asymmetry between "faithful" and "profuse" encourages the reader to develop the thought of each line:

Faithful, but few, the wounds of a friend,
but deceitful and profuse, the kisses of an enemy.

may be the most significant.[12] The poet projects a world that is true in many respects, and the reader is invited not only to enter and assess this world but also to consider the way in which the world created by the poet evaluates one's life within and one's view of the actual world.[13] Entrance into these worlds created by poets requires imagination. As Luis Alonso Schökel advises in his discussion of reading biblical poetry, "What has been written with imagination, must also be read with imagination, provided the individual has imagination and it is in working order."[14] Imagination is indispensable for reading the poetry in Proverbs, Job, Ecclesiastes, the Song, and the Psalter. Imagination helps the reader chew on the short lines and elliptical expressions in poetic discourse so as to taste their richness. It enables a person to see the gaps between parallel lines and fill them appropriately. It provides a person with the capacity to spot asymmetrical elements in parallel lines and extend certain sayings. And it allows the reader to plumb the depths of poetry's images and metaphors to perceive the way the poet has worked the miracle of King Midas, transforming ordinary words into treasures. Poetry does not operate under the normal rules of discourse. Certain rules do serve as a guide for reading biblical poetry, but they must be applied with imagination. Or better, they must be applied with "*truthful* imagination,"[15] which is the instrument through which a person is able to look at a poetic piece, look through a poetic piece, and discern its message(s).[16]

This is no easy task. But it is a fruitful task. The nature, function, and demands of poetry enable readers to perceive the form of life projected in Proverbs, Job, Ecclesiastes, the Song, and Psalms and to (re)capture a vision of the beauty of a life of faith seeking understanding. That is, an awareness of the nature, function, and demands of poetry provides a way to enter the world of these books and to hear their voice. As Flannery O'Connor observes, "It is from the kind of world the writer creates, from the kind of character and detail he invests it with, that a reader can find the intellectual meaning of a book."[17] The nature and function of poetry supply the reader with a compass to enter the world of the biblical text and to pursue its message.

The Category of Wisdom Literature

The wisdom books and the Psalms cultivate understanding through poetry, but the wisdom books, especially, are distinct in the Bible. Beginning in the nineteenth century, biblical scholars operated under the assumption that Proverbs, Job, and Ecclesiastes, as well as the deuterocanonical books of Wisdom of Solomon and Ben Sira, constitute a category or genre of "wisdom literature." This genre was thought to be a distinctive form of literature, with distinctive content, a distinctive basis of authority, a distinctive worldview, and a distinctive life setting (*Sitz im Leben*).[18] The Song of Songs, by virtue of its mention of Solomon, is at the periphery of the category: some contend that—given the Solomonic connection with Proverbs and perhaps Ecclesiastes—the Song is fully within the wisdom family; others argue that it has a unique place in the canon. However, beyond the issue of the Song, recent questions about the entire category "wisdom literature" have emerged, and assumptions about its distinctiveness have come under serious scrutiny. In fact, Will Kynes claims that "wisdom literature" is a scholarly construct, the product of mid-nineteenth-century German thinking.[19]

The *category* "wisdom literature" may be suspect, even dead, but the

Figure 1.3. Suffering seeking understanding. *Job—Out of the Depths I Cry to You* by Andreas Neumann-Nochten (2015).

RECEPTION HISTORY

Ben Sira and Proverbs

While the book of Ben Sira (often called Sirach) is not considered canonical Scripture by Jews or Protestants, Catholics and Orthodox Christians accept it as part of the Old Testament. Ben Sira was a Jewish sage. Writing in the early second century BC, he addressed the pressures of Greek life, religion, and thought on the Jewish community by extending and recontextualizing the wisdom of Proverbs. In addition to reinforcing the moral vision of Proverbs, Ben Sira introduces three striking developments. First, he links wisdom with salvation history, interpreting people and events across redemptive history through the lens of wisdom. Second, he associates wisdom with the law, uniting wisdom and the wise life with the covenant and its vision of life. And third, he identifies Lady Wisdom's dwelling place: Jerusalem (Zion). In so doing, Ben Sira attempts to demonstrate that wisdom is found in Jerusalem, not Athens.

RECEPTION HISTORY

Wisdom of Solomon

Whereas Ben Sira seeks to protect his audience from aspects of Greek philosophy, Wisdom of Solomon embraces certain tenets of Greek philosophy to develop texts and themes from Genesis, Exodus, Isaiah, Proverbs, and the book of Psalms. Donning the persona of Solomon, the author expands the Old Testament's description of wisdom and Lady Wisdom. According to Wisdom of Solomon, wisdom leads to eternal life. Lady Wisdom encompasses creation, and Lady Wisdom intervenes in history, enacting salvation.

Figure 1.4. Desire seeking understanding. Illuminated illustration for Song of Songs 4:8, "Come with me from Lebanon, my bride," in the Levy Maḥzor, a Hebrew liturgical book (1350). Cod. Levy 37, f. 169r.

concept of wisdom and the biblical texts once associated with the category remain in the capacious context of the canon.[20]

Kynes's diagnosis of and autopsy on the literary category "wisdom literature" has engendered fresh discussions on genre theory and intertextuality with reference to Proverbs, Job, and Ecclesiastes.[21] These developments are welcomed. The hope is that this book contributes to such discussions on Proverbs, Job, Ecclesiastes, and the Song. While the title of this book may give the impression that the wisdom books are distinct within the canon of Scripture, the content dispels any notion that Proverbs, Job, Ecclesiastes, and even the Song are an "alien body" or "an orphan in the biblical household."[22] As Christian Scripture, these texts are read in the context of the entire canon of Christian Scripture, where Scripture may interpret Scripture.

An Outline of the Book

The principle of Scripture interpreting Scripture governs the chapters that follow. These chapters follow a basic pattern. They move from introductory issues pertaining to the biblical book under discussion to specific theological themes. In accord with this pattern, chapter 2 explores the nature and structure of the book of Proverbs, as well as the form and organization of the materials in the anthology. Chapters 3 and 4 then attend to several theological themes in Proverbs, including wisdom, the acquisition of wisdom, the metaphor of the way, the fear of Yahweh, the character-consequence connection, Lady Wisdom, and wisdom and creation. Chapter 5 turns to the book of Job; it places Proverbs' vision of retribution in conversation with the book of Job, identifies the principal questions raised by the book, and sketches its content as well as its movement. Chapters 6 and 7 then focus on the themes of human limits, Yahweh's wisdom and justice, Job's integrity, the fear of God, and the motif of protest. Chapters 8 and 9 consider the book of Ecclesiastes. Following a review of the problem presented in the book, its literary texture, and the evaluative term *hebel* in chapter 8, chapter 9 reflects on Ecclesiastes's theological ontology/anthropology, epistemology, and axiology/ethics. Chapters 10 and 11 tour the world created by the Song of Songs. Chapter 10 assesses the interpretive registers of the Song, its relation to ancient Near Eastern love songs, and its association with Solomon, whereas chapter 11 examines the relationship between the lovers, landscapes of love, and the nature of genuine love. Chapters 12 and 13 address the book of Psalms. Within the framework of the relational context of the psalms, different interpretive approaches to the psalms, and the canonical shape of the book in chapter 12, chapter 13 probes the character of God and the nature of the life of faith.

The hope is that this book will contribute to the Christian pursuit of faith seeking understanding. Proverbs, Job, Ecclesiastes, the Song, and

RECEPTION HISTORY

Wisdom Literature

The category "wisdom literature" has thrived on its presumed distinctiveness within the canon of Scripture. Unlike the rest of the Old Testament, the so-called wisdom books show little to no interest in events associated with redemptive history or the covenant. These elements bind together the Pentateuch, the historical books, and the Prophets, setting the stage for the advent of Jesus, but they are missing in the wisdom books. Experience, observation, and good sense appear to serve as the basis of the wise person's authority. This stands in sharp contrast to the basis of the priest's and the prophet's authority in ancient Israel. The authority of the priest is rooted in the covenant with Levi and genealogical lineage (Mal. 2:4). The authority of the prophet is rooted in the divine call and confirmed by the fulfillment of the prophetic word as well as the prophet's conformity to the revelation of the covenant.

In light of the silence regarding redemptive history and the covenant, it is not surprising that many have concluded the wisdom books operate under a distinctive worldview. This worldview accounts for God's intervention in human life, but it privileges creation, the order of creation, and human life lived in accord with the order of creation. Taken together, the distinctive content, basis of authority, and worldview of the wisdom literature suggest that a distinctive group or class of people in ancient Israel—namely, the intellectual elite—composed these books.

RECEPTION HISTORY

The Beginning of "Wisdom Literature"

Certain canonical lists and codices bear witness to an association between the Solomonic books (i.e., Proverbs, Ecclesiastes, Song of Songs), but according to Kynes, the category of wisdom literature does not emerge from early traditions or canonical groupings. Rather, the category was born in the nineteenth century through the work of Johann Friedrich Bruch. Bruch distinguished the wisdom books from other texts in the canon by virtue of their presumed rationalism, empiricism, humanism, and universalism.[b]

CANONICAL CONNECTIONS

Intertextual Links

The chapters that follow attend to many intertextual links between the wisdom books and Psalms and other portions of canonical Scripture. A brief example from Proverbs and Job illustrates this kind of canonical conversation. Proverbs deploys a unique metaphor: tree of life (Prov. 3:18; 11:30; 13:12; 15:4). This metaphor sprouts from Eden; and its use across Proverbs indicates that east of Eden and in anticipation of the consummation of all things in the new heavens and the new earth one may access, touch, taste, and consume the fruit of a tree of life (Gen. 2:9; 3:22, 24; Rev. 22:2, 19). Job triggers the debate with his so-called friends by cursing the day of his birth (Job 3:3–11). This curse both resembles Jeremiah's curse on the day of his birth (Jer. 20:14–18) and seeks to reverse the creation of the cosmos in Genesis 1:3 (Job 3:4).

Figure 1.5. Fear seeking understanding. *Moses and the Burning Bush* by John Alexander.

Psalms each reveal the person and character of God, enriching faith. And each book offers an understanding of the self before the face of God. The Christian hope is to see the face of God (Rev. 22:4); may this book make a small contribution to that end, even if through a mirror dimly (1 Cor. 13:12).

CHAPTER TWO

Proverbs

Fear Seeking Understanding

Still waters run deep. This contemporary proverb exploits a natural phenomenon to capture a particular aspect of reality: things may not be what they seem, for clear surfaces may conceal profound depths. The truth of this proverb is manifest in relationships with people, who prove to be more complex than first meets the eye. And the truth of this proverb is demonstrated through the book of Proverbs. On the surface, the book's sayings sound simplistic, its advice tastes bland, and its vision of life feels idealistic. These general sentiments are epitomized by the following aphorisms—short, pithy sayings that convey a traditional and traditioned truth:

> The righteous will never be shaken;
>   and the wicked will not dwell in the land. (10:30)

> The righteous is delivered from trouble;
>   and the wicked takes his place. (11:8)

> The house of the righteous, much wealth;
>   but in the produce of the wicked, ruin. (15:6)

These representative sayings sound shallow, even unrealistic. However, probing below the surface of Proverbs' material reveals subtleties, ambiguities, and complexities that reflect the contingencies of human life (14:12; 19:21; 21:30–31; 27:1), the blurriness of human interactions (13:7; 14:10; 18:4; 20:6), and the inscrutability of God's involvement in ordinary affairs (16:1–9; 21:1). The seemingly still waters of Proverbs run deep, a depth concealed in pregnant imagery, elliptical expressions, twice-told proverbs, and apparent contradictions.[1] 📖

The pregnant imagery of the book's sayings is exemplified in Proverbs 27:17:

> Iron sharpens iron,
>   and a person sharpens the face of his neighbor.

Many interpret the image of iron sharpening iron positively. When this positive image is read together with the second line of the saying, the proverb captures the way a person sharpens the character of another. But this may not represent the best interpretation of the image.[2] The image in the first line comes from the process of iron smithing. In fact, this image conflates the entire process of iron smithing, which requires the smith to generate intense heat through charcoal or other fuels to extract the oxygen from the iron ore and make the iron soft so the impurities can be removed. These impurities are removed by striking the heated iron. When the smith removes the impurities, the iron is then shaped into weapons or tools with a hammer. The process is violent, suggesting that the image of iron sharpening iron is negative. This negative reading is reinforced by the language in the second line of the proverb. The expression "sharpens the face" is comparable to descriptions of sharp facial features elsewhere in the Old Testament: sharp eyes, a sharp lip, and a sharp tongue. These parts of the face attack others (Job 16:9; Pss. 52:2; 57:4). The same is true in Proverbs 27:17, where the violent process of iron smithing is applied to interpersonal relations. Just as one pounds iron into a sharp instrument for battle, so also one may pound one's neighbor, causing the neighbor to attack. Whether the image of iron sharpening iron is interpreted positively or negatively, it requires probing.

In addition to pregnant imagery, proverbs traffic in elliptical expressions. They omit words. This omission invites the reader to exercise moral reasoning by filling in the gap. The elliptical nature of the sayings in Proverbs is apparent in Proverbs 12:12:

> The wicked desires a snare for evil things;
>   but the root of the righteous gives.

What does the root of the righteous give? The verb lacks an object. The line is elliptical; it demands that the reader fill in the gap, but it provides some

LITERARY NOTES

Aphorisms

Aphorisms or proverbs are memorable utterances in popular use that convey a basic truth. The truth expressed through these utterances is limited and situational. It requires perceptive application in appropriate circumstances. This is apparent in the use of modern proverbs. "Too many cooks spoil the broth" is appropriate in certain situations, while "Many hands make light work" is appropriate in others. Imagination and discernment are necessary for the application of both modern and biblical proverbs.

guidance for this exercise. The righteous is depicted as a tree or plant with a root. This root produces something in accord with the character of the righteous person. In contrast to the wicked, the righteous gives fruit that nourishes others and satisfies their longings. The nature and effects of this fruit are supplied through the reader's moral imagination.

While rich imagery and elliptical expressions mark individual proverbs, "twice-told" proverbs and apparent contradictions introduce a dialogue among different sayings. Twice-told proverbs are proverbs or parts of a proverb that are repeated in modified form. These repetitions create a conversation among sayings. This conversation plays out across the following proverbs:

> From the fruit of his mouth, one is satisfied with good things,
>   and the work of one's hands returns to him. (12:14)

> From the fruit of his mouth, one eats good things,
>   but the throat of the treacherous, violence. (13:2)

> From the fruit of his mouth, one's belly is satisfied;
>   he is satisfied by the produce of his lips. (18:20)

The first lines of these sayings are twice-told proverbs. When placed in conversation with one another, they shape the reader's moral discernment. The repeated lines do not include a specific character type; rather, they focus on a generic person who produces something through speech. Both Proverbs 12:14a and 13:2a characterize the verbal fruit produced as "good." This is not the case with Proverbs 18:20. The quality of the fruit is unclear. It fills one's belly, but is it good? These twice-told proverbs train the moral palate (12:14; 13:2) and then call the reader to taste and see whether the speech of others is good (18:20).

The conversation staged by twice-told proverbs is comparable to the dialogue among proverbs that treat a common theme. In some cases, common themes are reinforced (e.g., 10:4; 12:24; 13:4; 21:5). In others, themes are modified or nuanced through tensions or apparent contradictions. The descriptions of the fool and the simple are representative of such nuances among sayings. Speech is foregrounded as a telltale sign of the fool. In fact, the fool is loquacious (12:23; 13:16), but so are those who serve as a perpetual fountain of wisdom (18:4). And when the fool keeps silent, he is regarded as wise (17:28). The simple are naive and inexperienced. They believe anything (14:15). They fail to perceive consequences (22:3), but they are also able to learn through the discipline of others (19:25; 21:11). These

The Instruction of Amenemope

Many argue that the "words of the wise" in Proverbs 22:17–24:22 (esp. 22:17–23:11) are dependent on or inspired by the Egyptian Instruction of Amenemope. Reading "thirty" in Proverbs 22:20, interpreters identify thirty sayings in the "words of the wise," which align with the thirty chapters in the Instruction of Amenemope. These thirty sayings do not track with the subject matter of the thirty chapters in Amenemope, but the striking similarities in expressions, imagery, and content intimate a relationship between these texts. It is important to note that if Proverbs 22:17–23:11 is dependent on or inspired by the Instruction of Amenemope, the Egyptian text has been recast into the theological worldview of the wise.[a]

characterizations of the fool and the simple illustrate the nuanced development of character types across the sayings in Proverbs. People are fuzzy and complicated, like the sayings in Proverbs.

Taken together, the evocative imagery, elliptical expressions, twice-told proverbs, and apparent contradictions in Proverbs confirm that still waters run deep. These poetic techniques are designed to cultivate the character and train the moral reasoning of the reader. The same is true of the structure and design of the book of Proverbs. The book's diverse materials coalesce to provide discrete perspectives on and responses to a basic question: What is the good life?

The Structure of Proverbs

Proverbs profiles the good life through its structure, which is an anthology. It is, in fact, a collection of collections, each introduced by a title attributing the material to a different individual.

1. The proverbs of Solomon, son of David, king of Israel (1:1)
2. The proverbs of Solomon (10:1)
3. The words of the wise (22:17)
4. These also are of the wise (24:23)
5. These also are proverbs of Solomon, which the men of Hezekiah, king of Judah, transcribed (25:1)
6. The words of Agur, son of Yaqeh, the burden, the oracle of the man (30:1)
7. The words of Lemuel, a king; a burden, which his mother taught him (31:1)

At minimum, these titles reveal the compositional contours of the book of Proverbs. Proverbs is a puzzle, consisting of multiple pieces that depict the multidimensional nature of the good life. The size, shape, and texture of these pieces differ, but their vision of the good life is uniform. This unity amid diversity is also reflected in the authorial attributions of the different collections. Taken together, the authorial attributions of the collections

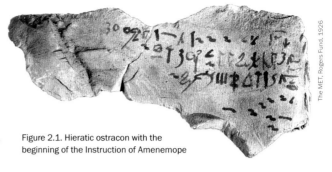

Figure 2.1. Hieratic ostracon with the beginning of the Instruction of Amenemope

indicate that Solomon is neither the author nor the compiler of all the collections. This does not mean, however, that the collections bear no relationship to Solomon. The canonical arrangement invites the reader to understand each collection against the backdrop of Proverbs 1:1 and through the biography of Solomon.[3] Read this way, the materials in the discrete collections appear consonant with Solomonic wisdom. The titles and attributions of the book's different collections not only orient the reader to the structural contours of the book and the question of authorship; they also stage an interpretive dialogue designed to hone the hermeneutical instincts and theological imagination of the reader.

The Form and Design of Proverbs

The form of the materials in Proverbs and the design of the anthology sharpen the perception and shape the thinking of readers. On formal grounds, the title of the book gives the impression that it is a collection of proverbs (1:1). But the diverse poetic forms in the anthology reveal that the book is not, strictly speaking, a book of proverbs. The diverse authorial attributions correspond with the variety of poetic forms across the collections, which include extended instructions (1:8–19; 31:1–9), epigrams (6:1–19; 30:11–33), and encomia (8:1–36; 31:10–31), as well as terse aphoristic sayings and admonitions (10:2; 23:9–11).

Regardless of the origins of these poetic materials, their literary form is designed to shape the reader in various ways.[4] They appeal to different aspects of the human self: the intellect, imagination, desires, emotions, and motivations. And they require interpretive dexterity. This requirement is heightened by the fact that, on compositional grounds, the materials in the collections

CANONICAL CONNECTIONS

Solomon and Proverbs

Three titles in Proverbs associate the collections with Solomon (1:1; 10:1; 25:1). These attributions recall 1 Kings 4:32, which indicates Solomon spoke three thousand proverbs. When Proverbs is read together with the account of Solomon in 1 Kings 1–11, the nature and dimensions of wisdom come into sharper focus. Both texts describe wisdom as a divine gift (1 Kings 3:12; Prov. 2:6), a skilled practice (1 Kings 7:14; Prov. 24:3–4), and the instrument of effective governance (1 Kings 3:9, 16–28; 5:1–7; Prov. 8:15–16; 16:10).

LITERARY NOTES

Poetic Forms in Proverbs

Instructions in Proverbs are lessons cast in the form of a father instructing his son. These instructions focus on specific issues (e.g., the dangers of seduction and the value of wisdom). They tend to move from an introduction to a lesson to a conclusion.

Epigrams are terse and witty poems that evoke a sense of surprise and then clarify the astonishing situation in an unexpected way.

Encomia are speeches that praise someone or something.

Admonitions are commands that prescribe or proscribe certain forms of behavior.

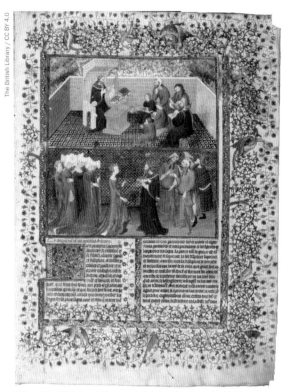

Figure 2.2. Miniature of Solomon dictating the Proverbs, in Guyart des Moulins, *Bible historiale* (France, fifteenth century), f. 285

evince neither a systematic design nor a logical progression of thought. While some proverbs exhibit deliberate arrangement into pairs or larger units (e.g., 16:1–9; 26:1–12) and the anthology is framed by collections with shared settings, language, and imagery (chaps. 1–9; 30–31), these signs of coherence are not enough to signal a comprehensive organization across the individual collections. The poetic materials in each collection demand that the reader taste and see their vision of wisdom and the good life. They create associative links with comparable proverbs and common themes treated across the book. In so doing, they train a person's moral reasoning and nuance one's vision of life by pushing the reader to perceive aspects of unity amid diversity. Like the titles and attributions of the collections in Proverbs, the form and organization of the materials function to form the character and structure the thinking of the reader.

This formation is facilitated by the sequence of the collections in Proverbs. At the microlevel, the materials in the individual collections do not show signs of deliberate design. But at the macrolevel, it appears that the collections are arranged in a manner comparable to modern educational curricula.[5] The preamble sets the expectations for the book (1:1–7, see discussion below), and the prologue serves as an extended introduction (1:8–9:18). The discourses of the parents, Lady Wisdom, and Woman Folly do not provide a detailed portrait of the good life. That is not their intention. Together, these discourses illuminate the indispensable value of wisdom, and they inspire the pursuit of wisdom (9:1–18).

Getting wisdom opens access to the first Solomonic collection (10:1–22:16). This access changes things. The reader is no longer the passive recipient of direct address. Aphorisms formulated in the third person bombard the reader, who is now responsible for discerning their wisdom. The first half of the collection eases the reader into this new educational experience (10:1–15:33). The vast majority of the sayings are antithetic;

they traffic in contrasts. These contrasts create a measure of pedagogical stability; the reader knows what is coming next. They offer a form of elementary wisdom, outlining the basic characteristics of different character types and the consequences that accompany the actions of these character types. This exercise in elementary wisdom sets the stage for the delivery of intermediate wisdom across the second half of this Solomonic collection (16:1–22:16). Antithetic sayings recede. New poetic forms emerge as the instruments of formation, training readers to think differently about certain subjects. Moreover, themes introduced in Proverbs 10:1–15:33 are modified, and fresh themes as well as different character types are foregrounded. Several sayings assert that poverty is not the product of vice; in fact, the poor may be virtuous (16:19; 19:1, 22; 22:1). Other sayings explore

Figure 2.3. The virtuous poor. *Parable of the Rich Man and the Beggar Lazarus* (ca. 1035–40) in Codex Aureus Epternacensis, f. 78r.

the topic of friendship (17:9, 17; 19:4, 6), which is absent from Proverbs 10:1–15:33. From a formal and a thematic perspective, Proverbs 10:1–22:16 moves from elementary to intermediate wisdom.

This formal and thematic movement also marks the curricular progression in the collections of Proverbs 22:17–24:34 and Proverbs 25–29. The former—"the words of the wise" (22:17)—returns to direct address, placing the reader under the instruction of another. These instructions cover matters of social relations and vocational wisdom. The admonitions of this collection are accompanied by motivations that appeal to self-preservation, honor and shame, or parental approval. They educate through moral motivations. That is, they employ the educational technique of carrot and stick. The admonitions thrust readers into a variety of social roles: messengers (22:21), citizens (22:24, 28; 23:20–21; 24:10–12, 15), dinner guests (23:1–3, 6–8), parents (23:13–14), drunkards (23:33–34), and military leaders (24:6). More than shaping the character and social relations of the reader, the admonitions in Proverbs 22:17–24:34 contribute to the goal of the "words of the wise"—namely, to nurture trust in Yahweh and to form a person into a reliable communicator who may flourish in the dynamic vocations of life (22:19, 21).

Whereas the "words of the wise" offer vocational wisdom, the collection of Proverbs 25–29—the second Solomonic collection (25:1)—delivers a course on advanced wisdom. Rich analogies and thematic clusters dominate this collection, forcing readers to sort out and synthesize the relationship between an image and its referent, as well as between various sayings and their shared subject matter (e.g., 25:3–5, 11–12; 26:1–12). Antithetical sayings also appear at the end of the collection, but in contrast to the antitheses across chapters 10–15, these comparisons usher the reader into a world populated by totalitarian kings, political lobbyists, and the harsh conflict between the righteous and the wicked (28:3, 15, 16, 28; 29:2, 4, 12, 16). The collection captures the messiness of life in the world by projecting a society that is conflicted.[6]

The final collections in the book of Proverbs bring its educational program to a fitting conclusion. The words of Agur dispense a pill that is difficult to swallow (30:1–33). In the event that the reader has progressed through Proverbs 10–29 and emerged from the course on advanced wisdom with the sense that they are wise, Agur says, "Think again." One never arrives in the life of wisdom. They never graduate. The course is never complete. The reason is simple: humans are finite and human wisdom is limited. The appropriate response to the completion of the curriculum in Proverbs 10–29 is humility. From this posture of humility, Proverbs 31:1–9 and 31:10–31 explore aspects of applied wisdom. The application of wisdom is conceptualized as the exercise of power for the benefit of others. Lemuel's mother sketches an ethic of leadership, according to which power is deployed to care for the marginalized rather than to satisfy one's personal desires (31:1–9). The poem on the valiant woman memorializes one who used her power and prowess to care for her household and to provide for the poor within the community (31:10–31). It is not surprising that this woman is depicted as the very embodiment of the fear of Yahweh (31:30).

The arrangement of the collections in the book of Proverbs invites a person to read them in succession. This succession mirrors the structure and movement of educational curricula. The book progresses from a preamble (1:1–7) and a prologue (1:8–9:18) to elementary wisdom (chaps. 10–15) and intermediate wisdom (16:1–22:16), then to vocational wisdom (22:17–24:34), advanced wisdom (chaps. 25–29), and applied wisdom (chaps. 30–31). The book of Proverbs is not a narrative. The materials lack coherence at the microlevel; but they exhibit coherence at the macrolevel. They outline an educational program in wisdom and virtue. In so doing, they map the progression of the reader's maturation in wisdom and virtue.

Proverbs' concern with education and formation aligns with its purpose to form "fearers of Yahweh."[7] The book nurtures a life of "fear seeking understanding."[8] Flourishing in relation to God and humans, creatures and creation is the goal of Proverbs, and the (trans)formation of character in accord with wisdom and virtue is the pedagogical means by which Proverbs achieves this goal. The content and poetic forms of the anthology shape the reader's being and behavior in various ways. This holistic educational program is distilled in the preamble of the anthology (1:1–7):

> [1]The proverbs of Solomon, son of David, king of Israel.
>
> > [2]For learning wisdom and instruction;
> >   for understanding insightful words;
> > [3]for acquiring instruction in prudent living:
> >   righteousness, justice, and uprightness;
> > [4]for giving to the uncommitted shrewdness,
> >   to the young, knowledge and discretion;
> > [5]so the wise may hear and increase instruction,
> >   and one with understanding may acquire guidance,
> > [6]for understanding a proverb and an allusive saying,
> >   the words of the wise and their riddles;
> > [7]the fear of Yahweh is the beginning of knowledge;
> >   wisdom and instruction fools despise.

The preamble functions as the syllabus for Proverbs. Like a syllabus, it delineates the book's learning outcomes, expectations, and the prerequisite for engaging the material. The learning outcomes are sketched across verses 2–4. Proverbs seeks to (trans)form one's character through the inculcation of wisdom and virtue. The terms associated with wisdom in verses 2–4 are not synonyms. They refer to different type of virtues: intellectual virtues (vv. 2, 4), practical virtues (v. 3a; cf. v. 5b), and moral virtues (v. 3b). The cultivation of these virtues is the goal of the book. But achieving this goal will be difficult. The poetic forms cataloged in verse 6 calibrate the expectations of readers. Understanding the materials in the book will require receptivity and acuity. These requirements correspond with the addressees of the book: the uncommitted and the wise. The uncommitted are neither wise nor foolish. They are inexperienced, and Proverbs calls them to receive its teaching and embrace wisdom. The wise are wise, and they are invited to engage the book's materials to increase in wisdom. These two addressees create positions that readers are to inhabit. That is, upon entering the

The Goal of Proverbs

In *Homily 12: On the Beginning of Proverbs*, Basil the Great argues that the book of Proverbs seeks to discipline one's passions, banish vice, direct desire, and develop an appetite for the good.[b]

book of Proverbs, one assumes the position of either the uncommitted or the wise. Regardless of the position assumed, the preamble concludes with the prerequisite for reading the book: the fear of Yahweh (v. 7). This posture is essential for achieving the objectives and learning outcomes of Proverbs.

Proverbs is a book devoted to education for character formation. This educational program is outlined in the preamble and has governed the ways Proverbs has been read in the Christian tradition. Proverbs answers the question "What is the good life?" by forming and conforming human creatures in relationship with God and in accord with the goodness of God's creation. The book seeks to form "fearers of Yahweh" and to inculcate "fear seeking understanding" by attending to several theological themes. These themes will serve as the focus of attention in the following chapters.

Christian Reading Questions

1. How have you read the book of Proverbs? As Christian Scripture, how does Proverbs differ from secular forms of wisdom?

2. What is biblical wisdom? How does biblical wisdom differ from modern conceptions of wisdom?

3. What are some of the techniques used by the book of Proverbs to teach readers? Personally, which of these educational techniques have you found most effective?

4. What is the fear of Yahweh? What does this expression entail?

CHAPTER THREE

Theological Themes in Proverbs (1)

Knowledge is power. This is a typical way of assessing knowledge. The sentiment captures something of the truth. In fact, it corresponds with an aspect of Proverbs' conception of wisdom. Wisdom, however, differs from knowledge. Proverbs illuminates this difference. According to Proverbs, knowing something does not constitute wisdom. Wisdom is manifest in an embodied form of life. This form of life is profiled across the book of Proverbs; it comes together through the themes of wisdom, the acquisition of wisdom, the "way" of wisdom, the fear of Yahweh, and the connection between character and consequences.

Wisdom

■ READ PROVERBS 4:20–27; 31:10–31 ■

The book of Proverbs focuses on wisdom, but what is wisdom? Aristotle—that wise philosopher—employed a helpful educational technique that provides clarity to this question. The technique is simple: learning by difference.[1] That is, one learns what something is by virtue of learning what it is not. So what is wisdom? According to Scripture in general and Proverbs in particular, wisdom is not the intellectual mastery of a body of knowledge, whatever it may be. In fact, biblical wisdom has no room for knowing "about" something. This impersonal conception of wisdom is foreign to the witness of Scripture. Proverbs only ever understands wisdom as personal or, better, as interpersonal. 📖 📖

Contrary to the practice of much Western epistemology, wisdom is not acquired by the autonomous self. Nor is it in utero within the human person, drawn out by the self or midwifed by another. This conviction clarifies why the autonomous self is subjected to such severe criticism in Proverbs. The following aphorisms are representative of this criticism:

> A fool's way, upright in his eyes;
>> but one who listens to counsel is wise. (12:15)

> Have you seen a person wise in his own eyes?
>> There is more hope for a fool than for him. (26:12)

> A rich person, wise in his own eyes,
>> but a discerning poor person sees through him. (28:11)

THEOLOGICAL ISSUES

Knowing and Knowing About

The distinction between knowing "about" something and interpersonal knowing is captured by Martin Buber's distinction between "I-It" and "I-Thou" relations. According to Buber,

> The *I* of the primary word *I-Thou* is a different *I* from that of the primary word *I-It*. The *I* of the primary word *I-It* makes its appearance as individuality and becomes conscious of itself as subject (of experiencing and using). The *I* of the primary word *I-Thou* makes its appearance as a person and becomes conscious of itself as subjectivity (without a dependent genitive). Individuality makes its appearance by being differentiated from other individualities. A person makes his appearance by entering into relation with other persons. The one is the spiritual form of natural detachment, the other the spiritual form of natural solidarity of connexion.[a]

THEOLOGICAL ISSUES

True and Sound Wisdom

The interpersonal framework for knowing is expressed by John Calvin, who opened his *Institutes of the Christian Religion* with the observation that "nearly all the wisdom we possess, that is to say, true and sound wisdom, consists of two parts: the knowledge of God and of ourselves."[b]

Wisdom is not innate within the human self. The opposite is the case. Wisdom is taught. It comes from outside of a person. It is received from another. More than revealing wisdom as a gift, this relational framework also recasts the nature of biblical wisdom. *Biblical* wisdom has very little to do with abstract, propositional knowledge. This is because biblical wisdom is an *embodied skill* or a *skilled practice*. According to Proverbs, wisdom is holistic; it encompasses one's intellect, desires, emotions, taste, sight, touch, and actions.[2] If one is "wise" or if one "knows" something, then one acts out that wisdom and knowledge in concrete, embodied, interpersonal actions.[3] If the proof of the pudding is in the eating, then the proof of wisdom is manifest in one's being and doing, in one's moral nature and virtuous actions. ⚖️⚖️

This holistic conception of wisdom pervades Proverbs. In the most general terms, wisdom is manifested in and through the character and actions of the book's intellectual and moral prototypes: the wise and the righteous. The wise and the righteous exemplify and embody wisdom and moral virtue in Proverbs.

There is this: one who chatters like a sword's
    stabs;
  but the tongue of the wise, healing.
    (12:18)[4]

The teaching of the wise, a fount of life,
  for avoiding the snares of death. (13:14)

The lips of the righteous nourish many;
  but fools die through senselessness. (10:21)

Doing justice, joy for the righteous,
  but ruin for evildoers. (21:15)

Figure 3.1. Stained glass window depiction of Lady Wisdom, Zrenjanin, Serbia

The poetic portraits of the wise and righteous demonstrate that the body is integral to the reception and exhibition of wisdom. While the embodied nature of wisdom is illustrated across Proverbs, Proverbs 4:20–27 and 31:10–17 foreground the importance of the body. The former instruction depicts the acquisition of wisdom as the gift of another. The body receives the wisdom of the other through its organs of reception: the ear, the eyes, and the heart/mind (4:20–21); it stores and protects wisdom in the headquarters of the heart (4:23); and the heart releases wisdom, directing the parts and movements of the body along the straight path (4:24–27). Proverbs 31:10–17 gives particular attention to the embodiment of wisdom through its portrait of the valiant woman. Wisdom is portrayed as a moral and physical power exercised on behalf of another. The power of wisdom is evinced through the valiant woman's pursuits and her body parts: her hands (31:13, 16, 19, 20, 31), her palms (31:19, 20), her loins (31:17), and her arms (31:17).[5] Whether expressed through formal instructions and eulogies or terse aphorisms and common character types, Proverbs assumes that wisdom is embodied.

In light of this, it is not surprising that Proverbs seeks to attune the parts of the human person to wisdom—namely, the intellect, desires, emotions, taste, sight, and

PHILOSOPHICAL ISSUES

Innate Wisdom

The conviction that wisdom is innate within the human self is the operative assumption of both Socrates and René Descartes, among others. In fact, Socrates describes himself as a midwife, as one who oversees the birth of a person's soul and of wisdom from within.[c]

PHILOSOPHICAL ISSUES

Wisdom as Embodied Skill

The vision of wisdom as an embodied, skilled practice is explored by Matthew B. Crawford, who sketches the nature and dynamics of skilled practices through the work of auto mechanics and organ makers, just to name a few kinds of workers. These accounts are described in his excellent works *Shop Class as Soulcraft: An Inquiry into the Value of Work* and *The World beyond Your Head: How to Flourish in an Age of Distraction*.[d]

touch.[6] From a post-Enlightenment perspective, the intellect is the natural home of wisdom. Proverbs countenances the intellect in its vision of wisdom (1:2, 4–6): it identifies the heart/mind as the organ that must be open to the instruction and discipline of others to acquire wisdom (cf. 2:2; 3:1, 5; 16:21).

> The wise of heart receives commands;
>> but one with foolish lips will be ruined. (10:8)

> Wisdom rests in the heart of the discerning;
>> and in the midst of fools she makes herself known. (14:33)

> The heart of the discerning acquires knowledge,
>> and the ear of the wise seeks knowledge. (18:15)

The intellect plays a formative role in Proverbs' vision of wisdom's acquisition. One's desires, however, can short-circuit this acquisition. Proverbs recognizes this, and many sayings seek to direct desire to wisdom and virtue by highlighting the worth of proper objects of desire. Lady Wisdom, for example, epitomizes all that is desirable: virtuous character, straightforward speech, the responsible exercise of power, reciprocal love, material benefits, an intimate relationship with Yahweh, and a beatific life (8:4–36). The portraits of the righteous person across the anthology not only fill out the character and content of the moral life; they also induce desire "*by showing what is desirable*."[7] Desire and the objects of one's desire are fundamental to wisdom in Proverbs. If you are what you love, the wise person is one who loves wisdom (4:6–8; 8:17, 36; 12:1).

Nonetheless, training desire in accord with wisdom is a tricky business. This may explain why Proverbs appeals to the emotional and sensory dimensions of the self in addition to the intellect and desire. The delight of wisdom (10:23), the weight of worry (12:25), the force of jealousy (27:4), the wounds of a friend (27:6), the taste of gossip (18:8), the "sweetness" of the wise person's lips (16:21), the pain of self-deception (30:12–14)—each, in different ways, gestures to Proverbs' recognition of the emotional, aesthetic, and tactile

Figure 3.2. *Jealousy* by Edvard Munch (1930)

facets of wisdom and the human self.[8] As an embodied skill, wisdom is manifested in and through one's character and actions. Put simply, wisdom is loving, knowing, tasting, sensing, seeing, and doing what is good, on the one hand, and it is hating, grieving, rejecting what is evil, on the other.

The Acquisition of Wisdom

■ READ PROVERBS 2 ■

This sketch of wisdom in Proverbs captures the concept's inclusive definition and holistic understanding of human creatures. This vision may feel out of reach (30:1–4). That is the outcome Proverbs seeks to elicit in its student feedback. This outcome, however, sits in tension with the book's optimism regarding the human agent's ability to acquire and embody wisdom (1:1–7). So how does one reconcile these *felt* realities? In two ways, both of which were intimated above: (1) by recognizing that wisdom is the gracious gift of the triune God; and (2) by recognizing that wisdom, by implication, is the gracious gift of other people. ⚖

While the nature of wisdom as a gift is implied across Proverbs, wisdom as the gift of God is expressed in explicit terms in Proverbs 2. In light of the syntax and logic of the chapter, the parental instruction may be summarized as follows:

> If you receive my words, cry out for insight, and seek understanding (vv. 1–4),
> "then you will understand" the fear of Yahweh and find the knowledge of God (v. 5),
> "for" Yahweh grants wisdom and stores up resourcefulness (vv. 6–7)
> "in order to protect" the paths of justice (v. 8);
> *[if you receive my words, cry out for insight, and seek understanding (vv. 1–4),]*
> "then you will understand" righteousness, justice, and uprightness (v. 9),
> "for" wisdom will infiltrate your heart (vv. 10–11)
> "in order to deliver you" from the way of the evildoer (vv. 12–15),
> "in order to deliver you" from the strange woman (vv. 16–19),
> "so that" you may walk in the way of the good (vv. 20–22).

If nothing else, this summary shows that wisdom is never acquired passively. It requires receptivity and an active search, motivated by a desire for wisdom. But desiring and seeking wisdom alone will not deliver the goods of wisdom. The reason is simple: it is Yahweh who grants wisdom (2:6). Wisdom is a gift from God. It is a gift because human beings are creatures, contingent beings constituted by and dependent upon another. This means that whatever humans need—in this instance, wisdom—must come from elsewhere. Ultimately, this wisdom comes from the God of all wisdom. As noted above, wisdom is not self-generated. Wisdom is the generous gift of a wise and generous God. In his generosity, the triune God gives wisdom to those who seek or ask for it (James 1:5). More than this, the triune God gives understanding of the knowledge of God (Prov. 2:5), of righteousness justice, and uprightness (2:9) in order to protect justice and bring deliverance (2:8, 12–19), so that the wise may walk in the way of the good (2:20–22). 📜

But this theological vision of wisdom's acquisition as gift represents only a portion of Proverbs' pedagogical story. In addition to Proverbs' recognition that wisdom is the gift of God, the anthology describes the acquisition of wisdom as gift through ordinary, providential means. That is, the book describes acquisition of wisdom through the instruction and example of others. This interpersonal framework creates the necessary conditions for the acquisition of wisdom in Proverbs. Across the anthology, wisdom is acquired through receptivity to interpersonal instruction (12:15; 13:14; 15:31), as well as through the company one keeps (12:26; 13:20), discipline (12:1; 13:1; 22:15), wise speech (15:7; 16:21, 23), and reproof (15:12; 17:10; 19:25; 21:11), which functions as

the means by which one "acquires a mind" (15:32). The resounding witness of Proverbs is that wisdom is acquired and the moral self is formed *in relationship*.

This interpersonal vision of wisdom's acquisition is bound up with "submission to external authority."[9] External authorities serve as a source of wisdom. The acquisition of wisdom, however, requires relational submission or, better, trust.[10] This requirement is foregrounded in the discourses of Proverbs 1:8–9:18. Here one encounters different voices: the parents and Lady Wisdom (e.g., 1:22–33; 2:1–22; 3:1–12; 8:4–36; 9:4–6), on the one hand, and sinners (1:11–14), the "strange woman" (7:14–20), and Woman Folly (9:16–17), on the other. These voices project different moral worldviews. They are characterized in different ways. But they sound the same.[11] More specifically, they make comparable promises. And these comparable promises raise a question: Whom should one trust? Both the sinners and Lady Wisdom promise wealth (1:13; 8:18, 21). The sinners, the strange woman, and Lady Wisdom promise relationship and satisfaction (1:14; 7:14–20; 8:17–21). Sifting these comparable promises, discerning the real from the pseudo, and perceiving the consequences of one's commitments are dependent on wisdom. Yet the acquisition of wisdom is dependent on the authority to whom one submits, the voice one trusts.

The "Way" of Wisdom

■ READ PROVERBS 4:10–19; 9:1–18 ■

Trust in and submission to an authorized authority is fundamental to the acquisition of wisdom in Proverbs 1–9.[12] The parents nurture trust in and submission to their voice by interpreting the character, speech, moral worldview, and consequences of deceptive voices across Proverbs 1–9. Moreover, the parents cultivate a way of seeing and being-in-the-world throughout the discourses in Proverbs 1–9. This vision of the world is

Ground Metaphors

As George Lakoff and Mark Johnson argue, a ground metaphor provides a clear, structured concept that clarifies and structures another concept. The metaphor LIFE IS A PATH clarifies and structures a person's behavior, orientation, movements, and end. It provides a way of understanding life and the world. According to Lakoff and Johnson, the concepts that people use to think and to act are metaphorical through and through (e.g., ARGUMENT IS WAR, TIME IS MONEY). They use small capitals for these metaphors to mark them as prominent metaphorical concepts.[9]

constructed through a network of interrelated symbols that coalesce to depict the orientation, embodiment, domain, and destination of a wise and virtuous life. The image of the path serves as the "nuclear symbol" in Proverbs 1–9.[13] That is, the concept LIFE IS A PATH constitutes the root or *ground metaphor* of Proverbs 1–9.[14] This root/ground metaphor is organically and conceptually related to the images of wisdom and folly, life and death, women and houses. Each deserves specific comment.

The conceptual metaphor LIFE IS A PATH entails that the nature of one's life is embodied in and manifested through movements along a particular way. What's more, the metaphor means that one's being and behavior are oriented to a particular end: life or death. These entailments pervade the discourses of Proverbs 1–9. The way of wisdom and life is depicted as straight, clear, and open (3:23; 4:11–12, 18; 11:5). The way of folly and death, by contrast, is portrayed as crooked, dark, and dangerous (2:12–15; 4:19; 21:8; 22:5). The intimate relationship between the path metaphor and these images suggests that a person's way or path is much more than a lifestyle or course of life; it includes one's character, conduct, and the consequences associated with one's behavior. Similar to Aristotle's ethical theory, in Proverbs wisdom and character determine the path or direction one travels through life: character determines the goal or direction of a person's choices and behavior, while wisdom identifies the means for achieving that goal in specific situations. Together, character and wisdom participate in a teleological activity to achieve a particular end: life or death.[15]

Despite the common concepts and images used to describe the way of wisdom and life as well as the way of folly and death, it is important to note that Proverbs does not envision two specific footpaths in life. The ways of wisdom and folly are not that straightforward. The wise and the fool may travel on several "paths" or "ways" (1:19; 2:19, 20; 3:6, 17; 4:26; 5:6; 8:32). These different paths represent different behaviors or choices that may be characterized as wise or foolish, that lead to life or death. Like the diverse choices and experiences of everyday life, the network of these paths is complex, like the web of a big city's streets, rather than the single road that passes through a small rural town. The use of the plural "paths" intimates that the metaphor LIFE IS A PATH does not refer to "preordained routes" in Proverbs 1–9; rather, it represents "the directions that individuals take: footprints, as it were, rather than footpaths."[16] Put differently, the use of the plural "paths" refers to the direction or orientation of one's life: toward wisdom and life or toward folly and death. As noted above, this direction is determined by character and actualized through wisdom, each of which is shaped and cultivated by the materials within Proverbs.

The metaphor LIFE IS A PATH is related to the concepts of wisdom and folly, life and death. The metaphor is also intimately related to the women and their respective houses in Proverbs 1–9. As with the path metaphor, the women traverse ways that lead to distinct destinations: Lady Wisdom to life (8:35; 9:6), the strange woman and Woman Folly to death (2:18; 5:5–6; 7:22–23; 9:18). In fact, the women's homes are depicted as the gateways to these destinations (2:18; 7:27; 8:34–35; 9:13–18). Also similar to the path metaphor, the women are distinguished by particular virtues or vices: Lady Wisdom is marked by wisdom, righteousness, and justice (8:8, 14, 20); the strange woman and Woman Folly are marked by seduction, deception, and folly (2:16; 5:3; 6:24; 7:5, 21; 9:13). The intimate relationship between the path metaphor, on the one hand, and the women and their respective homes, on the other, suggests that "the way" functions as a nuclear symbol, a governing metaphor through which to understand the "satellite images" of wisdom and folly, life and death, women and houses.[17] Together, the metaphor and its satellite images exist in dialogical relationship with one another, illuminating the multifaceted dimensions of the embodied, holistic nature of wisdom, virtue, and the good life in Proverbs.

While the path metaphor is implicit in the speeches of the women and the description of their homes across Proverbs 1–9, the concept informs the characterization of them and their homes. The way or path in their

Figure 3.3. *Wisdom Hath Built Her House* icon, Novgorod (1548)

discourses is cast in a different form than in the parental lectures. Rather than projecting a road that symbolizes the direction or orientation of one's life, the direction or orientation of one's life is concretized or incarnated through the character and speech of the women in Proverbs 1–9. The women deliver their discourses in the public thoroughfares: in the streets, intersections, and thresholds of life (1:20–21; 7:8, 12; 8:2–3; 9:3, 14–15). Those who fall prey to the seductive rhetoric and empty promises of the strange woman are characterized as those who "turn aside to her ways" (7:25), which stands in sharp contrast to the father's command to "turn aside" (4:15) from the path of the wicked. Whereas those who delight in evil travel on "crooked paths" (2:15), Lady Wisdom's speech is marked by righteousness; none of her words are "crooked" (8:8). Whereas Wisdom calls the uncommitted to "walk straight in the path of understanding" (9:6; cf. 4:14), Woman Folly attempts to divert "those who make their ways straight" (9:15). Far from being abstract metaphors about the direction of one's life, the female characters in Proverbs 1–9 embody the nature of these directions (wisdom and folly) and illustrate their telos (life and death). Their discourses move away from a general discussion of the direction or orientation of a person's life to the way in which character and wisdom (or the lack thereof) manifest themselves in a form of life.

Together, the nuclear metaphor of the way and its satellite images of life and death, women and houses illuminate the coherence of the didactic materials across Proverbs 1–9 and capture the essence of their pedagogical agenda. The relationship between the path metaphor and the women in Proverbs 1–9 links the parental lectures and their concern with "the way" to the discourses of the women and their embodiment of different ways. The parents provide instruction in the home. The women deliver their speeches in streets and invite the uncommitted into their homes (7:14–20; 9:1–6, 13–18). The parent uses conventional language to highlight the value of wisdom, to interpret the seductive rhetoric of diverse characters, and to diagnose the ways in which they walk. The discourses of the women mimic one another, and the figures incarnate particular ways, inviting the uncommitted to interpret their speech, to decipher the consequences of their actions, and to choose a mate, a house, a banquet, and a fate. The path metaphor and its satellite images are deployed to shape the character, desires, and worldview of the reader. That is, they are intended to cultivate wisdom and virtue. The parent nurtures the intellect and cultivates instrumental virtues by describing the value of wisdom and the way in which it enables one to interpret people, determine the consequences of one's choices, and proceed down the way of life. The women, on the other hand, cultivate desire, either for what is good and leads to life or for what is evil and leads to death.[18]

The Fear of Yahweh

▓ READ PROVERBS 1:1–7; 9:10 ▓

The acquisition of wisdom and its manifestation in a beatific life is contingent on the fear of Yahweh.[19] This expression frames the book of Proverbs (1:7; 31:30), orienting the reader to the theological nature of the whole book. But the relationship between the fear of Yahweh and wisdom is unclear. According to Proverbs 1:7, "The fear of Yahweh is the *re'shit* of knowledge." The term *re'shit* is polysemous. The verse may mean the fear of Yahweh is *the beginning* of knowledge/wisdom (a temporal referent), or it could mean such fear is wisdom's *first principle* (a logical basis); it could also mean the fear of Yahweh is the *firstfruit* of wisdom (a consequence). This last meaning seems to suit the description of wisdom's acquisition in Proverbs 2:1–5, where the active pursuit of wisdom culminates in understanding the fear of Yahweh.

However, Proverbs 9:10 seems to say the reverse, calling this idea into question:

> The *tehillat* of wisdom is the fear of Yahweh,
> and knowledge of the Holy One is understanding.

While many translate *tehillat* as "beginning," others think it means "first point" in the lifelong process of wisdom's acquisition.[20] In light of the grammar of Proverbs 15:33, both senses remain possible, for the proverb equates the fear of Yahweh with instruction in wisdom. Do these intertextual reverberations suggest that the precise relationship between wisdom and the fear of Yahweh is undecidable? If nothing else, the ambiguity of these texts suggests that the "fear of Yahweh" may not be the temporal beginning of wisdom.

The fear of Yahweh is not distinct from wisdom; it is the firstfruits or the initial manifestation of wisdom.[21] This connection between the fear of Yahweh and wisdom mirrors a connection that exists between ontology and epistemology—that is, the connection between *being* and *knowing*. According to Job Jindo, there is a certain kind of knowledge that accompanies fear and creates a mode of being. That knowledge is perspectival rather than propositional; it is the perception of one's status in the cosmos in relation to Yahweh, rather than an intellectual understanding of particular facts.[22] By accepting one's status in the cosmos in relation to Yahweh, a person assumes a posture of understanding that enables them to see themselves and to experience the world in a particular way. Put in terms of Proverbs, people recognize the reality and the implications of the Creator-creature

Figure 3.4. *Wisdom*, by Nigerian artist Olusola David Ayibiowu (2008), depicts a woman asking God for wisdom.

distinction. As creatures, humans are finite beings, dependent on the divine. This epistemological insight leads to a state of fear, to an ontological state, which Jindo regards as "a basic norm that constitutes the normative mode of human existence."[23] On this account, epistemology determines the ontology of the self. Perspectival knowledge of one's place in the cosmos in relation to Yahweh creates a state of fear, an ontology of the self that "validates one's mode of being and living as human."[24]

Jindo's description of the interrelationship between wisdom and the fear of Yahweh entails that the fear of Yahweh is a mode of being, not a virtue. It is a consciousness of one's place in the cosmos in relation to Yahweh that directs a person's inner faculties and external actions. The fear of Yahweh is the fundamental norm for human beings; and it serves as this norm because it situates human agents in their divinely designed places within the cosmos.[25]

This conception of wisdom and the fear of Yahweh explains why a person can grow in understanding of the fear of Yahweh (Prov. 2:5). The magnitude of one's fear is proportional to the quality of one's knowledge of God.[26] This conception of wisdom and the fear of Yahweh accounts for the severe limits of human wisdom and power (16:1–9; 21:2, 30–31). It may also explain the problem with certain character types in Proverbs, such as the fool, the wicked, the scoffer, and the lazy. If the fear of Yahweh refers to a mode of being that is inseparable from a certain type of perspectival knowledge, then the problem with these aberrant character types is not their lack of propositional knowledge; it is their lack of perspectival knowledge, which would allow them to see themselves and the world through a particular way of thinking. This is seen most clearly through the terminal condition of "one who is wise in his own eyes." This type of individual engages "in a fatal act of self-perception. . . . It is finally the *failure of self-knowledge* that defines the fool. Because such a person does not know himself, he is prone to seeking glory beyond his limits."[27] The failure of self-knowledge leads to a mode of being that is incongruous with humanity's nature, place, and function in the cosmos.[28] No wonder these sorts of characters cannot learn. They know neither their place in the world nor themselves in relation to Yahweh.

The Character-Consequence Connection

■ READ PROVERBS 1:8–19 ■

The knowledge of one's creaturehood, dependence on Yahweh, and place in the cosmos creates the necessary conditions for the acquisition and maturation of wisdom in Proverbs.[29] But the acquisition of wisdom and the cultivation of virtuous character do not guarantee success. This observation seems to fly in the face of many of the anthology's aphorisms, which appear to umbilically link one's character or actions with the appropriate consequences:

> No calamity will befall the righteous;
>> but the wicked are filled with evil. (12:21)

> Evil pursues sinners;
>> but the righteous will be rewarded with good. (13:21)

> One who is gracious to the poor lends to Yahweh,
>> and he will repay him for his deed. (19:17)

> The reward of humility, the fear of Yahweh,
>> wealth, and honor and life. (22:4)

> Whoever digs a pit will fall into it;
>> and whoever rolls a stone—it will come back on him. (26:27)

These representative sayings seem to project a deterministic yet synthetic "sphere of action," where acts are organically connected to consequences.[30] This inbuilt "act-consequence connection" means that retribution or reward for particular deeds is part of a mechanistic system; certain actions trigger specific outcomes. The wise and righteous perform acts in accord with their character, achieving success. The fool and the wicked perform acts in accord with their character, engendering punishment.

While many sayings appear to endorse such a system of retribution and reward, others demonstrate that Proverbs is aware of different patterns:

> The wicked makes a deceitful wage;
>> but one who sows righteousness, a true reward. (11:18)

> In the transgression of lips, an evil snare;
>> but the righteous escapes from trouble. (12:13)

> An abundance of food—the fallow ground of the poor;
>> but the reality is this: it is swept away without justice. (13:23)

> Do not lie in wait as a wicked person against the dwelling of the
>> righteous;
>> do not destroy his resting place;
> though the righteous may fall seven times, he will rise,
>> while the wicked will stumble in evil. (24:15–16)

> When the righteous increase, the people rejoice,
>> but when the wicked rule, people groan. (29:2)

The wicked and the violent gain wealth (10:2; 11:16, 18), and the righteous require deliverance (11:6, 8, 9; 12:13). The righteous fall (24:15–16), while the wicked rise to rule over people (28:12, 28; 29:2, 16). The poor are poor, but they are not necessarily culpable for their poverty (13:23).

These observations not only undermine a strict connection between acts and consequences; they also suggest that "character-consequence" is a more appropriate designation for retribution and reward in Proverbs.[31] One's character, rather than specific acts, serves as a wide-angle lens with which to consider retribution and reward. What's more, this wide-angle lens creates space to consider the agents involved in retribution and reward. These agents vary among the materials in Proverbs. Some texts attribute the connection between character and consequence to individuals or society in general (11:10, 26; 27:18). Others identify Yahweh's active role in the administration of retribution and reward (12:2; 15:25; 22:12). Still others deal in passive constructions, leaving the timing and agency behind the connection open to different formulations (11:25; 13:13; 22:9). Proverbs acknowledges the exceptions to the predictable patterns of life, as well as the ambiguities of retribution and reward, and the anthology relates these realities to the contingencies of human existence. In light of the limits of creaturehood and the incalculable activity of God, "there always lies a great unknown" between character, act, and consequence (16:1, 9; 27:1).[32] This great unknown may be the "minority report" in Proverbs. Nonetheless, the minority report qualifies the predictable patterns and orders of life, forcing readers to exercise their moral reasoning and develop a nuanced perspective of being-in-the-world.[33]

Conclusion

Proverbs offers a dense description of wisdom, its acquisition, and its manifestation in a way or form of life. According to Proverbs, wisdom is a holistic, embodied, skilled practice; it is "cognitive *and* emotional *and* aesthetic."[34] It presupposes "a *praxis* rooted in the knowledge of *individual* creatures, things, persons, circumstances."[35] Wisdom is knowing the good, loving the good, and doing the good. It is a form of being, a way of life in relationship with Yahweh and in accord with the grain of Yahweh's good creation, and it is received and cultivated in relationship. In light of this, it is not surprising that Proverbs personifies wisdom. Wisdom is a person. Her personal profile and the intimate connection between wisdom and creation are treated in the next chapter.

CHAPTER FOUR

Theological Themes in Proverbs (2)

Wisdom is vindicated by her deeds (Matt. 11:19). The proof of wisdom is not in the knowing; it is in the doing. The last chapter sketched the relational and embodied nature of wisdom in Proverbs. This chapter extends these motifs by exploring Lady Wisdom and the intimate connection between wisdom and creation. Lady Wisdom offers relationship; the connection between wisdom and creation orients one to embodied behaviors that align with the order of creation.

Lady Wisdom

■ READ PROVERBS 1:20–33; 8:1–36 ■

Given the relational context of wisdom's acquisition, it is not surprising that wisdom is personified as someone who desires relationship.[1] Against the backdrop of her startling rebuke (1:20–33), Lady Wisdom delivers an evocative encomium in Proverbs 8. Her words of praise are designed to woo prospective devotees through a captivating portrait of her character (8:6–9, 12–13, 20–21), social value (8:14–16), personal benefits (8:10–11, 17–19), and cosmic preeminence (8:22–31). The portrait depicts a vision of life suffused with truth, trust, justice, righteousness, stability, safety, wonder, joy, and delight. Its rhetorical richness awakens desire and enchants the moral imagination.

According to her account, Lady Wisdom possesses all that is desirable. She embodies that which Proverbs seeks to inculcate in readers: integrity/uprightness (8:6; cf. 1:3), righteousness (8:8, 18, 20; cf. 1:3), justice (8:20; cf. 1:3), knowledge (8:10; cf. 1:4), wisdom (8:11; cf. 1:2), shrewdness (8:12;

cf. 1:4), discretion (8:12; cf. 1:4),
the fear of Yahweh (8:13; cf.
1:7), and understanding (8:14;
cf. 1:2). By embodying the fundamental virtues proffered in
the anthology, Lady Wisdom is
presented as a legitimate object
of love.

Lady Wisdom's self-praise,
however, is not an exercise in
vain rhetoric. She legitimizes
her character, credentials, and
function in the present world
(8:12–21) through an account of
her preeminence and position in
the primordial world (8:22–31).
This account divides into three
parts, each of which assumes

Figure 4.1. *Wisdom* by Titian (1560)

a distinctive vantage point: Lady Wisdom's emergence before creation
(8:22–26), her presence at creation (8:27–29), and her activity after creation
(8:30–31).[2]

Lady Wisdom preceded creation. In fact, she says she was the first of
God's works (8:22; cf. Job 15:7–9). She was begotten in the nothingness
before Yahweh created time and the cosmos (Prov. 8:22–26). Wisdom's
temporal and qualitative preeminence explains her preeminent position
during Yahweh's creation of the cosmos (8:27–29). When Yahweh established the heavens (8:27a), carved the horizon (8:27b; cf. Gen. 1:2), made
firm the clouds (Prov. 8:28a), fixed the foundations of the deep (8:28b),
circumscribed the sea (8:29a), and marked out the foundations of the earth
(8:29b), Lady Wisdom was present as an eyewitness ("I was there," 8:27).
Her presence at Yahweh's construction of the cosmos not only enhances
her authority; it also means she understands the patterns and boundaries
Yahweh ingrained in the created world.[3] Yet Lady Wisdom's preeminent

---

THEOLOGICAL ISSUES

Wisdom, Christ, and Creation

The verbs associated with creation and birth in Proverbs 8:22–26 stood
at the center of early Christian christological debates. The participants in
these debates agreed that Lady Wisdom's emergence in primeval time
refers to God the Son, but they disagreed on *how* it does so. Arius argued
that Proverbs 8:22–25 indicates that the Son was created: there was a
time when he was not. Athanasius, by contrast, offered two different
readings of Proverbs 8:22–25 to maintain that the Son was coeternal
with the Father. Athanasius's first reading relates Proverbs 8:22–24 to
the incarnation of the Son and Proverbs 8:25 to the eternal generation
of the Son (i.e., the Son is eternally begotten, not made or created).
His second reading relates Wisdom in Proverbs 8:22 to the creation
of humanity in Genesis 1:26–28. More specifically, Athanasius links
Wisdom with the image of God. Humans were created in the image of
Wisdom—that is, in the image of *the* image of God: the Son (2 Cor. 4:4).[a]

Figure 4.2. *The Ancient of Days* by William Blake (1794)

position is not restricted to Yahweh's creation of the cosmos. Her presence at Yahweh's side extends beyond the construction of the cosmos to the period after creation (8:30–31). From eternal generation to the present, Wisdom has faithfully resided at Yahweh's side, rejoicing in the goodness of Yahweh's creation and delighting in humankind (8:30–31).

Play and delight characterize Lady Wisdom's relationship with Yahweh, creation, and humanity, and they serve as a bridge between them. They also function as the climax of Lady Wisdom's case in Proverbs 8. In view of her credentials (8:12–13), function in the present world (8:14–16), gifts (8:17–21), emergence in primordial time (8:22–26), presence at creation (8:27–29), and position at Yahweh's side (8:30), Lady Wisdom possesses all that is desirable: virtue, the principles of statecraft, wealth, an intimate relationship with Yahweh, knowledge of the fundamental structures of the world, faithfulness, and perpetual access to the divine. Humans are the object of her affections, her prized preoccupation within the cosmic playhouse constructed by Yahweh. Lady Wisdom's play in the presence of Yahweh and her delight in the moral and aesthetic beauty of the cosmos coincide with her play in the inhabitable world and her delight in humankind. She communes with Creator and creatures, expressing a joy that traverses the transcendent and immanent realms and incorporates Creator and creature in a harmonious celebration of creation's goodness.[4]

Lady Wisdom's self-portrait in Proverbs 8 is rife with theological significance. When her words are read in the broader context of the anthology, Lady Wisdom bears a striking resemblance to the valiant woman (31:10–31). The valiant woman is described by terms and expressions used elsewhere only for Lady Wisdom. Like Lady Wisdom, the valiant woman is difficult to obtain (31:10; cf. 1:28; 8:17). She is more precious than corals (31:10; cf. 3:15; 8:11). She is the proprietress of a substantial household (31:15, 21, 27; cf. 9:1, 3). She is a source of security (31:11; cf. 1:33), and she fears Yahweh (31:30; cf. 1:29; 8:13).[5] The family resemblance between these figures leads some scholars to say that the valiant woman is a symbol or an allegory of wisdom.[6] Others push back, demonstrating that the valiant woman embodies the activities of real women in particular periods of Israel's history. Still others contend that the impressionistic portrait of the valiant woman projects an impossible ideal.[7] 🝙 📜

The truth, it seems, is somewhere in between. The valiant woman resembles Lady Wisdom, but she is neither a symbol nor an allegory. The realism of her activities is not dependent on a particular period of Israelite history, and these activities are not an impossible ideal. When the predominance of perfect verbs are rendered rightly in the depiction of the "perfect woman," the poem may be understood as the activities and achievements of a real kind of woman, who embodied and practiced these activities across her life.[8] It is a poem that praises her "lifetime achievement," "not her daily planner."[9] She was and is a real type of woman. As such, she serves as the positive counterpart to another type of woman—that is, the "strange woman" (2:16; 5:3; 7:5). Furthermore, she instantiates the moral character of the wise and righteous, as well as the power and value of Lady Wisdom.

In addition to the resemblance between Lady Wisdom and the valiant woman, Wisdom's self-portrait illuminates her intimate and enigmatic relation to Yahweh, for it portrays Wisdom in a manner comparable to Yahweh's depiction elsewhere in the Old Testament. Wisdom's words are true (8:7; cf. Exod. 34:6; 2 Sam. 7:28) and right (Prov. 8:9; cf. Neh. 9:13; Pss. 19:8; 33:4; Isa. 45:19); she speaks "in accord with righteousness" (Prov. 8:8; cf. Pss. 11:7; 19:9; 33:5; 65:5; Isa. 45:19); and wickedness is an abomination to her lips (Prov. 8:7; cf. 12:22).[10] Similar to Yahweh, Wisdom possesses and implements those skills that contribute to the establishment of an ordered society: counsel, resourcefulness, and strength (8:14; cf. Job 12:13, 16; Isa. 11:2). Relationship with Wisdom also brings life (Prov. 8:35–36; cf. 14:27; Jer. 21:8),[11] and like Yahweh, Wisdom transcends creation (Prov. 8:22–31; cf. Gen. 1:1–2:4; Ps. 104). Proverbs 3:19–20 describes Wisdom's relation to creation in instrumental terms, and 8:22–31 expresses this relationship through presence,

HISTORICAL MATTERS

The Valiant Woman as a Real Woman

Utilizing biblical and epigraphic evidence, Christine Roy Yoder has demonstrated that the activities of the valiant woman are comparable to the socioeconomic activities of real women in Palestine during the Persian period. Women within the Achaemenid Empire operated in specialized professions, manufactured textiles, traded in the marketplace, owned and supervised slaves, and owned and managed properties. This suggests that the portrait of the valiant woman was shaped in light of the social roles and activities of real women in the Persian period. Some argue that the same is true of Lady Wisdom. Her portrait was shaped by the role and activities of real women in the Persian period. Lady Wisdom, on this account, provided a family-centered model of community and served as a figure who reconciled the realities of life under Persian rule with the order of the cosmos.[b]

CANONICAL CONNECTIONS

The Valiant Woman and Wise Women

Many have placed the accounts of Lady Wisdom and the valiant woman in conversation with texts that describe wise women in ancient Israel: Rebekah (Gen. 27:1–17), Deborah (Judg. 4–5), Michal (1 Sam. 19:11–17), Bathsheba (1 Kings 1:11–27), Abigail (1 Sam. 25), the wise woman of Tekoa (2 Sam. 14), and the wise woman of Abel-Beth-Maacah (2 Sam. 20:14–22).[c]

Lady Wisdom and Ancient Goddesses

From the perspective of the history of religions, many argue that Lady Wisdom possesses characteristics reminiscent of goddesses elsewhere in the ancient world. Among them, the Mesopotamian goddess Ishtar, the Egyptian goddess Maat, a Hellenized form of the Egyptian goddess Isis, and an unknown Canaanite goddess are the most popular. These comparisons assume that Lady Wisdom developed under the influence of these foreign goddesses, providing ancient Israel with a literary substitute for the unorthodox practice of goddess worship.

observation, delight, and dance. Wisdom is among the tools or powers employed by the divine architect to construct a sure, enduring cosmos (3:19), and Wisdom is also an independent, exuberant eyewitness within Yahweh's stable world (8:22–31).

These distinctive accounts of Wisdom's relation to creation, combined with her intimate association with Yahweh and Yahweh's prerogatives, raise questions concerning her nature and function in Proverbs 8, each of which has theological and especially christological implications. Many scholars address these questions, with or without regard for their theological consequences, by exploring the origin(s) or sociohistorical context of Wisdom's literary creation. While these investigations are not unimportant, they contribute little to an understanding of Wisdom's literary and theological portrayal.

As a personified figure, Wisdom does not appear to have a single referent.[12] This is not surprising, since personification is a rhetorical convention that provides a general, conceptual framework within which multiple images and roles may be subsumed and concretized in a composite figure.[13] Wisdom's literary persona may integrate and gesture to images and concepts reminiscent of goddesses, lovers, mothers, counselors, teachers, prophets, and real women,[14] but her multifaceted description refuses classification into one category alone. Wisdom wears many hats, none of which capture the fullness of her literary identity.

If one looks beyond Wisdom's wardrobe and focuses on her literary and theological functions, then her characterization and contribution to Proverbs become clearer. As a personified figure, Wisdom absorbs and embodies the various aspects of wisdom presented in the parental lectures.[15] She is a divine gift who grants gifts in filial relationship with Yahweh and within creation (2:6; 8:17–21, 22–31). She is the emanation of Yahweh's mouth and the frolicking daughter brought forth from his womb (2:6; 8:22–31). She is the substance of parental instruction and the constant companion of Yahweh (2:2, 10; 4:5, 7; 5:1; 7:4; 8:30). She provides direction on the path of the righteous and walks along the way of righteousness (2:20; 8:20). She is the authorized object of love and the one who loves her devotees (4:6; 8:17). Wisdom is inextricably linked with the wisdom of the parental lectures, and she is inextricably linked to Yahweh.

The nature of this link, however, is unclear. Despite the insightful observations of many proposals concerning Wisdom's identity, it appears that she is neither a personified divine attribute nor a mediator, at least in the conventional sense of the term. If anything, Lady Wisdom is a divine hypostasis. She is depicted as a distinct, personal agent. She speaks for herself. She shares the prerogatives of Yahweh. She presents herself as one who subsists through time, both beside Yahweh and before Yahweh.[16] Her intermediate position between Yahweh and humanity provides a person with access to the wisdom, will, and presence of God.[17] As with the personification of other divine attributes, Wisdom is portrayed as a distinct, personal being.

When her poetic portrayal is viewed within the conceptual world of the Old Testament, it appears that Lady Wisdom participates in the unique being and identity of the one God of Israel, who creates through wisdom, speaks through his word, enlivens through his Spirit, and reveals himself through intimate, covenant relationship with his people.[18] The Old Testament reveals a unique God who is not the God of Unitarians, but who exists "in a class of his own," who remains distinct from "all other reality," yet graciously relates to his creatures in a way that allows for "distinction within the unique identity of the one God."[19] Wisdom's testimony across Proverbs 8 bears witness to this distinction within the unique identity of the one God of Israel. And Wisdom's poetic portrait focuses attention on the wonder, supremacy, delight, and goodness of God's wisdom.

While the precise nature of Wisdom's relationship with Yahweh and creation defies simple classification, her multifaceted portrayal may be more of an asset than a liability. The semantic range of the terms used to describe her and the poetic cast of her presentation in Proverbs 8 create space within which to understand and appreciate the diverse ways in which Wisdom has been received and appropriated, from the Second Temple period to the New Testament period and beyond. According to Ben Sira, Wisdom was created before all things (Sir. 1:4; 24:9; cf. Prov. 8:22–26; see the sidebar "Ben Sira and Proverbs" in chap. 1). As the emanation of Yahweh's mouth (Sir. 24:3; cf. Prov. 2:6), she is manifest in, even equivalent to, the Torah (Sir. 24:23). For Wisdom of Solomon, Wisdom was present at Yahweh's construction of the cosmos (Wis. 9:9; cf. Prov. 8:27–29; see sidebar "Wisdom of Solomon" in chap. 1), but far from merely observing Yahweh's creative work, Wisdom participated in the process as "the fashioner of all things" (Wis. 7:22 NRSV) and as the one by whom God "formed humankind" (9:2 NRSV). This brief account

The Word and Wisdom

The prologue of John's Gospel depicts the Word (*logos*) in terms and concepts reminiscent of Proverbs 8. As with Wisdom in Proverbs 8:22, the Word was with God in the beginning (John 1:1–2; cf. Gen. 1:1). As in Proverbs 8:35, the Word possesses life itself (John 1:4). In contrast to Lady Wisdom's passive observance of creation in Proverbs 8:27–29, the Word is the active agent of creation (John 1:3). This active agency indicates John's depiction of the Word includes elements that are closer to Wisdom's portrayal in Ben Sira and Wisdom of Solomon.

Colossians and Proverbs 8

Colossians 1:15–20 praises Christ's preeminence with terms and expressions reminiscent of Proverbs 8. Jesus is the firstborn of all creation, the beginning, and the one who existed before all things. The language and the rhetoric of the Colossian hymn mirror the language and the rhetoric of Proverbs 8. But like John 1, the christological hymn describes the Son as the one in whom all things were created, which corresponds with Wisdom's activity in Wisdom of Solomon and Philo.[f]

Jesus, the "Wisdom of God"

Paul's description of Jesus as "the wisdom of God" (1 Cor. 1:24; cf. v. 30) bears witness to the apostle's use of wisdom as a theological category. Proverbs 8 plays an important canonical role in the formation of this theological category, but in the context of 1 Corinthians 1:18–3:23, it is important to note that this "wisdom" is thoroughly subversive. As Richard Hays rightly notes, throughout this text Paul counters the Corinthians' boasting in their distinguished knowledge and powerful eloquence "by performing an ironic counter-reading of wisdom in light of the cross." The death of the crucified Messiah "confounds all human wisdom and redefines wisdom in a new and paradoxical way."[g] In light of Paul's argument, it appears that Proverbs 8 does not make a direct contribution to the discussion; rather, Greco-Roman conceptions of wisdom and Paul's theological interpretation of the Christ event drive the argument.

of Wisdom's reception indicates that both Ben Sira and Wisdom of Solomon develop aspects of Wisdom latent in Proverbs 8. The former equates Wisdom with Torah and identifies her dwelling in Jerusalem to describe the way in which God directs and cares for his people (Sir. 24:8–12, 23). The latter grants Wisdom an active role in creation, elevating her to the position of "God's chief agent."[20] The Wisdom figure of Ben Sira and Wisdom of Solomon resembles the Wisdom of Proverbs 8, but she is also different: differing landscapes and particular pigments have altered the portrait of Wisdom's place, function, and persona within the divine economy.

These alterations provide a necessary context for exploring Wisdom in the New Testament. While certain New Testament texts portray Jesus and the gospel message in terms and concepts redolent of Proverbs 8, these texts are closer to Ben Sira and Wisdom of Solomon than to Proverbs 8.

The point is that Proverbs 8 does not serve as a *direct* intertext with New Testament texts that contribute to Christology; rather, Proverbs 8 as developed and refracted through particular texts in early and late Judaism serves as the well from which New Testament authors draw to express their christological convictions. This does not mean, however, that Proverbs 8 contributes nothing to the witness of the New Testament. To the contrary, the terms and concepts that describe the evocative and enigmatic Wisdom are redeployed in several New Testament texts to demonstrate that the ultimate embodiment and expression of God's preeminent wisdom is found in the person of Jesus Christ.

The conceptual resonances of Wisdom's primordial existence, presence at creation, and intermediary position between Yahweh and humans do not indicate that Wisdom and Jesus are one and the same. Rather, these resonances suggest that "Christ is the hidden reality underlying and fulfilling the cosmic and personal imagery of Wisdom in Proverbs 8."[21] Christ is the referent or *reality* of Lady Wisdom's poetic portrait in Proverbs 8. If this is the case, then early, pro-Nicene readers of Proverbs 8 (e.g., Athanasius; see the sidebar "Wisdom, Christ, and Creation" earlier in this chapter) were not fanciful interpreters; rather, they were wise theological interpreters who penetrated the surface of the text to see the reality of Christ in Wisdom's words.[22]

The fact that Proverbs 8 offers only a faint witness to New Testament conceptions of Jesus and expressions of Christology does not mean that it has nothing to say to the church. Lady Wisdom's self-portrait links the primordial world with the present, the transcendent with the immanent, the order of the cosmos with the order of human life, and Wisdom's delight before Yahweh with her delight in humankind. This wondrous vision enlivens and enchants one's worldview; it indicates that freedom, joy, and mirth are found in intimate relationship with Yahweh and Wisdom within the boundaries of God's good creation.[23] Wisdom's exuberant rejoicing awakens the pathos appropriate for God's wonderful works. Here joy and life are found within God's good boundaries. And here the order and stability of creation are the arena of delight rather than the domain of drudgery.

Lady Wisdom's praise expresses the reality that wisdom is available and accessible. In contrast to wisdom in Job 28, Lady Wisdom's whereabouts are neither hidden nor unknown. She cries out to all from the centers of social life, summoning devotees to listen to her and to darken her door. The one who seeks her will find her (Prov. 8:17). The one who cries aloud for wisdom will receive it (2:1–6). And whoever lacks wisdom may ask God, who promises to grant it to those who trust in him.

Wisdom and Creation

■ READ PROVERBS 3:13–20 ■

Lady Wisdom's eyewitness account of Yahweh's construction of the cosmos in Proverbs 8 is counterbalanced by Yahweh's instrumental use of wisdom in creation in Proverbs 3:19–20:

> Yahweh founded the earth by wisdom;
>> he established the heavens by understanding;
> by his knowledge the deeps burst open,
>> and the clouds drip dew.

Merism

A merism is a figure of speech that brings together two opposing things to convey a comprehensive reality. For example, "the heavens and the earth" is a merism for all existence. "Head and foot" is a merism for the totality of a person's being. And "day and night" is a merism for continual time.

These verses describe Yahweh's comprehensive creation and intelligible design of the cosmos through two couplets, each of which includes a merism. The first couplet gives particular attention to the way in which Yahweh utilized wisdom and understanding to form a stable cosmos (v. 19). The divine architect used wisdom and understanding to construct a sure, enduring world. The second couplet highlights Yahweh's providential care for and preservation of the cosmos by means of knowledge (v. 20). The couplet narrows its vision to specific moments of creation during which Yahweh separated the waters from the dry land and flicked the meteorological switch, allowing the clouds to dispense water to nourish the earth. Wisdom, understanding, and knowledge are presented as the instruments of Yahweh's cosmic handiwork. These instruments indicate that creation has a meaningful order that is morally instructive.

The instructive nature of creation is developed in Proverbs 24:3–4, which reiterates the form and sequence of prepositional phrases from 3:19–20:

> By wisdom a house is built,
>   and by understanding it is established;
> and by knowledge rooms are filled
>   with all wealth, precious and pleasant.

Just as Yahweh founded the earth "by wisdom" (3:19a), established the heavens "by understanding" (3:19b), and filled particular spheres "by his knowledge" (3:20a), so also human homes are fashioned "by wisdom" (24:3a), established "by understanding" (24:3b), and filled "by knowledge" (24:4a). The unique sequence of these repeated prepositional phrases indicates that human house building and cultural formation mimic Yahweh's construction of the cosmos and provisioning of creation.[24] The divine architect provides a paradigm for human house building,[25] and the tools used by Yahweh in the construction of the cosmos are the tools that humans should employ in the construction of a home.

The intimate relationship between Yahweh's creation of the cosmos and the creation of human homes is also reflected in the building accounts of the Old Testament tabernacle and temple. As microcosms of the universe, the tabernacle and temple reflect the cosmos, but they are also constructed in the same manner as the cosmos and human homes. In line with Proverbs 3:19–20 and 24:3–4, Exodus 31:3 indicates that Yahweh filled Bezalel with wisdom, understanding, and knowledge to construct portions of the tabernacle (cf. 35:31, 35; 36:1). First Kings 7:14 follows the same sequence of phrases in its declaration that Hiram was filled with wisdom, understanding, and knowledge to construct elements of the temple. Just as human house building mimics the work of the divine builder, so also do the constructions of the tabernacle and temple. Each builder uses the same tools, and each text presents these tools in the same order. These striking similarities indicate that human wisdom and building are rooted in the divine wisdom manifested in the construction, ordering, and filling of the cosmos.[26] Those who acquire wisdom, then, reflect God's wisdom, imitate his creation order, and manifest his provision for the cosmos through their work and care for others.

The relationship between Yahweh's creation of the cosmos and the creation of human homes also establishes a relationship between the created order and the moral order. This relationship is sketched in the Noahic or, better, cosmic covenant (Gen. 8:22; 9:1–17), and it is implied in a variety of sayings across Proverbs. The wisdom of the wise son, for example, is manifested through his sensitivity to created time and work in accord with the rhythm of creation (Prov. 10:5). This sensitivity to the calendrical pattern of creation is also evident in the ant (6:6–11). A comparable sensitivity is exemplified by the righteous, who know the particularity and appetite of

Figure 4.3. *God as Architect*, the frontispiece of Bible Moralisée (ca. 1230)

Austrian National Library / public domain

CANONICAL CONNECTIONS

The Tabernacle and the Temple

The building accounts of both the tabernacle and the temple correspond to the creation account in Genesis 1:1–3:24, indicating that these sacred spaces function as microcosmic representations of the created world. Among the correspondences, the following are the most significant:

1. Just as God creates the cosmos in seven days, the instructions for the construction of the tabernacle are cast in seven divine speeches (Exod. 25:1–30:10, 11–16, 17–21, 22–33, 34–38; 31:1–11, 12–18). And in accord with the days of creation, the temple is built in seven years (1 Kings 6:38).
2. Just as God stations the cherubim east of Eden to guard the temple-garden, cherubim are represented on the veil separating the most holy place from the holy place (Exod. 26:31; 1 Kings 6:23–29).
3. The tree of life in Eden corresponds with the menorah or lampstand in the tabernacle and temple (Gen. 2:9; 3:24; Exod. 25:31–40).

their livestock (12:10). Sensitivity to the rhythmical patterns of creation and the uniqueness of creatures informs wise behavior (cf. 26:1; 27:18). More than this, sensitivity to certain patterns of creation and the uniqueness of creatures may also attune one to other patterns and creatures, such as when to speak or how to speak to certain people, when to act and what to do in particular circumstances. These patterned judgments permeate the book of Proverbs, and to some extent, they are informed by the patterns of the created order and the moral order.

In addition to the interrelationship between the construction of the cosmic house and that of human homes, as well as the interrelationship between the created order and the moral order, Proverbs relates the wise life to the form of life in Eden. This relationship is forged through Proverbs' use of the unique expression "tree of life" (3:18; 11:30; 13:12; 15:4). As a metaphorical and indefinite expression, it does not match *the* tree of life in Genesis 2–3, but it is nourished by the semantic field cultivated in Eden. The "fruit of the righteous," desire fulfilled, and soothing speech are a tree of life (Prov. 11:30; 13:12; 15:4). Each offers sustenance, healing, refreshment, and restoration. The same is true of Lady Wisdom (3:18):

> She is a tree of life to those who embrace her,
>   and those who hold fast to her are blessed.

As a tree of life, Lady Wisdom offers a life of flourishing, wholeness, delight, and shalom. What's more, Lady Wisdom provides a form of life that corresponds to the shape of life in Eden.[27] Whereas the way to the tree of life was blocked (Gen. 3:22–24), Lady Wisdom provides access to a tree of life (Prov. 3:13, 17–18). Whereas the tree of life was banned from human touch, Lady Wisdom is a tree of life that one must grasp (3:18).[28] East of Eden and prior to the consummation of the new heavens and the new earth, Lady Wisdom confers a beatific life that reflects the life and blessings enjoyed in Eden.

Conclusion

The theological themes sketched above orient one to the ways in which the book of Proverbs seeks to form fearers of Yahweh and to nurture a vision of the good life. This project in education for character formation is bound up with fear and faith seeking understanding.[29] While this form of education is significant for the Christian life and faith in many ways, three of those ways deserve specific comment.

Wisdom as a Gift

The first is the nature of wisdom as a gift. Wisdom is a gift; it is a gift from God and a gift from others. This means that the acquisition of wisdom requires trust in and submission to an authorized guide, and it means that wisdom is acquired in and through interpersonal relationship with the other. This vision of wisdom's acquisition is expressed by Esther Meek, who argues that "every act of knowing requires normative guidance, both from worldview commitments and working maxims. But they also involve, most fundamentally, . . . authoritative guidance from other persons. . . . Authoritative guides do not fabricate or teach us to fabricate the real, rather, they teach us to see what is there. Without human teaching, humans do not learn to talk and thus do not learn their world."[30]

Meek notes that, like Proverbs, wisdom is mediated by authoritative guides. Proverbs assumes that wisdom is acquired through trust in and submission to Yahweh, the parents, the wise, and dialogue with the anthology's aphorisms. And Proverbs acknowledges that the acquisition of wisdom is hindered by trust in and submission to unauthorized guides. The question is not whether a guide is required to acquire wisdom; the question is whom one trusts and to whom one listens. Guides are freely available, especially in our contemporary context. They include family and friends, websites and podcasts, and television and advertisements, to name just a few. Like the guides in Proverbs, these guides invite us to view our lives and the world in particular ways. The guide one trusts and listens to influences *how* and *what* that person thinks and how that person lives. Proverbs recognizes these realities. It recognizes that we are constantly bombarded by different voices, directing us to view ourselves and our world in particular ways. And it provides us with authorized guides, who cultivate discernment and enable us to determine which voices to heed.

This vision of wisdom's acquisition as gift is not limited to Proverbs; it pervades the canon of Scripture. Across redemptive history, the triune God guides his people into a wise and good life. He reveals his will in covenant relationship and through commands. He speaks to and guides his people through authorized guides: prophets, priests, kings, and sages.[31] And in climactic fashion, he speaks to and guides his people in the person of his Son (Heb. 1:1–2). Like the prophets, priests, kings, and sages, the Father speaks to his people in his Son and by his Spirit. One of the most striking features of the Synoptic Gospels is that God the Father speaks on only two occasions: at Jesus's baptism and transfiguration. On both occasions, the Father discloses that Jesus is his Son, the one he has chosen, the one he loves and with whom he is well pleased (Matt. 3:16–17; 17:5; Mark 1:9–11; 9:7; Luke

Figure 4.4. Adam and Eve listening to an unauthorized guide. *Adam and Eve* by John Martin (n.d.).

3:21–22; 9:34–35). But at the transfiguration, the Father provides an invaluable command: the disciples must *listen* to Jesus (Matt. 17:5; Mark 9:7; Luke 9:34–35). The Father identifies Jesus as the authorized guide, the voice the Christian should trust, listen to, and follow.

The canon also bears witness to people's failure to trust in, listen to, and follow the triune God's authorized guides. The woman, for example, trusts in and submits to the serpent's explanation of the tree of the knowledge of good and evil. She listens to the voice of an unauthorized guide, who directs her to see the tree and God in a particular way.[32] The same is true of the man. By listening to the voice of the woman and eating from the tree, he listens to and trusts in the guidance of the serpent. This explains the rationale offered in the curse of the man and the woman: "Because you [Adam] *listened* to the voice of the woman and ate . . . , cursed is the ground" (Gen. 3:17). Among other things, the fall is the result of the man and the woman's listening to and enacting the directives of an unauthorized guide. On other occasions in the Bible, people acknowledge the triune God's authorized guides, but they do not follow or enact their guidance (2 Kings 17:7–15; Jer. 7:12–15; 29:15–19). In so doing, they fall short of the acquisition of wisdom and the enjoyment of the good life.

Together with the canonical witness, Proverbs indicates that wisdom comes from outside of the self; it is a gift acquired in fiduciary relationship with authorized guides.[33] This explains why listening is among the quintessential characteristics of the wise person (Prov. 12:15; 15:31, 32). It also explains why the wise do not trust in their own wisdom (3:5, 7; 26:12; 28:26); they do not consider themselves as wise in their own eyes.

Always Room to Grow

This posture of humility provides the necessary context for the second way in which Proverbs is significant for the Christian life and faith. According to Proverbs, a person never arrives in the wise and good life;[34] while a person cannot grow in righteousness (see the sidebar "Growing in Righteousness?"),[35] the wise and the righteous can always grow in wisdom (9:9). This is the reality of creaturehood, for absolute, even certain, knowledge is above the standing of finite creatures. This reality should not evoke a sense of despair; rather, it should produce trust in and humble dependence on the triune God. Humility and trust are the hallmarks of a wise and good life. They are modeled by Agur's confession and prayer (30:1–9), and they pervade Paul's prayers in the New Testament, in which he expresses humble dependence on God, asking that God would grant the Christian community wisdom, understanding, and knowledge to animate their cruciform lives (Eph. 1:17; 3:10; Phil. 1:9; Col. 1:9–10, 28; 2:2–3, 23; 3:16; Philem. 6).[36] All the treasures of wisdom and knowledge may be hidden in the Lord Jesus (Col. 2:2–3), but Christians will never fully grasp or possess these treasures. To arrive in the wise and good life, to grasp the whole of wisdom, and to obtain absolute knowledge would be a breach of creaturehood. Put simply, it would mean that one is God. Proverbs precludes this vision of the wise and good life. The wise know that they can always grow in wisdom, because the wise know who they are in relationship with God.

As a gift acquired through interpersonal relationship with the other and received from a humble posture, wisdom is accessible. It is accessed through the example of others (Prov. 12:26; 13:20; 31:10–31), and it is mediated through the teaching of others.

Proverbs as a Pedagogical Resource

The forms of teaching within Proverbs constitute the third way in which the book

THEOLOGICAL ISSUES

Growing in Righteousness?

Among the character types in Proverbs, the righteous person is the book's moral exemplar. The righteous reflect God's righteousness. The most striking feature of the righteous is that Proverbs never indicates that the righteous can grow in the ethical virtue that marks their character. This intimates that the righteousness of the righteous is a fixed state or an imputed virtue. While Proverbs does not venture an account of justification, the theological judgment underlying the depiction of the righteous informs the doctrine of justification.

Figure 4.5. *Humility* by Peter Candid (before 1586)

is significant for the Christian life and faith. The anthology provides a pedagogical resource for a life of fear and faith seeking understanding. It provides a pedagogical resource for sanctification. Contrary to much contemporary use of Proverbs, the book's pedagogical value is not limited to tidbits of self-help or advice regarding sex, parenting, work, wealth, and speech. The book offers pedagogical models. These models employ different pedagogical techniques. Some involve rebuke (1:20–33; 20:22; 24:1–2). Others deal in erotic desire (5:15–23), terror (6:20–35), and seduction (7:1–27). Still others utilize paradoxes (11:24; 13:7, 23; 14:12; 16:25), false leads (14:12, 34; 16:25; 29:10), enigmatic analogies (25:3–4, 11–20), and the juxtaposition of asymmetrical lines, which require the reader to exercise moral reasoning by filling in particular gaps (28:10–11, 16, 20, 25–27).[37]

Some of these forms of pedagogy are analogous to hand-holding or spoon-feeding. Others necessitate the exercise of imagination and perception. But all forms of pedagogy in Proverbs are designed to (trans)form character, intellect, imagination, desires, emotions, and motivations in accord with wisdom and virtue. Just as Jesus employs parables and other forms of teaching to instruct his disciples in the way of life in the kingdom of heaven, so also Proverbs employs different pedagogical techniques to instruct Christian disciples in the way of the wise and good life. The book is an invaluable pedagogical resource for Christian discipleship.

CHAPTER FIVE

Job

Suffering Seeking Understanding

Why do bad things happen to good people? How ought a person to live amid the silence of God and the absence of answers to the perplexing circumstances of life? Does the experience of profound suffering reveal that God is not omnipotent or loving or just or good? Do the Holocaust, the genocides in Rwanda and Bosnia, the nuclear catastrophes at Chernobyl and Fukushima, domestic and international terrorist attacks, human trafficking, and mass shootings bear witness to the reality that God is either indifferent to his creatures or not in control of his creation? These are important questions. They are questions lodged in contemporary communal consciousness, and they are questions raised by the book of Job.

Job—the epitome of piety and the fear of God (Job 1:1; Ezek. 14:14, 20)—experiences profound suffering: the loss of his wealth, servants, children, and health (Job 1:13–19; 2:7–8). The boils on Job's body advertise God's curse (2:7; cf. Deut. 28:35). Job's worldview is shattered (Job 3). He is placeless, ostracized by both friends and family (19:13–22; 30:1–15). His friends lay the blame for his suffering at his feet. Job lays the blame on God. But God remains silent in response to Job's protests and questions. Job's suffering raises perennial questions about the character of God and his relationship to his creatures and his creation. While the book raises a multitude of questions, it does not answer many of them. That is not the point of the book, for answers to life's disconcerting atrocities elude humans. If nothing else, the book of Job affirms our questions. It maintains that questioning God is part of the life of faith, and it provides a theological framework within which to understand our questions by staging a performance of suffering seeking understanding.

Key Questions of the Book of Job

■ READ JOB 1:1–11 ■

Suffering and understanding are strange bedfellows, especially against the witness of the moral majority in Proverbs. Proverbs acknowledges that even the wise, righteous, and good life is gray: the wicked flourish (10:2; 11:16), the righteous fall (24:15–16; 25:26), and the depths of God's providential governance cannot be plumbed by finite creatures (16:1–9; 21:1). This acknowledgment of contingency and creaturely limits, however, tends to be lost to the predominant witness of Proverbs: the wise and the righteous flourish, while the fool and the wicked suffer.

The expectations created by much of Proverbs are difficult to reconcile with what Job experiences. The connection between character, action, and consequence unravels. God's nature and character are subjected to severe scrutiny. Job's suffering engenders hard questions about the order of the world, the order of life, and God's providential governance of these orders. More specifically, Job's suffering creates the conditions for understanding the nature of genuine faith and God's wisdom, justice, and providential governance of all things.

God's wisdom, justice, and providential governance are challenged in a pair of questions, both of which are posed by "the *satan*" (*hassatan*). The

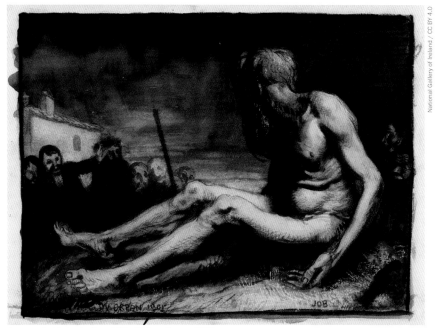

Figure 5.1. *Job on the Dunghill* by William Orpen (1905)

first concerns the nature of genuine faith: Is disinterested piety possible? That is, can a person fear God "without benefit" (Job 1:9)?[1] This question is closely related to the second: Is the retribution principle a suitable policy for God's governance of the world? By blessing the righteous, does God subvert the very righteousness that he desires in his servants, incentivizing forms of behavior driven by the expectation of reward rather than the reality of genuine relationship (1:10)?[2]

Job's piety and God's policies are introduced in the opening chapter and explored throughout the rest of the book. Contrary to the interests of Job and his friends, the book is not about why pious people suffer. While it does raise this question, it does not answer it. Instead, the book focuses on God and on how one ought to understand God in a world marked by innocent suffering.[3] As Job maintains his integrity to the end (27:2–6), he demonstrates that a person can fear God without benefit (*hinnam*, 1:9; 2:3). The sequence of the divine speeches suggests that Yahweh's governance of the world is directed by his wisdom (chaps. 38–39), not by a mechanical system of retribution and reward (chaps. 40–41). God is not a cosmic vending machine, doling out rewards and punishments in accord with some strict system. He is just, but his justice is governed by his wisdom.[4] His world is ordered, but it is also unsafe.[5]

The Structure, Content, and Movement of the Book of Job

The orderly yet unsettled nature of God's world is reflected in the structure of the book. The book begins and ends with a prose frame (1:1–2:13; 42:7–17), but the bulk of the book is a series of poetic dialogues between Job and his friends (Eliphaz, Bildad, Zophar, and Elihu; chaps. 3–37) and between Job and God (38:1–42:6). The tone and content of the prose frame sit in tension with those of the poetic dialogues. More specifically, the Job of the prose frame seems to conflict with the Job of the poetic dialogue. The protagonist moves from the position of praise and acceptance of God's providential ordering of all things (1:21; 2:10) to one who questions and challenges God's governance (3:2–26; 9:22; 24:1–12). Together with these points of tension, the arrangement of the book raises several questions, three in particular:

1. The poetic dialogue between Job and his friends is cast in three cycles, where each friend has a pass at Job (chaps. 4–14; 15–21; 22–27). But Zophar is missing from the third cycle of the dialogue. Does he deliver a third and final speech?

2. Who is the speaker in Job 28, the poem about wisdom?

3. Who is Elihu (chaps. 32–37)? Where did he come from? Why is he not reprimanded with the other friends in the epilogue (42:7–9)? Should his speeches be placed earlier in the book?

LITERARY NOTES

The Poetry in Job

Many interpret the shift in genre and tone from the prose introduction in Job to the poetic dialogue as an indication of different authors and a window into the compositional development of the book. Regardless of the number of authors and compositional history of the book, Tod Linafelt argues that the poetry across the book's center plays an indispensable role in the advancement of the plot. Poetry possesses literary resources unavailable to prose, and these are leveraged to reveal Job's interior life and to allow Job, the friends, and God to express their responses in realistic and creative ways.[b]

HISTORICAL MATTERS

Zophar's Third Speech

The narrator of Job does not assign Zophar a third and final speech, so many commentators have searched for and marked off Zophar's third speech. For example, David Clines argues that while the Hebrew text ascribes Job 27:7–23 to Job, these verses represent Zophar's last speech. The identification of Zophar's third speech creates symmetry across the dialogue: each friend delivers three speeches across the three cycles of the dialogue. If the absence of Zophar's third speech is interpreted from a literary perspective, its omission signals the breakdown of the dialogue between Job and his friends.

Scholars have answered these questions in different ways (see the sidebars). These answers are helpful from a historical and compositional perspective, for they stimulate the reader's theological imagination.

But if one takes the arrangement of the book of Job at face value, then it appears the drama consists of six parts:

1. The prose frame (chaps. 1–2; 42:7–17)
2. Job's soliloquies (chaps. 3, 29–31)
3. The dialogue between Job and his friends (chaps. 4–27)
4. The poem on wisdom (chap. 28)
5. The speeches of Elihu (32:1–37:24)
6. The speeches of Yahweh (38:1–42:6)

The relationship among these parts gives the book of Job a dramatic character. The dramatic movement of the book is apparent in their interrelationship.

The Prose Frame

READ JOB 2:1–13; 42:7–17

The first component of the drama is the prose frame (1:1–2:13; 42:7–17). While many people characterize the story narrated across this frame as naive or shallow, it is a subtle and indispensable element for any reading of the book.[6] More than introducing the questions that drive the poetic dialogue (1:9–11), the prologue's movement from heaven (1:6–12) to earth (1:13–22) and back again (2:1–6, 7–13) reveals the occasion and cause of Job's suffering through the medium of dramatic irony. The reader receives information that remains hidden from the characters in the unfolding drama. Without this information, the reader would likely accuse Job as his so-called friends do.

The prologue also elicits numerous questions: Who is the *satan*? Why is this figure absent from the remainder of the book? Does the *satan* claim that Job will bless God or curse God in response to his afflictions? In like manner, does Job's wife call him to "curse God and die" or to "bless God and die"? And what is one to make of Job's interior life? His cultic activity on behalf of his children is rooted in the suspicion that they have cursed God in their hearts (1:5). Following the first round of afflictions, the narrator makes a summary statement: "In all this, Job did not sin or charge God with wrongdoing" (1:22). And following his response to his wife, the narrator states, "In all this, Job did not sin with his lips" (2:10). But with the focus on Job's interior life, did he sin in his heart? Answers to these questions are not clear. This is appropriate, for answers to life's questions are ambiguous in the book of Job.

Robert Frost: Job 43

Robert Frost fills the gap created by the absence of the *satan* in the remainder of the book of Job. Frost's *A Masque of Reason* is a short play that he designates as chapter 43 of Job. Among other things, Frost imagines the following exchange between Job and God:

JOB. No, for I have yet
To ask my question. We disparage reason.
But all the time it's what we're most concerned with. . . .
Come, after all these years—to satisfy me.
I'm curious. And I'm a grown-up man:
I'm not a child for You to put me off
And tantalize me with another "Oh, because."
You'd be the last to want me to believe
All Your effects were merely lucky blunders.
That would be unbelief and atheism.
The artist in me cries out for design.
Such devilish ingenuity of torture
Did seem unlike You, and I tried to think
The reason might have been some other person's.
But there is nothing You are not behind.
I did not ask then, but it seems as if
Now after all these years You might indulge me.

Why did You hurt me so? I am reduced
To ask flatly for the reason—outright.

GOD. I'd tell you, Job—

JOB. All right, don't tell me then
If You don't want to. I don't want to know.
But what is all this secrecy about?
I fail to see what fun, what satisfaction
A God can find in laughing at how badly
Men fumble at the possibilities
When left forever to guess for themselves.
The chances are when there's so much pretense
Of metaphysical profundity
The obscurity's a fraud to cover nothing. . . .

GOD. . . .
I'm going to tell Job why I tortured him
And trust it won't be adding to the torture.
I was just showing off to the Devil, Job,
As is set forth in Chapters One and Two.
(*Job takes a few steps pacing.*) Do you mind?
(*God eyes him anxiously.*)[c]

Bless or Curse?

The Hebrew text of Job 1:5, 11, and 2:5, 9 reads "bless" where most English translations read "curse." The text-critical notes for these texts suggest that "bless" should be read as a euphemism for "curse." This is not surprising, for a Hebrew reader would never say aloud "curse God." The context of each verse suggests that a euphemistic reading aligns with Job's sacrifices (1:5), the *satan*'s declarations (1:11; 2:5), and Job's response to his wife (2:9–10). But others argue that the reading "bless" remains in play. The matter is undecidable.[d]

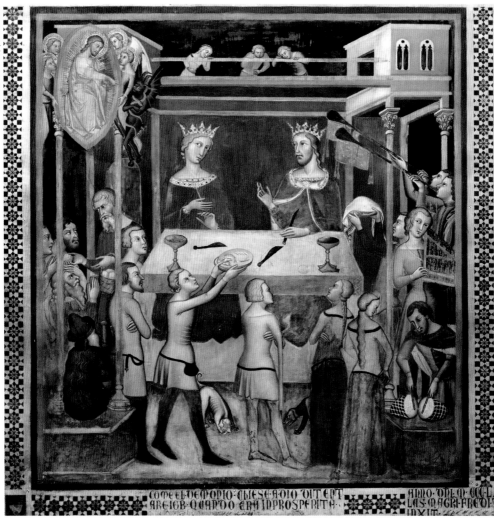

Figure 5.2. *The Devil Bargains with God over Job's Faith* by Bartolo di Fredi (ca. 1335–45)

These answers may appear clearer in the second part of the prose frame, the book's epilogue (42:7–17), but they are not. While the closing section brings the drama to something of a resolution, it also leaves many questions unanswered. How has Job spoken truthfully to or about God (42:7–8)? Having marginalized the retribution principle as the means by which Yahweh governs the cosmos (38:1–40:2; 40:6–41:34), why does God appear to reactivate the principle and restore Job's fortunes twofold (42:10)? In addition to the birth of more children and the restoration of his wealth, is Job's body restored? Questions remain, but new horizons also open. Job is consoled and welcomed into a community that accepts his experience of all the calamity that Yahweh has brought upon him (42:11).

Job's Soliloquies

■ READ JOB 3 ■

Just as the prose frame serves as an envelope around the entire book, Job's soliloquies serve as an envelope around the dialogue with the friends (chaps. 3; 29–31). These soliloquies constitute the second part of the book. After seven days and seven nights of silence with his friends (2:13), Job unleashes a curse on the day of his birth (3:1–10; cf. Jer. 20:14–18) and a lament that portrays a topsy-turvy world he wishes to inhabit (Job 3:11–26). In the former, he seeks to reverse creation; in the latter, he creates a world that aligns with his experience and offers rest. In addition to breaking the seven days and seven nights of silence, this curse and lament trigger the dialogue with the friends. Job's response prompts the friends' responses.

This is not the case with Job's closing soliloquy (chaps. 29–31), where Job delivers an extended testimony that includes his past status (chap. 29), his present predicament (chap. 30), and an oath of innocence (chap. 31). In the past, Yahweh's lamp shone above Job's head (29:2–3). Job dwelt securely, with his children by his side, and presided over assemblies at the city gate (29:5–10). He clothed himself with justice and righteousness, serving as eyes for the blind, feet for the lame, a father for orphans, and a refuge for the widow (29:11–17). But things have changed. The community that honored Job has turned on their righteous representative. Job is now an outcast or, better, an animal (30:29). He is the recipient of social humiliation, verbal assaults, and divine silence (30:9–23). This situation moves Job to do something unprecedented in the Old Testament—that is, to examine his interior and exterior forms of life and to call God to level explicit punishments against him for any sin he has committed. As Job nears the conclusion of his oath of innocence, he expresses his intention to sign a formal lawsuit against God (31:35–37). Then the narrator says Job's words are ended (31:40) and indicates that, in response to this extended soliloquy, the friends cease to answer Job (32:1).

The Dialogue between Job and His Friends

■ READ JOB 4–5 ■

An extended dialogue between Job and his friends makes up the third section of the book, and it includes three cycles of speeches (chaps. 4–14; 15–21; 22–27). Eliphaz, Bildad, and Zophar appeal to tradition to

Figure 5.3. *Job Rebuked by His Friends* by William Blake (1805)

explain Job's suffering (8:8; 15:9–10, 17–18) and encourage him to renounce his ritual mourning.[7] Their explanations epitomize the best answers to pious suffering available in the ancient world. In different ways, they chalk up Job's predicament to just retribution (4:7–9; 18:5–10; 20:12–16),[8] divine inscrutability (11:7–9; cf. 15:7–9), and the innate sinfulness of human beings (4:17–19; 15:14–16; 25:4–6). These explanations, however, fail to satisfy Job and account for his experience. It is not surprising that as the dialogue progresses the friends transform from sympathetic comforters to ferocious faultfinders, nor is it surprising that they have less to say. The diminishing length of their speeches not only reflects their diminishing relationship with Job; it also indicates that they have neither a suitable explanation nor a viable solution for Job.

The Poem on Wisdom

■ READ JOB 28 ■

The friends' inability to resolve Job's problem is reinforced by the poem on wisdom, the fourth section of the book (chap. 28). The poem juxtaposes humanity's power and unmitigated success with humanity's failure. Humanity can explore the depth and breadth of the earth to uncover hidden treasures, but it cannot find the place of wisdom. No speaker is assigned to the poem, but Job 28 plays a significant role in the book's broader context. Its account of God's superior wisdom casts judgment on the wisdom offered in the dialogue (chaps. 4–27).[9] Its cosmic panorama anticipates that of the divine speeches (chaps. 38–41). And its final verse echoes the narrator's evaluation of Job in 1:1, forming an inclusio around this half of the book (28:28). The poem acknowledges human wisdom and power, but it places them in their proper limits. The poem also reveals the unexpected place of wisdom's residence (28:26–27), and it indicates that wisdom is only discovered through relationship with the one who knows where wisdom is to be found.

The Speeches of Elihu

READ JOB 32:1–33:33; 35:1–16

As noted above, Job's closing soliloquy silences the friends (chaps. 29–31). The cessation of the friends' responses creates the conditions for an interloper, the young Elihu, to intervene. Elihu's speeches make up the fifth section of the book (32:6–37:24), but in many respects his contribution to the book of Job is a mystery. Does he extend the argument of the friends? Does he mount a distinct response to Job? Some say yes. Others say no. The truth is probably somewhere in between. Filled with the spirit of God (32:8), Elihu assumes the role of a mediator who seeks to vindicate Job (33:32). But in the end, he justifies God. Elihu reinforces and develops the value of divine discipline (33:12–30; cf. 5:17–27). He criticizes Job for his stubborn insistence on his innocence (33:9–11; 34:37; 35:2). And he attempts to remove God from Job's line of questioning by arguing that humans have no effect on God (35:5–8). Elihu goes so far as to claim that God will neither listen to nor respond to Job (35:12–14). Among other things, Elihu gets this wrong: God does appear to Job and respond to the sufferer. Ironically, Elihu sets the scene for this response; the rhetorical questions and concern with God's rule over creation at the end of his discourse give way to the rhetorical questions and concern with God's wise rule over creation in the first divine speech (37:14–24; 38:1–39:30).

The Speeches of Yahweh

READ JOB 38:1–41; 40:6–41:34

The divine speeches and Job's brief responses make up the final, climactic section of the book (38:1–40:5; 40:6–42:6), but there is little agreement about the suitability of Yahweh's "answer" to Job. This answer is delivered through two speeches. The first is riddled with rhetorical questions, each attesting to Yahweh's wise governance over the inanimate and animate world (38:1–40:2). The second focuses on two untamable beasts, each of which thrives within its respective boundaries under Yahweh's good governance (40:6–41:34). Whether or not one assesses Yahweh's answers as appropriate responses to Job's protests, Job's final confession suggests the "answers" are sufficient (42:1–6). Job acknowledges his epistemological limits, how he transgressed the intellectual boundaries of creaturehood (42:2–3). And he receives comfort concerning his ritual state of mourning: he moves on, consoled by Yahweh but forever changed by his experience of suffering and his eyewitness experience of Yahweh (42:4–6).

As a book that stages a performance of suffering seeking understanding, the drama of Job explores a variety of significant theological themes. These themes will be the focus of our attention in the next two chapters.

Christian Reading Questions

1. How should Christians think about God in a world plagued by suffering?
2. How does God's justice relate to God's wisdom?
3. How would you comfort someone who is suffering? How would you *not* comfort someone who is suffering?
4. How is the wisdom of the book of Job similar to and different from the wisdom of Proverbs?

CHAPTER SIX

Theological Themes in Job (1)

Humans are fragile, finite creatures. God is wise and just. These theological truths intersect in the book of Job as Job and his friends consider the nature of wisdom and the nature of humanity. They probe the depths of God's wisdom and his unsearchable judgments. More specifically, they explore the relationship between God's wisdom and God's justice. Whereas the Old Testament prophets scrutinize the relationship between God's justice and God's mercy, the book of Job examines divine wisdom and divine justice. Does divine justice provide the point of orientation for understanding divine wisdom? Or does divine wisdom provide the point of orientation for understanding divine justice? Can humans, given their nature, comprehend the riches of the wisdom and knowledge of God? Can they know the mind of God and understand God's justice? The book of Job raises these questions. This chapter will consider them by attending to two prominent theological themes: humanity's limits and Yahweh's wisdom and justice.

Humanity's Limits

■ READ JOB 11–12, 28 ■

The theme of human limitations features prominently in the book of Job. While this motif is explored in different ways, two of these ways deserve specific comment: wisdom's (in)accessibility and the theological anthropology of Job and his friends.

Wisdom's (In)accessibility

When heard alongside Proverbs' claim that wisdom is available to any who pursue it (e.g., Prov. 2:1–5), the book of Job's testimony concerning wisdom's (in)accessibility is both shocking and profound. In Job 12:13–25, Job describes wisdom as accessible to humans; but according to chapter 28, wisdom is hidden. Contrary to Zophar's contention that God's wisdom is inaccessible—higher than the heavens, deeper than Sheol, longer than the earth, and broader than the sea (11:7–9)—Job maintains that wisdom is manifest *in creation*. In fact, Behemoth (cf. 40:15–24), the birds of the air, the earth itself, and the fish of the sea can teach the friends, for these creatures know the wisdom revealed through Yahweh's mysterious hand (12:7–9). This wisdom, however, is shocking; its shock derives from Lady Wisdom's function in Proverbs 8:14–16.

Proverbs 8:14–16	Job 12:13–21
Mine are counsel and resourcefulness; I am Understanding; strength is mine. By me kings reign, and rulers decree justice. By me princes rule, and nobles, all judges of justice.	With him are wisdom and strength; counsel and understanding belong to him. . . . With him are strength and resourcefulness; the deceiver and the deceived belong to him. He leads counselors away naked and makes judges fools. He loosens the bond of kings and binds a belt on their loins. . . . He pours contempt on nobles and loosens the belt of the strong.

THEOLOGICAL ISSUES

Wisdom and Human Tradition

Zophar's description of the transcendence and hiddenness of wisdom suggests that divine wisdom is inaccessible to humans (Job 11:7–9), but his use of a traditional trope concerning wisdom's transcendence and hiddenness betrays the ground of his argument. Like the other friends, Zophar's wisdom or knowledge is dependent on human perception and tradition (5:27; 8:8–10; 15:10). Tradition serves as the quarry from which the friends extract conventional truths to build their arguments. As Carol Newsom notes, "Tradition is itself a form of transcendent wisdom [for the friends], since it overcomes the finitude of the individual."[a]

LITERARY NOTES

"Yahweh" in Job

The divine name, Yahweh, appears outside the prologue, divine speeches, and epilogue only in Job 12:9 (cf. 1:1–2:13; 38:1–42:6; 42:7–17). This prompts many scholars to emend the divine name here to the more generic designation, "God." From a text-critical perspective, "Yahweh" is attested by several ancient versions, and it represents the more difficult reading. What's more, Job 12:9 echoes Isaiah 41:20:

Job 12:9	Isaiah 41:20
Who among all these does not know that the hand of Yahweh has done this?	so that they may see and know and consider and understand together that the hand of Yahweh has done this and the Holy One of Israel has created it.

Together with text-critical considerations, this echo suggests that the divine name should be retained.[b]

The depiction of wisdom's accessibility in Job 12:13–25 is disorienting when heard against Wisdom's words in Proverbs 8:14–16 (cf. Isa. 11:2). Both Lady Wisdom and Job affirm that wisdom is manifest *in creation*, but they do so to make very different points. Whereas Lady Wisdom praises herself as the instrument through which societal leaders establish order, Job praises God and his wisdom as the instruments through which societal leaders are deceived. Job turns wisdom's place and function in creation upside down: it is revealed not through the order of the social world but through the disorder of the social world. According to Job, this disorder is extensive; it includes rulers, judges, kings, priests, advisors, elders, nobles, and the strong, as well as entire nations and their leaders (Job 12:17–25). It is a startling claim, even more so when Job's conception of the topsy-turvy nature of wisdom *in creation* is heard in concert with the *absence of wisdom in creation* in Job 28.

The poem on wisdom in Job 28 offers a profound perspective on the whereabouts and the (in)accessibility of wisdom. This perspective is particularly intriguing when considered alongside those of Job 12 and Proverbs 3:19–20 and 8:22–31. In Proverbs 3:19–20, wisdom is the instrument by which Yahweh formed and filled the cosmos according to a stable and discernable design. Wisdom is revealed through the very structure of the world; it constitutes "the stuff of reality itself."[1] Wisdom's testimony in Proverbs 8:22–31, by contrast, attests to her passive role in Yahweh's construction of the cosmos: she was faithfully beside Yahweh, delighting and rejoicing in his handiwork (8:30). Wisdom bears witness to the reality that she is separate from creation; she precedes and transcends it (8:22–29). To these poetic portraits of wisdom and creation, Job 28 provides yet another rendering. Wisdom and creation, as well as God and humanity, remain in view. But wisdom's whereabouts, (in)accessibility, and unique relation to God, creation, and humanity produce a puzzling portrait.

This portrait develops across three sections (Job 28:1–11, 12–19, 20–28). The search for precious commodities and, by extension, the search for wisdom pervades these sections. Three motifs recur in each section: the place/source of the precious commodity, the way/access to the precious commodity, and the discovery/acquisition of the precious commodity.[2]

Figure 6.1. Representation of Gilgamesh fighting the bull from the heavens. Votive plate (ca. 2255–2219 BC).

The first section focuses on human power manifested in humanity's capacity to perforate the boundaries of the created order, discover items, extract their valuable materials, and bring these hidden materials to light (28:1–11). By virtue of their prowess, humans explore particular places: a mine and a place for gold (v. 1), the dust and rock (v. 2), and the earth, its rocks, and its dust (vv. 5–6). They create access to ways that are inaccessible, clearing paths to uninhabited regions and putting an end to the darkness of hidden portions of the earth (vv. 3–4). While these portions of the earth are hidden from the birds of the air and the proud beasts of the earth (vv. 7–8), they are accessible to humans. From these places, humans discover items and extract precious commodities: silver, gold, iron, copper, and sapphire (vv. 1–2, 6). These discoveries place humans on an even playing field with God. Just as God moves mountains (9:5), so also humans "overturn mountains at their [geographical] roots" (28:9). Just as God causes water to flow from a rock (Exod. 17:5–7), so also humans cause water to flow from a rock (28:10). Humans, by their cognitive and physical powers, overcome all obstacles and bring hidden things to light (v. 11).

The second section of the poem questions and qualifies this portrait of power, moving from human power to human limits (28:12–19). Questions in verse 12 foreground these limits: "But where is wisdom to be found? And where is the place of understanding?" The latter question assumes that wisdom resides in a place. Humans may be able to perforate the places of creation, uncover items, draw out their value, and bring them into the light, but according to verses 12–19, humans are unable to find wisdom. In fact, they cannot even identify its place. The reason is simple: humans do not know the place of wisdom because wisdom "is not to be found in the land of the living" (v. 13). It is not located in the earth, from which humans access, discover, extract, and bring to light precious commodities. Contrary to Job 12:13–25, wisdom does not reside *in creation*, and contrary to Proverbs 3:19–20, wisdom is not necessarily apparent *in creation*. Wisdom is more elusive. It is located neither in the deeps nor in the sea. Both are ignorant of wisdom's whereabouts (Job 28:14). What's more, wisdom can be neither acquired nor compared with the precious commodities that humans extract from the earth (vv. 15–19; cf. vv. 1–2, 6, 10–11). It's priceless. Its place is unknown to humans. Its location escapes human discovery, and it cannot be purchased.

This pessimistic conclusion sets the stage for the third and final section of Job 28 (vv. 20–28), which depicts the place of wisdom and the relationship between God, wisdom, and humanity in unique and profound detail. The stage is set by a repetition and modification of the question in verse 12: "So where does wisdom *come from*? And where is the place of understanding?" (v. 20). The place of wisdom remains in view, but the question in verse 20 is different, for it focuses on the source of wisdom. The nexus of place and source shifts this developing portrait of wisdom and creation, as well as of God and humans, to a different plane of discovery. Verse 23 discloses this plane; whereas humans do not know the way to wisdom (v. 13), God perceives its way and knows its place (v. 23). God's perception of the location and the way to wisdom is attributed to his sight. While humans put an end to darkness (v. 3a), search out the farthest limits of the earth (v. 3b), see every precious thing (v. 10), and bring hidden things to light (v. 11), God looks to the ends of the earth and sees everything under the heavens (v. 24). The spatial superiority of God's sight is complemented by its temporal preeminence. When God gave to the wind a weight, apportioned the waters by measure, made a decree for the rain, and appointed a way for the thunderbolt, then he saw, appraised, established, and searched out wisdom (vv. 25–27). The spatial and temporal preeminence of God's sight explains his perception of the location and way to wisdom. But it does not explain the relationship between God, wisdom, and creation.[3]

In contrast to Proverbs 3:19–20, the poem of Job 28 does not depict wisdom as the instrument by which God created the cosmos. But like Proverbs 8:22–31, the poem indicates that wisdom is present *during* God's construction of the world. Following his creation of the storm (Job 28:25–26), God perceives wisdom in the meteorological phenomenon (v. 27; cf. 38:1). God sees wisdom as an *other*, not as an *object* to be acquired (cf. 28:1–11). More specifically, God perceives that "wisdom is the storm's ground-plan."[4] This discovery is then disclosed to humanity so that they may live in accord with it: "And he said to humankind, 'Look, the fear of the Lord—that is wisdom, and turning aside from evil is understanding'" (v. 28). Wisdom is not possessed by the powers of autonomous humans (vv. 1–11); wisdom is revealed and received in relationship with God.[5] This interpersonal framework is consistent with the relational context of wisdom's acquisition in the book of Proverbs. Wisdom is the gift of another. What's more, wisdom is manifested through embodied practice, by turning aside from evil; it is not the objective mastery of a body of knowledge.

This revelation of wisdom aligns with Proverbs, but when read with the rest of the book of Job, this revelation of wisdom is deeply ironic. Its irony derives from the relationship between Job 1:1 and Job 28:28. According to the narrator, Job fears God and turns aside from evil (1:1); and the fear of the Lord is wisdom, and understanding is turning aside from evil (28:28). While Job possesses and embodies wisdom, this wisdom does not grant him understanding of his experience. Job's wisdom is genuine, but it is limited. It is wisdom appropriate to finite creatures.

Theological Anthropology

In addition to exploring the theme of wisdom's (in)accessibility, the book of Job considers the theme of human limits. It does so through the theological anthropology of Job and his friends. As the designation suggests, theological anthropology considers the nature of humans and what it means to be human from a theological perspective. Among other things, theological anthropology contemplates the relationship between body and soul, the purpose of human life, and the relationship between humans and creation, as well as gender and free will. Theological anthropology plays a formative role in ancient Near Eastern texts about pious sufferers, and it plays a formative role in the book of Job as well. Among the traditional explanations for pious or innocent suffering in the ancient world, the congenital sinfulness of humanity may be the most prominent. This belief pervades Sumerian and Akkadian literary works that reflect on the dogma from both anthropocentric and theocentric perspectives. From an anthropocentric frame of reference, the sufferer in the Sumerian Man and His God provides a clear distillation of the human condition: "They say—the wise men—a word true and right: 'Never has a sinless child been born to its mother . . . a sinless man has never existed from old.'"[6]

This conception of humanity is reiterated in the Akkadian prayer Against Congenital Guilt, as well as in the pleas of Who Has Not Sinned? The former gives

particular attention to the notion of generative transmission, as the sufferer declares, "O Shamash, abatement is within your reach: Dispel, drive off the guilt of my mother and father."[7] The latter contends that all human beings foster sin. This is captured by the petitioner's reflections: "Who is there who is guilty of no sin against his god? Which is he who kept a commandment forever? All human beings there are harbor sin."[8]

Certain ancient Near Eastern texts also reflect on the human condition from a theocentric frame of reference. In accordance with the Mesopotamian worldview, all the codes of human conduct were woven into the fabric of the cosmos by the gods.[9] Sin was not only an innate characteristic of humanity; it was also perceived as a divine norm established in the structure of the cosmos. When the descriptions of humanity across representative ancient Near Eastern texts are read together, it seems that the notion of humanity's congenital sinfulness is rooted in three basic theological assumptions: generative transmission, the fragility and limitations of humans, and the inscrutable design of the gods.

These assumptions also inform the anthropological perspectives woven throughout the poetic dialogue of the book of Job. The parties within the dialogue appeal to these assumptions in a selective fashion to construct a distinctive vision of the human condition. This is especially apparent in the speeches of Eliphaz and Bildad. According to these friends, humanity's material constitution, natural birth, and subordinate status within the hierarchical structure of the cosmos confirm humankind's innate sinfulness and indignity before God:

> Can a mortal be in the right before God?
> Can a human be pure before his Maker?

> Even in his servants he puts no trust,
>   and his messengers he charges with error;
> surely, those who dwell in houses of clay,
>   whose foundation is from dust,
> they are crushed before the Maker. (4:17–19)

> What is a mortal that one should be pure,
>   and one born of a woman that one should be in the right?
> If (God) puts no trust in his holy ones,
>   and the heavens are not pure in his eyes,
> how much less one who is abominable and corrupt,
>   a human who drinks iniquity as water. (15:14–16)

> How can a mortal be in the right before God?
>   And how can one born of a woman be pure?
> Even the moon is not bright,
>   and the stars are not pure in his eyes;
> how much less a mortal, who is a maggot,
>   and a human being, who is a worm. (25:4–6)

Both Eliphaz and Bildad's vision of the human condition is comparable to the fundamental tenets of Mesopotamian thought, but it is unique in at least one respect. While these friends appeal to generative transmission and the fragility and limitations of humanity to validate their anthropological conclusions, they fail to account for divine design. In contrast to the theocentric perspective of their Mesopotamian counterparts, they contend that God is not responsible for the innate sinfulness of humanity; rather, humans are personally responsible for their immoral disposition and common trouble. Far from charging God with defective design or divine malfeasance (8:3; cf. 11:7–12), Eliphaz and Bildad attempt to neutralize Job's objections by emphasizing aspects of the ancient dogma concerning humanity's nature. They focus on human culpability at the expense of God's design of the cosmos.[10]

Job offers a rival perspective on the human condition. Whereas Eliphaz and Bildad associate humanity's material constitution with moral corruption (4:17–19), Job correlates it with its mortal condition (1:21; 10:8–9). Eliphaz and Bildad attribute humanity's fallibility to generative transmission (15:14–16; 25:4–6); Job simply says humanity's woman-born status confirms its ephemeral nature (14:1–6). Eliphaz and Bildad give particular attention to humanity's subordinate status within the cosmos to highlight its imperfection (4:17–21; 15:14–16; 25:4–6). Job, by contrast, associates humanity's dreadful status with the malicious design of God (7:1–3, 17–18; cf. 10:17; 14:14). Job's attention to the mortal condition of humanity and his exploration of divine design serve as the fundamental pillars on which he constructs his alternative anthropology. For Job, the human condition is not characterized by innate sinfulness; rather, it is marked by mortality (1:21; 14:1–6), trouble (3:10; 7:3), harsh servitude (7:1–2), and an obscure destiny (3:23; 19:8), each of which is the product of divine design.

Although the friends promote a view of divine design characterized by justice and retribution (15:17–35; 18:1–21; 20:1–29), Job's vision of divine design moves beyond the stale principles of the retributive system to God's perplexing relationship with his creatures. In contrast to the friends' impersonal conception of humankind, Job incorporates a series of metaphors to explore God's enigmatic design and personal involvement in the human predicament. Job describes God as the divine sculptor (10:8–9), cheese maker (10:10), weaver (10:11), and parent (10:12), who formed humans

Figure 6.2. *The Hand of God* by Auguste Rodin (ca. 1907). In this sculpture, "Rodin presents the inchoate figures of Adam and Eve cradled in God's hand. The composition is an homage to his revered 'master' Michelangelo, the Renaissance artist whose unfinished figures materializing out of rough stone symbolize the process of artistic creation. In this work, Rodin boldly equates the generative hand of God with the ingenious hand of the sculptor" (The MET website).

from clay, shaped their constitution in the womb, knit together their bodies, endowed them with the breath of life, and determined their destiny. This intimate description of God's personal involvement in the creation of humanity creates the context for Job's vivid account of God's mysterious agenda. The sensitive, divine hands that fashioned humankind now seek to pulverize the mortal vessel (10:9), puncture the organs fashioned in the womb (6:4; 16:13), and mutilate the body (16:12–14). The images concerning God's intimate attention to the prenatal development of the human embryo (10:8–12) are reconfigured in the light of his unsettling surveillance of humans (7:17–19), inattention to the bestial existence of the oppressed (chap. 24), and vicious treatment of Job (16:7–11). In fact, the implicit charter of royal dignity bestowed on humans is recast as a diabolical decree that anesthetizes them from their true lot: harsh servitude and psychological anguish under God's totalitarian regime (7:1–6, 17–19; cf. Gen. 1:26–28; Ps. 8:4–8).[11]

Job's reconfiguration of metaphors concerning the creation of humanity,[12] coupled with his focus on human mortality and divine design, produces a distinctive vision of the human condition. While the friends assess humankind in accordance with the anthropocentric vision of their Mesopotamian counterparts, Job assesses humankind in accordance with the theocentric vision of his Mesopotamian counterparts. Job maintains that humanity is not intrinsically sinful; rather, humans are the victims of cruel providence and arbitrary evil woven into the fabric of the cosmos. Job incorporates the theocentric dimension of Mesopotamian thought concerning the human condition, but he modifies the perspective to eliminate human culpability. That is, he adopts the Mesopotamian conception of divine, cosmic design but excludes humanity from the faulty elements of this structure. For Job, humans are not morally defective by virtue of their creaturehood (10:1–17; cf. Eccles. 7:29).[13] They are mortal, finite creatures. Mortality and finitude are part of the goodness of creaturehood. They are not the product of sin.[14] Although humans possess the proclivity to sin and humankind may be characterized as impure before God (Job 14:4), evil is not an innate characteristic of humanity. Rather, evil is an innate characteristic of the world. On this account, it seems that before humans are considered guilty through participation, they are victims of inscrutable, divine design.[15] This vision captures Job's anthropological perspective and provides an explanation for Yahweh's concern with cosmic design, rather than the human condition, in the divine speeches (chaps. 38–41).

For those who hold to the view of total depravity, Job's theological anthropology may miss the doctrinal mark. If nothing else, it privileges humanity's limits and its mortal, ephemeral condition. These aspects of humanity are not the product of sin. They "are constitutive of human being" and the goodness of creaturehood.[16] This is the theological anthropology that Job embodies and expresses in his concluding confession:

> I know that you can do everything,
>> nothing you propose is beyond you.
> [You said,] "Who is this that obscures my design without knowledge?"
>> Indeed, I spoke without understanding,
>> of things beyond me, which I did not know.
> [You said,] "Hear now and I will speak,
>> I will question you and you will cause me to know."
> I have heard of you by the hearing of the ear,
>> but now my eye sees you.

> Therefore, I retract (my lawsuit),
>   and I am comforted concerning dust and ashes. (42:2–6) 📖

Job's climactic confession is a profound acknowledgment of creaturehood. He embraces the limits of human power and knowledge. More specifically, he acknowledges the limits of human knowledge concerning divine design. Yahweh's design, his governance of the world in wisdom and justice, eludes Job. It's above his pay grade as a creature. The recognition of this reality engenders dependence on Yahweh. It breeds trust in Yahweh. And it yields comfort from Yahweh. While Yahweh neither provides a rationale for Job's suffering nor questions Job's moral integrity, his speeches attune Job to his creaturehood and enable him to embrace his limits and his dependence on Yahweh.

Yahweh's Wisdom and Justice

■ READ JOB 38:1–42:6 ■

The embrace of human limits, the goodness of creaturehood, and the dependence on Yahweh that Job's theological anthropology represents are realized and acknowledged through the divine speeches (38:1–42:6). As noted above, these speeches raise many questions about the suitability of Yahweh's "answer" to Job. For some, this answer is less than satisfying. This disappointment is expressed by Slavoj Žižek, who writes:

> Far from providing some kind of satisfactory account of Job's undeserved suffering, God's appearance at the end ultimately amounts to a pure argument of authority grounded in a breathtaking display of power: "You see all that I can do? Can you do this? Who are you, then, to complain?" So what we get is neither the good God letting Job know that his suffering is just an ordeal destined to test his faith, nor a dark God beyond the Law, the God of pure caprice, but, rather, a God who acts like someone caught in the moment of impotence—weakness, at least—and tries to escape his

LITERARY NOTES 📖

Job Confesses

The climax of Job's confession in Job 42:1–6 is riddled with interpretive difficulties. Three issues confront the reader in verse 6:

1. The verb "I retract" lacks an object. If one supplies an implied object, the options range from "myself" and "my words" to "my life" and "my lawsuit."

2. The verb "I am comforted" can also be translated as "repent" or "moved to pity." The rendering "repent" is found elsewhere in the Old Testament without an explicit object, but in all these instances, Yahweh is the one repenting, not a human. The rendering "moved to pity" is possible. With this sense, Job feels sorry for humanity, which must live under the rule of Yahweh.

3. The expression "dust and ashes" occurs only three times in the Old Testament (Gen. 18:27; Job 30:19; 42:6). Elsewhere it describes the nature of humanity (Gen. 18:27) and Job's shameful state (Job 30:19).

It appears that Job retracts his lawsuit against God and expresses comfort concerning his mourning in 42:6. In light of the fact that Job repents in verses 2–3, verses 4–6 appear to introduce another movement in Job's confession. Here Job throws out the lawsuit that he signed in 31:35, bringing the matter of his legal case against God to a resolution. And here Job expresses consolation concerning his state of ritual mourning. Job has been in dust and ashes since 2:8. Now he renounces dust and ashes. He leaves his state of ritual mourning.[9]

predicament by empty boasting. What we get at the end is a kind of cheap Hollywood horror show with lots of special effects.[17]

That is one way of understanding the divine speeches. We get something else from Kathryn Schifferdecker, who contends, "The world is not a safe place, but it is indeed an ordered one. Forces of chaos and wildness are given a place in the world, but they are also given boundaries so that they cannot overwhelm it. . . . Job must acknowledge God's sovereignty; but he must also live with the knowledge that God's sovereignty does not exclude forces indifferent toward, and even dangerous to, humanity. Job must submit to God and learn to live in the untamed, dangerous, but stunningly beautiful world that is God's creation."[18]

The world is not a safe place. Chaos, wildness, and wonder are part and parcel of God's world. This may be hard to square with the world projected in the book of Proverbs, though Proverbs does acknowledge that life in the world is unpredictable: the wicked rule and prosper (Prov. 10:3; 28:12, 28; 29:2), while the righteous fall and fail (24:16; 25:26). The apparent tension between Proverbs' orderly world and Job's chaotic world may signal humanity's inability to make sense of the world. More importantly, it may signal humanity's misunderstanding of God and his relationship to his creation. This is the case with Job. Job's understanding of divine justice through the doctrine of retribution shapes his perception of God, the world, and humanity's relationship with God and the world. God's concern with creation and various creatures across the divine speeches suggests that Job's understanding of his governance of and relationship to the world requires modification. This modification is expressed through the ordering of the divine speeches. The first speech emphasizes God's wisdom (Job 38:1–40:5), and the second explores his justice (40:6–42:6). Whereas Job views God's wisdom through the lens of divine retribution and reward, God contends that his justice must be viewed through the lens of his wisdom. This modification results in a different vision of God's governance of the world.

Yahweh delivers this vision of divine governance through the "storm-wind" (38:1; 40:6). The speaker and the medium of the divine speeches are striking in the broader context of the book. With one exception (12:9), whenever Job or the friends mention God in the poetic dialogue, they use the generic designations *El*, *Eloah*, and *Elohim* ("God") or *Shaddai* ("Almighty"). They do not use the personal, covenantal name of Israel's God, Yahweh. But *Yahweh* speaks to Job, and the speech and sight of Yahweh play a formative role in the transformation of Job's worldview and social location (42:2–6). The same is true of the medium of Yahweh's speech. He appears to Job through the storm-wind. Elsewhere in the Old Testament,

Yahweh appears in a storm-wind to execute judgment (Isa. 40:24; Jer. 23:19; 30:23; Ezek. 13:13). In fact, Job assumed that if God accepted his subpoena, the divine would crush him with a "storm" (Job 9:17). But this is not the case. Yahweh does not manifest his presence through a storm-wind to judge or to crush Job; he manifests his presence through this medium to inspire wonder. While wonder at Yahweh's wonder-full world is the focus of attention in the divine speeches, the subject matter of each speech is distinct.

Figure 6.3. *Job Confessing His Presumption to God Who Answers from the Whirlwind* by William Blake (ca. 1803–5)

Yahweh's Wisdom

The first divine speech attends to Yahweh's wisdom as seen in his astonishing care for the inanimate and animate world. The speech proceeds through a barrage of rhetorical questions. These questions are not designed to assess Job's knowledge. They are designed to exalt God's wisdom, which Job has questioned (e.g., 9:5–7, 24).[19] Yahweh, therefore, asks Job, "Who is this who darkens providence by words without knowledge?" (38:2). Job has darkened Yahweh's providential ordering of things. As a result, Yahweh sheds light on this providence by taking Job on a rhetorical tour of the cosmos, a journey intended to show Job that Yahweh's governance of the world is neither random nor hostile to its spheres, structures, or the creatures that inhabit them.[20] This tour moves from the inanimate to animate world—from the foundation of the earth, the sphere of the stars, the boundaries of the sea, the position of the clouds, the order of the morning, the shape of the earth, the springs of the sea, the gates of the underworld, the place of light and darkness, the storehouses of snow, and the path of the thunderbolt to the lion, the raven, the mountain goat, the wild donkey, the wild ox, the ostrich, the horse, the hawk, and the eagle. Far from representing impersonal geographical and meteorological phenomena, Yahweh's description of the inanimate world is riddled with the language of birth, family, and the home.[21] And far from symbolizing exotic

Figure 6.4. The Babylonian Map of the World (ca. 700–500 BC)

creatures that occupy the peripheral realms of the earth, Yahweh's account of the animate world is filled with the language of vulnerability and strength, the bestial and the beautiful. On this tour of the inanimate and animate world, Yahweh asks two types of questions, each of which serves a distinct rhetorical purpose.[22]

The first are "who" questions: Who set the measurements of the earth's foundation? "Who stretched a line upon it?" (38:5). "Who cut a channel for the torrent of rain and a path for the thunderbolt?" (38:25). These questions assume the parenthetical comment "surely you know" (38:5, 21). Job knows the answers to these questions: "You, Yahweh." And these answers result in a renewed sense of God's wisdom and power.

The second type of question alerts Job to the other side of the coin. If the "who" questions remind Job of Yahweh's wisdom and power, the others remind Job of the limits of human wisdom and power. This type of question takes different forms, ranging from "have you" and "do you" to "can you" questions: "Have you ever commanded the morning, caused the dawn to know its place?" (38:12); "Do you know when the mountain goats give birth? Do you watch over the writhing of the doe?" (39:1); "Can you tie the wild ox in a furrow with ropes? Or will it till the valleys after you?" (39:10). The expected answer to each of these questions is either "No I don't, but you do, Yahweh," or "No I can't, but you can, Yahweh." Neither question seeks to humiliate Job. Each draws Job into a dialogue with Yahweh; each leverages what Job knows to reorient his perspective on God's providential governance of the world and, ultimately, to reestablish Job within this world.

The rhetorical questions across the first speech contribute to this goal in at least two ways. The first is through Yahweh's passing reference to retribution. The retribution principle is a fundamental theological conviction in the poetic dialogue. It governs the friends' view of God's action in the world and their assessment of Job's predicament; and it is the source of both comfort and confusion for Job. Contrary to expectations, Yahweh does not focus on retribution and reward in his extended account of his wise governance of the world. But retributive justice does receive a cursory treatment, and what

Yahweh excludes from this cursory account of retribution is revealing. Yahweh manifests his wisdom by exposing and punishing the wicked (38:15; cf. 40:8–14). Nothing is said, however, of rewarding the righteous.[23] Job and the friends assume that retribution and reward are umbilically linked to God's wisdom and justice. Yahweh intimates that only the punishment of the wicked is linked to his wisdom and justice. This changes things. While the matter is mentioned briefly, it contributes to Job's reorientation and reintegration in the world.

The same is true of God's treatment of wild animals, which constitutes the second contribution of the rhetorical questions to Job's reorientation. These wild animals defy human domestication and control. They do not serve the interests or promote the well-being of humanity. Yet each has a particularity, place, and integrity within Yahweh's wondrous world. The ostrich, for example, is unaware that she may crush her eggs (39:14–15). She treats her young as if they were not her own (39:16). This is not surprising, for God has not given her a share in wisdom (39:17). Instead, God has given her a share in wonder: she flaps her wings wildly and laughs (39:13, 18). She is not ashamed. She occupies an honorable and dignified, albeit mysterious, place in Yahweh's world. If the ostrich exemplifies the mysterious nature of Yahweh's wisdom, other wild animals exemplify their dependence on Yahweh. Yahweh hunts prey for the lion (38:39), provides for the raven (38:41), and exercises providential care over the delivery of the mountain goats (39:1–3). Yahweh's attention to the structure of the inanimate world and those creatures that occupy the margins of the animate world destabilizes Job and broadens his vision of the world. This spacious yet dangerous world bears witness to Yahweh's wisdom and creativity more than his control.[24] It is the world that Job inhabits, a world in which he is invited to rediscover his place as a creature with its own particularity and integrity.

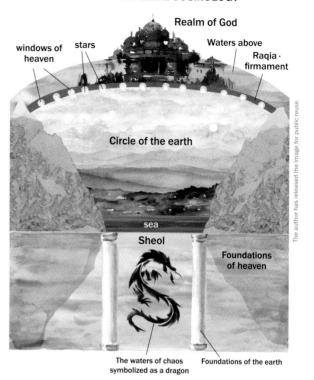

ANCIENT ISRAELITE COSMOLOGY

Realm of God

windows of heaven   stars   Waters above

Raqia · firmament

Circle of the earth

sea

Sheol   Foundations of heaven

The waters of chaos symbolized as a dragon   Foundations of the earth

The author has released the image for public reuse.

Figure 6.5. Based on a figure from Ben Stanhope, *(Mis)interpreting Genesis: How the Creation Museum Misunderstands the Ancient Near Eastern Context of the Bible* (Louisville: Scarab, 2018), 88.

Yahweh's Justice

The second divine speech contributes to the goal of comforting Job and reintegrating him into Yahweh's wise and wonderful world, but it shifts to focus on Yahweh's justice. Justice is foregrounded in Yahweh's second charge against Job: "Will you even pervert my justice? Will you condemn me so that you may be right?" (40:8). Yahweh invites Job to exercise justice by humbling the proud and crushing the wicked (40:9–14). This invitation reinforces and extends Yahweh's passing reference to retribution in the first divine speech (38:15). Again, the punishment of the wicked is mentioned, but the reward for the righteous is missing; it appears that the latter falls outside of the parameters of Yahweh's justice. In view of Job's silence in response to his invitation, Yahweh directs Job's gaze to two monsters: Behemoth and Leviathan (40:15–24; 41:1–34). Like the wild animals in the first divine speech, these undomesticated monsters epitomize a pride and particularity appropriate to their place in the world.[25] Since Job passes on the invitation to adorn himself with "majesty" (i.e., "pride") and "dignity" (i.e., "height," 40:10), so as to bring low the "proud" (40:11–14), Yahweh invites him to consider a pair of proud beasts.

These proud beasts occupy a liminal space.[26] They are between the zoological and the mythological. To adapt and extend an observation by David Clines, if everything in the drama of the book of Job sets the scene for Yahweh's climactic response in the divine speeches, surely this response must

Figures 6.6 and 6.7. Two different depictions of Leviathan: left, "Book of Flowers" (1120) by Lambert of St. Omer; right, "North French Hebrew Miscellany" (ca. 1278–98)

be more than talk about the hippopotamus and the crocodile.[27] Behemoth and Leviathan may be classified as zoological specimens, but according to the second divine speech, they are much more than this. They are powerful monsters that evoke terror. Behemoth typifies strength and stability. Elsewhere in the Old Testament, Leviathan is a mythological creature of chaos whom Yahweh defeats (Ps. 74:13–14; Isa. 27:1). But this is not the case in the second divine speech. Just as Behemoth is created by Yahweh (Job 40:15), so also Leviathan is a creature (41:25). Behemoth and Leviathan pose no threat to Yahweh. In fact, these monsters are not the object of Yahweh's judgment; rather, they are creatures that elicit divine admiration (cf. Ps. 104:26). Behemoth is the first of Yahweh's ways (Job 40:19), a preeminent creature without equal. This preeminence is exhibited

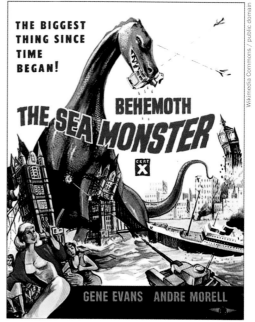

Figure 6.8. British movie poster for *Behemoth, the Sea Monster* (1959)

through the power of Behemoth's body parts: the strength in its loins, the power in the muscles of its belly, the stiffness of its tail, its bones of bronze, and its limbs of iron (40:16–18). Behemoth is the epitome of physical strength (40:24). This strength corresponds with Behemoth's self-confidence; it is not afraid of the threats in its environment (40:23), nor is it a threat to its environment. The mountains bring their produce to Behemoth (40:20); it lounges under the lotus plants, which offer the monster shade (40:21–22). Behemoth's power is appropriate to its place in the world.

Like Behemoth, Leviathan is depicted as a creature without equal (41:33). Leviathan's depiction merges mythological language with imagery reminiscent of divine theophanies elsewhere in the Old Testament to produce a portrait of irrepressible power. Not only does this creature's power have a place in Yahweh's world; its pride also has a place in Yahweh's world. It oversees all that is "lofty," and it is king over all who are "proud" (41:34). This admiration of Leviathan's position and pride is corroborated by Yahweh's description of this beast. It cannot be captured, controlled, or coerced (41:1–9); its limbs, back, eyes, mouth, nostrils, neck, flesh,

RECEPTION HISTORY

Behemoth and Leviathan

The liminal and open nature of Behemoth and Leviathan is attested throughout reception history, in which the rendering of these beasts ranges from natural animals and ancient Near Eastern chaos monsters to Satan, representations of heretics, delicacies consumed at the eschatological feast, political symbols, and monsters that engender the sublime.[h]

and heart are forcible and frightening (41:12–25). Its body is invulnerable (41:26–32).

In contrast to Yahweh's description of Behemoth, his description of Leviathan opens in the second person with a series of questions that focus on Job's inability to tame this monster (41:1–8). And in contrast to the depiction of Behemoth, the depiction of Leviathan includes images associated with Yahweh elsewhere in the Old Testament. Just as Leviathan manifests its fury through sparks of "fire" (41:19) and "coals" from its mouth (41:21), as well as "smoke" from its nostrils (41:20), so also Yahweh manifests his wrath through "smoke" from his nose and "fire" and "coals" from his mouth (Ps. 18:8). These intertextual links associate Yahweh with Leviathan. This association is strengthened by the witness of Job 41:10–11. If the Hebrew text as it stands is retained, Yahweh declares, "No one is so fierce to rouse it [i.e., Leviathan]; and who is the one who can stand before *me*? Whoever confronts *me*, I will repay! Under the whole of heaven, he belongs to *me*!" More than representing a creature of Yahweh, Leviathan is likened to Yahweh. Job cannot control Leviathan. In the same way, Job cannot control Yahweh.

What, if anything, does Yahweh's account of these monsters have to do with Yahweh's justice? In light of Job's refusal to execute his own form of justice by humbling the proud and crushing the wicked (40:6–14), Yahweh parades two paragons of power and pride before the sufferer. According to Yahweh, Behemoth and Leviathan have a place in Yahweh's world, and the power and pride appropriate to each have a place in Yahweh's world. Yahweh's ordered creation includes these creatures. It also includes Job. His power and pride have an appropriate place in Yahweh's ordered world. This construal of order may be at variance with modern conceptions of order, but it is not at odds with Yahweh's rendering of the order of creation. This fits with Schifferdecker's observation, which we noted above: Yahweh's world is ordered, but it is not safe. Job's understanding of God's just governance of the world is determined by a particular understanding of the retribution principle. This understanding of the retribution principle ensures that God's just governance of the world is both ordered and safe, for the wicked are punished and the righteous are rewarded. However, across the divine speeches, Yahweh intimates that the reward of the righteous is not constitutive of his justice. In the second divine speech, Yahweh demonstrates that unsafe forces or creatures occupy a particular and integral place in his just governance of the world. This is captured by Brian Doak, who observes, "God confirms Job's suspicions, while at the same time refuting the Adversary (who posited a rather mechanical, one-sided scheme). This is the shock of the book. It is not shocking to think that God is a creator, or that God is high above us, with ways not our own ways, and so on. It is shocking to think that we might look at nature's fractures and see God's pleasure."[28]

Job has misconstrued God's justice and, by implication, God's governance of the world by reducing his justice and governance to a mechanical system of retribution and reward. Yahweh reframes and reforms Job's misunderstanding of his justice and governance of the world not only by including seemingly chaotic forces or creatures in the economy of his creation but also by filtering these chaotic forces and his just governance of the world through the lens of his wisdom. God governs the world in wisdom. Full stop. His just, providential governance of the world in general and individual human lives in particular should only ever be understood through his wisdom. This changes things. And this changes things for Job.

Conclusion

The book of Job helps readers think through the perplexing nature of life in this world. It explores the accessibility of wisdom in relationship with God and the inefficacy of human wisdom for understanding the vicissitudes of life. The theological anthropologies of Job and the friends consider the nature of human existence and the implications of creaturehood. And the divine speeches cast a theological vision within which to understand human life in Yahweh's wild and wonderous world. The themes of human limits and Yahweh's wisdom and justice serve as a lens through which to think about God and human life in light of the reality of suffering. Job's integrity, fear of God, and protests provide a window into how one might live faithfully in the face of suffering. These themes are the focus of attention in the next chapter.

CHAPTER SEVEN

Theological Themes in Job (2)

The divine speeches play a formative role in the book of Job. These speeches function in at least two ways. They disorient Job, placing him in the broader environment of God's wise and wondrous world, and they reorient Job, inviting him to find his place in God's wild and wondrous world. The divine speeches provide Job with that for which he longed: God. In light of this, it is not surprising that they provide comfort. Job searches for both God and comfort throughout the book. This search is conducted under three theological themes: Job's integrity, the fear of God, and Job's protest.

Job's Integrity

■ READ JOB 29–31 ■

While Yahweh's speeches change things for Job, one thing remains unchanged across the book: Job's integrity. If anything links Job's preaffliction and postaffliction states, it is his integrity. Integrity is the quality that defines Job's character.[1] The way in which Job persists in his integrity provides an answer to the *satan*'s question: Does Job fear God without benefit (1:9)? Integrity is among the virtues attributed to Job throughout the prologue. He is introduced as a man who is blameless (1:1), and when the heavenly court convenes, Yahweh reiterates the narrator's evaluation: Job is blameless (1:8). This evaluation creates the conditions for the *satan*'s question and Job's initial affliction. The *satan* strips Job of all the social and symbolic emblems that provide identity and meaning, leaving him naked (1:13–22). From a social perspective, Job is placeless. His wealth and his children are gone. When the heavenly court convenes again, Yahweh reaffirms and develops his earlier evaluation: Job is blameless, even one who is still holding fast to his integrity (2:3). As with Yahweh's first evaluation, this assessment sets the stage for the second affliction, the attack on Job's health. Covered with boils and sitting on an ash heap, Job scrapes himself, epitomizing a man at odds with himself, outside of and unidentifiable by society and unrecognizable to his friends. Job's wife then provides a climactic twist to the dilemma. If understood as a question, she asks, "Are you still holding fast to your integrity?" (2:9).

Figure 7.1. *Job Mocked by His Wife* by Georges de La Tour (ca. 1625–50)

Job's blamelessness and integrity appear to unite his preafflicted state with his postafflicted state. From a social perspective, Job's existence is discontinuous with his preafflicted life, and from a physical perspective, he may be "bare life,"[2] stripped of all markers of self-identification and estranged even from himself. But what is Job from a moral perspective? The repeated statements about Job's blamelessness and integrity throughout the prologue suggest that, while Job is destroyed, at least one thing remains: his integrity. It is striking that the word for "integrity" (*tummah*) occurs only two times elsewhere in the book: in Job's oath at the end of the dialogue (27:5) and in the context of his extended oath in chapter 31. When read within the context of the developing legal metaphor in the book (see the section titled "Legal Case" below), Job concludes the

HISTORICAL MATTERS

The Divine Council

Belief in the divine council or heavenly court was common across the ancient world. Like an earthly council or court, the heavenly council was an assembly of the gods, which convened to weigh in on certain matters and to determine the outcome of events. A Mesopotamian account of the flood, Enuma Elish, includes a gathering of the divine council to determine the fate of both humanity and the earth. The notion of a heavenly council in the Old Testament is inherent in the divine epithet "Yahweh of hosts"—that is, "Yahweh of the heavenly armies." The heavenly council depicts Yahweh as king, presiding over an assembly of divine beings who execute his decrees and disseminate his messages. This heavenly council may serve as the backdrop for Genesis 1:26–28 (cf. Deut. 32:8). It is explicit in the prologue of Job as well as in Micaiah's encounter with Ahab and Ahab's prophets in 1 Kings 22.

dialogue by swearing to tell the truth, the whole truth, and nothing but the truth:

> As God lives, who has denied my justice,
>   and the Almighty, who has made my life bitter;
> indeed, so long as my breath is in me,
>   and the life breath of God in my nostrils,
> my lips will not speak falsehood,
>   and my tongue will not utter deceit.
> Far be it from me to declare you are right;
>   until I die, I will not put away my integrity [*tummah*] from me.
> I hold fast my righteousness and will not let it go;
>   my heart does not reproach me for any of my days. (27:2–6)

Despite his laments and protests, Job claims to maintain his integrity. His laments and protests may even be construed as an expression of his integrity or honesty. It is something he refuses to abandon (27:5). According to 31:6, Job's integrity is something that he wishes God knew: "Let me be weighed in a just balance, and let God know my integrity" (NRSV). If nothing else, Job's integrity is a quality of his character that constitutes his selfhood in both the prologue and the dialogues.

Job's persistence in both his moral blamelessness and his personal integrity fuels his discourses. This interplay between the moral and personal aspects of Job's integrity makes ethical evaluations of Job difficult. Virtue ethics, however, provides resources for understanding how these two aspects of integrity may coexist. According to Christine McKinnon, integrity is among those qualities that is "not reducible to acts or to dispositions to act," nor does it "dispose [a person] to act in predictable ways."[3] Rather, integrity is a quality that reveals one's orientation toward and commitment to one's being. Accordingly, a person of integrity may be thought of as "one who takes his moral image seriously. . . . The person of integrity is less concerned with how others judge" him than with his relation to himself.[4] On this account, Job is not necessarily dependent on the community or its sociosymbolic system of meaning. The social aspect of integrity is the context in which Job exhibits its personal aspect: his orientation toward and fidelity to his own being. Job's commitment to his moral image and being indicates that he takes his life seriously.[5]

In view of this sketch of integrity, it appears that integrity is a "master virtue," requiring robust self-examination that successfully takes one's life seriously.[6] To some degree, it appears that this is what Job does. The dialogue depicts Job caught in a vortex of self-examination, in which he increasingly acknowledges the bodily, social, moral, and personal dimensions of his wholeness and wretchedness, which cannot be understood within traditional social structures because of the "without benefit" nature of his integrity.[7] The boils on Job's body advertise God's curse (2:7; Deut. 28:35), and his abandonment by family, friends, and community bears witness to his social shame (Job 19:13–20). Job has nothing to show for his moral integrity. Yet he retains his integrity and wholeness and even puts his life in jeopardy to hold fast to his integrity (13:14). Discussions of integrity in virtue ethics provide insight into the dual nature of Job's integrity and reveal the fittingness of Yahweh's "answer" to Job in the divine speeches. Just as the animals and monsters across the divine speeches manifest their integrity through their determination to be themselves, so also Job manifests his integrity through his determination to remain faithful to himself.[8] These animals and monsters are not concerned with how traditional social structures judge them; in the same way, Job should not be concerned with how traditional social structures judge him.

The Fear of God

Job's integrity is bound up with his fear of God. Both the narrator and Yahweh establish the intimate relationship between Job's blamelessness, integrity, and fear of God in the prologue (1:1, 8; 2:3). This vision of virtue and relationship with God raises a basic question: How, if at all, is Job's fear of God comparable to Proverbs' understanding of the fear of Yahweh?

Proverbs' account of the fear of Yahweh is multifaceted. The fear of Yahweh is the "beginning" or "first principle" of wisdom (Prov. 1:7). The fear of Yahweh is the "firstfruit" or consequential product of wisdom's acquisition (2:1–5). The fear of Yahweh is the "first part" of wisdom (9:10). The fear of Yahweh is hating evil (8:13). It is instruction in wisdom, which is inextricably linked with humility (15:33), and it is a skilled practice, embodied across one's life (31:10–31). The fear of Yahweh is indistinguishable from wisdom in Proverbs. Like wisdom, it encompasses the whole of life.

The same is true of the concept in the book of Job, which reinforces and extends Proverbs' depiction of the fear of Yahweh. Like many biblical texts, however, Job has its own grammar or idiom. As noted above, the personal, covenantal name of the God of Israel appears sparingly. The narrator, Job, and the friends prefer the expression fear of "God" or fear of the "Lord" (Job 1:1, 8, 9; 2:3; 28:28; cf. 4:6; 6:14; 15:4; 22:4; 37:24), not the

Figure 7.2. Job and Satan in *The Nuremberg Chronicle* (1493), f. 29r

fear of "Yahweh." This distinctive idiom does not mean that the concept of the fear of God differs from that of Proverbs. Both share basic similarities. As in Proverbs, the fear of God is a mode of being that is manifested in embodied moral actions; it is wisdom shown through a turning away from evil (1:1, 8; 2:3; 28:28; Prov. 3:7; 14:16; 16:6, 17).[9] And as in Proverbs, the fear of God leads to appropriate self-perception; it allows one to recognize and embrace the limits of human wisdom (Job 37:24; Prov. 15:33).

The book of Job reinforces these aspects of the fear of Yahweh in its own idiom, and it also extends Proverbs' description of the fear of Yahweh through a dynamic intratextual dialogue of different voices, each of which contributes to the book's discourse on the fear of God. The narrator initiates this dialogue in the opening verse of the prologue: Job is a man who fears God and turns away from evil (Job 1:1; cf. 28:28). Yahweh reiterates this assessment before both of Job's afflictions (1:8; 2:3), and the *satan* isolates the fear of God in his challenge. The *satan* does not question the external characterizations of Job's character—that is, his blamelessness and uprightness. Instead, the *satan* questions Job's internal character: his fear of God (1:9). This is the posture the *satan* wishes to probe; it is investigated through the *satan*'s afflictions of Job. The narrator's comments intimate that Job maintains his fear of God across these afflictions (1:22; 2:10), and Eliphaz appears to confirm Job's fear of God in his first speech. According to Eliphaz, Job's fear and the integrity of his ways provide the basis for his hope and confidence (4:6). This may be true, but Job longs for "unreserved loyalty" from his friends, a loyalty that would venture to depart from the "fear of the Almighty" for the sake of friendship (6:14). The friends, however, prefer unreserved loyalty to their traditional theology over loyalty to Job. This may explain Eliphaz's comments at the beginning of the second and third cycles of the dialogue, where he changes his tune regarding Job's fear of God. Job's fear no longer serves as the basis of hope or confidence. Why? In light of Job's responses in the first and second cycles of the dialogue, Eliphaz concludes that Job has broken with the fear of God (15:4). In fact, Job's fear of God reproves him (22:4). Ironically, Elihu agrees with

Eliphaz's assessment, for he concludes his discourses with the claim that Job's self-righteousness and "wise heart" betray his lack of proper fear of God (37:23–24). What instigated this alternative evaluation of Job's fear of God? When, if at all, did Job turn from his fear of God?

As suggested above, both Eliphaz and Elihu construe Job's laments, complaints, and protests as evidence that he has parted ways with the fear of God. Job refuses to buy the traditional explanations *about* his suffering or his response to God *in* his suffering sold by Eliphaz and Elihu, respectively. According to them, Job departed from the fear of God at some point in the book's intratextual dialogue on the concept. But according to Yahweh and the narrator, Job has not departed from his fear of God. In fact, the description of wisdom as "fearing the Lord" and "turning away from evil" in Job 28:28 seems to indicate that, while Job is unable to understand his predicament, he possesses wisdom. He fears God. He has never departed from this fear. Why would Eliphaz and Elihu conclude otherwise?

The answer is found in the two ways in which the book of Job extends the concept of the fear of God. The first concerns how the fear of God negotiates the link between personal relationship and theological commitments. Job wishes that unreserved loyalty, undoubtedly an expression of the fear of God, would be so bold as to part with traditional understandings of the fear of God (6:14). That is, Job wishes that personal loyalty would trump doctrinal commitments when it comes to the suffering of a friend.[10] But this is not the case. Eliphaz and Elihu indicate that one's theological commitments override loyalty to one's friend. If the fear of God and wisdom are embodied actions on behalf of and for the sake of another, the friends and Elihu are found wanting. They claim Job has dispensed with the fear of God, but the irony is that they have failed to display the fear of God. They are "theological cowards."[11] The fear of God is not a doctrinal checklist to which one offers mental assent. Proverbs knows this. Job seconds it. But the book of Job exasperates and extends this understanding of the fear of God; it is expressed through interpersonal, other-centered loyalty rather than a personal grasping onto beholden theological positions.

The second way in which the book of Job extends the concept of the fear of God is through Job's laments, complaints, and protests. The friends as well as Elihu read these responses as a departure from the fear of God. This explains Eliphaz's shift in the second and third cycles of the dialogue (15:4; 22:4; cf. 4:6). But as noted above, neither the narrator nor God assesses Job's responses as a departure from the fear of God. To the contrary, Job's laments, complaints, and protests are appropriate expressions of both his integrity and his fear of God.[12] While these expressions of the fear of God may border on the extreme, Yahweh himself endorses them in the epilogue. According to Yahweh, Eliphaz and the friends have not spoken *to* him rightly (42:7–8). The friends speak about God, never *to* God. Job, by contrast, speaks *to* God across the book.[13] This relational posture and pursuit define Job's orientation. More than this, they manifest his fear of God. Yahweh affirms this manifestation of the fear of God as a legitimate expression of faith, an expression of faith that extends Proverbs' conception of the fear of Yahweh.

Job's Protest

■ READ JOB 16 AND 19 ■

Job expresses his integrity and fear of God through his protests. While these protests are delivered in different forms, two such forms deserve specific comment: Job's laments and his legal case.[14]

Lament

Lament is a traditional form of discourse with God. It is the most prominent form of discourse in Psalms and is an indispensable form of speech in the life of faith that names the reality and explores the experience of disorientation.[15] It is not surprising that Job embraces this form of discourse, but he uses it in an unusual way. When Job's laments are read together with the laments in the Psalter and in Lamentations, the differences and similarities are notable. Job uses language and imagery similar to other biblical laments. However, in the unique and "without benefit" conditions of his predicament, he twists traditional language and flips traditional imagery.

Like other biblical lamenters, Job asks why (3:11, 20; 10:18; cf. Pss. 22:1; 43:2; 74:1). He appeals for pity (Job 19:21; cf. Ps. 123:3), but he does not address his appeal to God. Job curses the day of his birth (Job 3:3–10; cf. Jer. 20:14–18), but he does not submit this curse to God, as Jeremiah does. Job depicts himself as a besieged city (Job 19:7–12; cf. Lam. 3:5–9), and he

describes his broken body to claim divine malfeasance rather than elicit divine compassion and
deliverance (Job 7:5; 10:8–12; 16:8; cf. Pss. 22:16–
17; 102:3–11).[16] What's more, Job parodies Psalm
8, portraying God's providential care as terrifying
oversight and scrupulous examination of humans
(Job 7:17–19; Ps. 8:4–6; cf. Job 19:9). 📖

Job acknowledges that his life is a breath (7:7;
cf. Ps. 39:5, 11), but in contrast to the psalmist,
Job adds that he remains without hope and will
never again see good. With the psalmist, Job asks
God to look away (Job 7:19; cf. Ps. 39:13). He
portrays his enemy as a predator, but whereas the
psalmists describe enemies as beasts that gnash
their teeth and rip the faithful to pieces (Pss. 7:2;
22:13; 35:16; 37:12), Job describes God as the
one who gnashes his teeth at him and tears him
in his wrath (Job 16:9). God is Job's personal adversary (16:9; cf. Pss. 3:1; 13:4; 27:2, 12) and even
wages war against Job. Drawing on language and
imagery reminiscent of the divine warrior motif
elsewhere in the Old Testament, Job depicts God
as a combatant who positions his archers around Job, pierces his kidneys
(Job 16:13; cf. Lam. 3:13), shatters him (Job 16:12; cf. Ps. 74:13–14), and
breaches him (Job 16:14; cf. Ps. 89:40; Isa. 42:13; Zeph. 1:14). Rather than
fighting on Job's behalf to enact deliverance, God attacks him. Rather than
using his "hand" to rescue Job (Exod. 7:5; Deut. 4:34; Isa. 41:20; 49:22),
God uses it to smite, strike, smash, crush, and harass Job (Job 5:18; 6:9;
10:8; 19:21).[17] 📜

Job's unusual use of traditional language and imagery from biblical laments corresponds with the unique and unusual nature of his "without
benefit" suffering. But this unusual use of traditional language and imagery
represents only half the story. Job also omits elements characteristic of
biblical laments and includes fresh components. He omits the affirmation
of trust, exchanging it for declarations of innocence (16:17; 23:10–12). He
omits a vow to praise, replacing it with oaths (27:2–6; 31:1–40).[18] These
alterations bear witness to the function of Job's laments. They are not
designed to move God to deliver him from his suffering. Rather, they seek
to evoke another response from God: Job's vindication. Job does not ask
for salvation from his suffering. He asks for justice. This desired response,
however, should not overshadow the fact that Job directs most of his

Parody in the Bible

Will Kynes reexamines the nature and function of parody in representative texts from the Old Testament,
including Psalm 8:4–6 and Job 7:17–19. Whereas
many understand parody as a literary technique that
draws upon a known utterance to subvert its authority
in a humorous fashion, Kynes defines parody as an
"antithetical allusion" that uses a known utterance
as a weapon to ridicule, reject, respect, or reaffirm
the thought of the known utterance. In light of this
typology, Kynes reads Job 7:17–19 as a "reaffirming
parody"—that is, as one that respects and reaffirms
Psalm 8:5. Job uses the status and dignity of humanity
sketched in Psalm 8:5–6 as a weapon to criticize God's
treatment (cf. Job 19:9).[b]

CANONICAL CONNECTIONS

The Divine Warrior

The biblical witness depicts God as a warrior, who
commands his heavenly army (2 Kings 6:6–23; Rev.
19:11–16), leads his people in battle, and fights on
their behalf (Exod. 15:3).

laments to God. Job's honest accusations are appropriate in this relational context. They not only express his integrity; they also indicate that he desires relationship with God.[19] The restoration of this relationship is the goal of Job's laments,[20] but in pursuit of this goal, Job searches for justice and vindication. This search is conducted through Job's legal case.

Legal Case

Job's legal case complements his laments, serving as a second form of protest and another means by which he tries to elicit a response from God.[21] This legal case develops through the dialogue and the speeches of Elihu and culminates in Yahweh's speeches and Job's climactic confession. Job's consideration of a lawsuit against God results from Eliphaz's argument concerning the material ontology and subordinate status of humans within the cosmic order (4:17–19).[22] According to Eliphaz, humanity's corporeal constitution and place in the hierarchical order of the cosmos entail that human beings cannot be righteous before their Maker (4:17). Eliphaz characterizes humans through a moral frame of reference. Job reframes this assessment from a legal frame of reference. From the moral perspective, Job acknowledges that his righteousness is on the line (6:29), and to clear his name and vindicate his moral righteousness, he contemplates a legal path: how a human can "be in the right" before God (9:2). More specifically, Job explores how a human could enter litigation against God (9:3). Eliphaz's attention to the ontological gulf that separates humanity from God is reframed by Job, who attends to the social equilibrium created by the rules that govern the law court. If Job files a lawsuit against God, then God must abide by the rules of the court. Job attempts to eliminate the ontological and the social distance that exists between him and God.[23] His legal case redraws the nature and rules of the playing field. It generates another way of understanding the "roles, norms, and values that govern relationship with God."[24] That is, it creates a context in which God is required to respond.

The idea is ingenious. But Job recognizes that it is riddled with difficulties. If Job files a lawsuit against God, will God respond to the subpoena (9:16)? Who will ensure that God plays by the rules of the law court (9:19, 32–35)? Who will force God to specify the charges against Job (10:2)? Put simply, who will arbitrate the case? Job searches for a mediator throughout the poetic dialogue. He entertains the idea of an arbiter (9:33). He imagines that the earth—as with Abel's blood (Gen. 4:10)—will testify along with a heavenly witness on his behalf (Job 16:18–19). He gropes for a (kinsman) redeemer who will persist in his case against God and win the verdict of not guilty (19:25). Job longs for a legal dispute with God that accords with the egalitarian rules of the court, but he is unable to find a suitable arbitrator. 🖎

Despite this, Job moves forward with his legal case against God. This decision closes the formal dialogue with the friends, initiates Elihu's response, and sets in motion Yahweh's discourses and ultimately Job's confession.

Job's legal case develops in three stages. The first is an oath in which Job swears to tell the truth (27:2–6). The second is Job's testimony, in which he moves from the past to the present (chaps. 29–30). In the past, Job enjoyed intimate friendship with God (29:4–5). As the embodiment of justice and righteousness (29:14), he presided over assemblies at the city gate, serving as eyes for the blind, feet for the lame, a father to orphans, and a refuge for the widow (29:7–17). He was loved by his community and feared by the wicked (29:21–25). But things have changed. Job's suffering has caused the community to turn on their righteous representative. Job is showered with shame (30:9–15) and assaulted by God (30:18–23). This testimony sets the scene for the third and final stage of Job's developing legal case: Job's extended oath of innocence, which clears him of all guilt (chap. 31).[25] Job signs the lawsuit, setting the legal process in motion:[26]

CANONICAL CONNECTIONS

Kinsman Redeemer

"Kinsman redeemer" is a kinship term within Israelite family law, denoting close relatives who are responsible for other members of the clan. Israelite family law sketches five responsibilities of the kinsman redeemer:

1. Redeeming a family's land that had been acquired by someone outside of the clan (Lev. 25:25–30)
2. Redeeming family members who had been sold into slavery (Lev. 25:47–55)
3. Monitoring a person who committed manslaughter against a member of the family or putting to death one who murdered a member of the family (Num. 35:19–27)
4. Receiving restitution for a deceased family member who was the victim of a crime (Num. 5:5–10)
5. Securing justice for a family member involved in a lawsuit (Job 19:15; Jer. 50:24)

While Job is not an Israelite, the book of Job was composed by an Israelite author for an Israelite audience. It leverages the responsibilities of the kinsman redeemer, especially the responsibility to secure justice for a family member involved in a lawsuit.

> Oh, that I had one to hear me!
>> Look, my signature! Let the Almighty answer me!
>> Oh, that I had the document written by my adversary!
> Surely, I would carry it on my shoulder;
>> I would tie it on me as a crown;
> I would declare to him the number of my steps;
>> like a prince I would approach him. (31:35–37)

Job's signature silences the friends (32:1), but it provokes Elihu, who plays the role of Job's (unwanted) arbiter. Elihu promises vindication, but rather than vindicating Job, he vindicates God and indicts Job for his self-righteousness. This indictment, however, does not close Job's legal case. Contrary to Elihu's claim that God will not answer Job (35:12–16), Yahweh answers the plaintiff from the storm. While legal language recedes in Yahweh's speeches, forensic terms at the conclusion of the first speech and the introduction to the second suggest that Job's legal case remains in view. Yahweh cross-examines Job. He characterizes Job as one who arraigns or contends (40:2) with God, as well as one who condemns God so that he might be right (40:8).[27] When read in view of Job's lawsuit, Yahweh's speeches may be construed as a cease-and-desist order. They invite Job to withdraw his legal case, an invitation Job accepts. He renounces his legal pursuit. Yahweh's responses comfort and console Job; his presence makes litigation unnecessary.

Together with his laments, Job's legal case is an expression of his integrity and fear of God. This case is directed against God, it has to do with God, and it is indispensable in Job's pursuit of God. This orientation toward God indicates that, despite Job's misguided attempt to arraign God, his legal case aligns with his genuine faith. It is among the ways in which Job seeks understanding through suffering.

Conclusion

If Proverbs casts a vision of fear seeking understanding, the book of Job stages a performance of suffering seeking understanding. The understanding Job seeks, however, is not the understanding that he receives. Job never learns the reason for his loss or the physical and psychological dimensions of his suffering. Instead, he learns about God, specifically how to think about God *in* suffering and within a world marked by suffering.[28] This exercise in theological understanding neither invalidates personal experience nor silences one's challenges to God; it places painful experiences and unanswered questions in the context of God's wisdom and providential governance of all things. It situates forms of verbal protest in relationship with God. According to the book of Job, when theology crashes into personal experience, neither is scrapped. Together, they forge genuine faith.[29] While the book of Job has many things to say about the Christian life, three deserve specific comment.

Genuine Faith

The first is the nature of genuine, courageous faith. Job demonstrates that one can fear God "without benefit" (1:9)—that is, devoid of ulterior motives and the expectation of beneficial treatment in relationship with God. Job embodies a courageous form of faith, one that pushes the boundaries of traditional understandings of the fear of God. This type of faith embraces lament and pursues a legal case against God. This form of faith pulls every weapon out of the rhetorical arsenal to move God to respond. It refuses to accept shallow theological answers to the enigmas of human life, to take the easy way out and embrace false repentance, and to give up on relationship with God altogether. This expression of faith explains why James refers to the perseverance of Job (James 5:11). Like Job, the Christian is called to persevere. Just as the testing of Job's faith produces perseverance, so also the testing of the Christian's faith produces perseverance (1:3). Perseverance is not only the product of testing; it is also the stance that characterizes the Christian life. According to the book of Revelation, the faithful are marked by perseverance (Rev. 1:9; 2:2, 19; 3:10; 13:10; 14:12). Job is a model of perseverance. More than this, Job is a model of one who relentlessly seeks God, seeks wisdom, and seeks justice.

The pursuit of justice, unfortunately, is peripheral for many modern Christians. This sad reality is due to many things. At minimum, it is due to progressive revelation and the expectation of judgment in the afterlife. This gives many an excuse to not pursue God and the manifestation of his justice in the manner of Job; it gives many modern Christians an opportunity to "punt" to the eschaton and God's definitive judgment. This is not entirely wrong, but it lacks the clarity, conviction, and desire for God's kingdom to come and his will to be done *on earth* as it is in heaven (Matt. 6:10). Job holds out hope for a heavenly encounter *coram Deo*, "before the face of God" (Job 19:26–27). This hope, however, never deflates Job's persistent pursuit of God and his justice. He is an exemplar of genuine and courageous faith.

God's Providence

Job's faith is a persevering faith, but this type of faith does not offer comfort. Comfort is received through the second contribution of the book: its doctrine of God. The divine speeches focus on certain aspects of the doctrine of God—specifically, God's wisdom, acts of creation, sovereignty, and justice, but they privilege God's providence. John Webster notes, "Providence concerns God's continuing relation to the world he has created";[30] and Herman Bavinck specifies that providence refers to "that act of God by which from moment to moment he preserves and governs all things."[31] God's astonishing care for the inanimate and animate world is expressed through the language of providence. Yahweh knows the way to light's dwelling place and the home of darkness (38:19–20); he frequents the storerooms of snow and hail (38:22–23); he satisfies the thirst of the wastelands, causing them to flourish (38:25–27); he knows the paternity of the rain and the dew, as well as the nativity of the ice and frost (38:28–29); he guides the constellations (38:32); he provides prey for the lion and the raven (38:39–41); he watches the writhing of the doe (39:1); he releases the wild donkey and furnishes it with a dwelling place in which to express its freedom (39:5–8); he gives the horse its strength and clothes its neck with a mane (39:19); he endows Behemoth with physical power (40:15–16); and he preserves the existence of Leviathan (41:33).

All these aspects of divine providence are inextricably related to one another. God's relation to the inanimate and animate world is described in terms of his preservation *and* his governance *and* the genuine concurrence of divine and creaturely agency. Job has darkened Yahweh's providence (38:2), so Yahweh explains it. This explanation is strange, for it focuses on Yahweh's providential care for and preservation of the strange. But following Mary Midgley, this explanation provides both Job and Christians with what they need: "We need the vast world, and it must be a world that does not need us; a world constantly capable of surprising us, a world we did not program, since only such a world is the proper object of wonder."[32]

PHILOSOPHICAL ISSUES

The Sublime

Biblical scholars draw on the concept of the sublime in their reading of the divine speeches. Edmund Burke distinguished the beautiful from the sublime in his work *A Philosophical Enquiry into the Origin of Our Ideas of the Sublime and Beautiful*. As Burke argues,

For sublime objects are vast in their dimensions; beautiful ones comparatively small: beauty should be smooth and polished; the great, rugged and negligent: beauty should shun the right line, yet deviate from it insensibly; the great in many cases loves the right line; and when it deviates, it often makes a strong deviation: beauty should not be obscure; the great ought to be dark and gloomy: beauty should be light and delicate; the great ought to be solid, and even massive. They are ideas of a very different nature; one being founded on pain, the other on pleasure; and however they may vary afterwards from the direct nature of their causes, yet these causes keep up an eternal distinction between them; a distinction never to be forgotten by any whose business it is to affect the passions.[c]

Put simply, beauty evokes love, whereas the sublime evokes fear. Sublimity names an aesthetic experience in the face of overwhelming objects or events.

Immanuel Kant adopts and develops Burke's distinction between beauty and the sublime. More specifically, Kant identifies two types of sublime experience: the mathematical sublime and the dynamical sublime. The mathematical sublime concerns the magnitude of an object or event, which eludes a person's mathematical measurement and escapes their aesthetic grasp. The dynamical sublime is an experience in which a person is confronted with a powerful object or event that overcomes the resistance of their will. According to Kant, the mathematical sublime reveals a person's desire for total comprehension, whereas the dynamical sublime reveals a person's desire for freedom of the will.[d]

These types of the sublime may serve as a heuristic guide for reading the divine speeches in the book of Job. In the first speech, Job is confronted with the mathematical sublime. In the second speech, he is confronted with the dynamical sublime. Taken together, the divine speeches expose Job's demand for total comprehension and freedom of the will. They illuminate his finitude through a vast world and before powerful monsters.

The vast world painted by Yahweh illuminates his wise providence, shedding light on what Job has darkened. This portrait of the world comforts and consoles Job by providing perspective on the anomalies, atrocities, and harsh vicissitudes of human life. It also offers consolation to Christians "by instructing them in how to read the world as an ordered, not random, reality—ordered by divine love and directed by divine power for God's glory and the creature's good."[33]

The vision of Yahweh's wisdom and providential care offers Job the comfort the friends have failed to provide. This failure leads to the book's third contribution to the Christian life—namely, genuine friendship.

Genuine Friendship

Samuel Balentine is right to a degree: "The Book of Job is about friendship."[34] The matter of friendship lingers across the book, binding together its parts.[35] While Proverbs acknowledges that friendships vary (Prov. 17:17; 18:24; 19:4, 6), Job illustrates how friendships change. If genuine friendship is marked by the virtues of love, loyalty, and perseverance for the sake of another (Prov. 17:9, 17; 18:24; 27:5, 6, 10), Job's friends are marked by a love for and loyalty to, as well as a perseverance in, their theological positions. Theology trumps relational commitment. Job's friends divorce orthodoxy from orthopraxy. They blame Job rather than console him. In so doing, they serve as a cautionary tale regarding the nature of friendship. They are caricatures. Eliphaz, Bildad, and Zophar serve as a counterpoint to genuine, biblical friendship. These so-called friends also create the conditions for exploring the restoration of broken friendships. The epilogue demonstrates that forgiveness is available for friends who fail to speak and to act rightly on behalf of another (Job 42:7–9). Job's relationship with his friends is not only restored; his experience of suffering is also accepted by a community that honors him and integrates him into its life (42:11).

The friends' failure to embody genuine friendship in their relationship with Job creates a relational vacuum that is filled by an unexpected figure in the book: God. Whereas the speeches of the friends are ineffective in comforting Job, Yahweh's speeches provide consolation. Whereas the friends are inhospitable to Job's protests, Yahweh allows Job to vent his anger and sorrow before inviting him to find his place in Yahweh's wise and wonderfull world. Friendship with God was unthinkable in both ancient Near Eastern and classical thought. The book of Job gestures to this intimate relationship between unequal parties with radically different natures. And the canon of Scripture develops this intimate relationship between the triune God and finite creatures. Those who fear Yahweh experience the friendship

Friendship in Classical Thought

According to Aristotle, social and economic equality form the foundation of friendship. Comparable character or virtue nurtures friendship. These ties that bind together friends indicate that divine-human friendship is impossible from an Aristotelian perspective. Aristotle articulates this reality in his extended discussion of friendship:

> However, equality does not seem to be the same in friendship as it is in just actions; for in the case of just actions equality is primarily that which is in accord with merit, quantitative equality being secondary; but in friendship quantitative equality is of primary and equality of merit only of secondary importance. This becomes evident if a wide gap develops between the parties in respect of virtue or vice, or of affluence or anything else; because they no longer remain friends, and do not even expect to do so. This is most evident in the case of the gods, because they are the furthest above us in respect of all good things; but it is obvious also in the case of royalty, because those who are far inferior do not expect to be their friends either, nor do people of no account expect to be friends of those who are outstandingly good or wise.[e]

of God (Ps. 25:14; cf. Job 29:4). From this theological perspective, it is not surprising that Abraham is a friend of God (Isa. 41:8; James 2:23) and that Jesus calls his disciples friends (John 15:14–15). Divine-human friendship is not the product of human initiative; it is created through divine initiative (1 John 3:1–2). Job is the recipient of Yahweh's friendship. Yahweh manifests his loyalty to Job by speaking to him and providing him with the comfort for which he longed.

CHAPTER EIGHT

Ecclesiastes

Finitude Seeking Understanding

What does it mean to be human? This is the fundamental question that the first-person speaker in Ecclesiastes—Qoheleth ("assembler," "Teacher" [NRSV])—seeks to answer.[1] Considering this question raises many more. What is a human being? What is good for humans in a world where the value of pursuits and activities is ambiguous at best and inconsequential at worst? Should humans embrace or seek to transcend their limits? Is human existence only meaningful and authentic when it is "being toward death"?[2] Put theologically, How, if at all, should one perform the practice of memento mori, "remember you must die"? What happens if people follow Immanuel Kant—"*Sapere aude!* Have courage to use your *own* understanding!"—and attune their lives to the chorus of the Enlightenment?[3] These are difficult questions. They are the same sort of questions that Qoheleth both asks and explores. In so doing, he exemplifies a particular stance on being-in-the-world: finitude seeking understanding.

What Is Qoheleth's Problem?

■ READ ECCLESIASTES 4:1–16; 9:1–6 ■

Finitude is characteristic of creaturely life. Qoheleth stares the reality of finitude squarely in the eye. He faces the frustrations that riddle finite human experience, and he dispenses some harsh conclusions that are difficult to absorb. According to Qoheleth, human wisdom is unable to determine the future and to decipher the work of God. Humans cannot grasp the temporal conditions of the world they inhabit. Human memory

Figure 8.1. Replica (by Vladimir Kakuc, 1959) of *Dance of Death* fresco by Janez iz Kastva (1490)

is amnesic. Wealth produced by hard work is vulnerable to loss. Fools occupy positions of power. Social institutions fail to enact justice. The oppressed are lonely. Death comes to all, regardless of moral or social status. From different angles, through different topics, and in different ways, Qoheleth circles around a set of human pursuits, activities, and circumstances to press the point that humans are contingent. This reality of creaturehood creates the conditions for asking a basic question: What, then, is good for finite creatures? Readers of Ecclesiastes wrestle with Qoheleth's concern. For some, it is ontological and anthropological. For others, it is epistemological. For still others, it is axiological and ethical. The arguments for each are compelling because each captures a facet of Qoheleth's concern.

Ontology and Anthropology

One facet of Qoheleth's concern is ontological and anthropological. He ruminates on the nature of humanity, the nature of the world, and the nature of God. Whereas human generations go and come, the earth retains a permanence that exceeds creaturely contingency (1:4).[4] Human being is given by the Creator (12:1), and the human life breath returns to the divine Giver at death (12:7; cf. 3:19–20). In contrast to human activities, God's activities remain forever (3:14). Humans are finite; but God has "hard-wired the infinite within human subjectivity," creating an ontological condition that compels humans to transgress the limits of creaturehood (3:11).[5] Put differently, humans desire to transcend their mortal existence and possess divine, immortal existence (1:14; 2:11, 17, 26; 4:4, 16; 6:9).

PHILOSOPHICAL ISSUES

Ontology and Anthropology

Ontology is a branch of philosophy that considers the nature of being rather than specific beings. Ontology is a part of metaphysics, which explores first principles and things beyond the physical world, like time and space.

Anthropology is a broad area of research that studies human cultures and societies as well as the biological and physiological features of human beings.

Qoheleth's reflections exhibit a concern with ontology in general and anthropology in particular. This concern is captured by C. L. Seow, who contends:

> Qohelet always begins his reflection with humanity and the human condition. He concludes at every turn that mortals are not in control of the things that happen in this world. They are not in control of their destiny. This is why Qohelet says that everything is *hebel* [vanity]. He does not mean that everything is meaningless or insignificant, but that everything is beyond human apprehension and comprehension. But in thinking about humanity, Qohelet also speaks of God. People are caught in this situation where everything is *hebel*—in every sense of the word. God is transcendent and wholly other, but humanity is "on earth." Yet God is related to humanity, and God has given humanity the possibilities of each moment. Hence people must accept what happens, whether good or bad. They must respond spontaneously to life, even in the midst of uncertainties, and accept both the possibilities and limitations of their being human.[6]

Epistemology

Seow's summary distills Qoheleth's ontological-anthropological concern, and it gestures to another concern that is umbilically linked to Qoheleth's theological anthropology—namely, epistemology. The fact that "everything is beyond human apprehension and comprehension" taints the proverbial perfume of creaturely existence (cf. 10:1). More than acknowledging the ontological distinction between humanity and the divine, Qoheleth's reflections plumb the severe limits of human wisdom and the epistemic disparity between human knowledge and God's knowledge. According to Qoheleth, God has set eternity in the human mind so that humans cannot discover the work that God has done *from beginning to end* (3:11).

LITERARY NOTES

A Chasing of Wind

Thomas Bolin captures the human desire for immortality and divinity through his interpretation of the refrain in Ecclesiastes that all is *hebel* and a chasing of wind (1:14; 2:11, 17, 26; 4:4, 16; 6:9). According to Bolin, this refrain conveys the notions that "all is mortal, but strives for immortality" or that "all is human, but strives for divinity."[a]

Epistemology

Epistemology is a branch of philosophy that attends to the sources, substance, and justification of knowledge. It seeks to provide an account of what can be known and how it may be known.

Axiology, Ethics, and Aesthetics

Axiology is the study of value and those things that are considered valuable; it includes ethics and aesthetics. Ethics is a branch of inquiry that focuses on moral principles that inform a person's behavior.

God has made good days and bad days so that humans cannot perceive anything *after them* (7:14). The works of the righteous and the wise are in the hand of God, and no one knows anything *before them* (9:1). Put simply, humans cannot discern the work that God has done under the sun (8:17; 11:5). This work operates in a temporal framework too broad for human apprehension, and it exists in a causal nexus that eludes human comprehension. The limits of human wisdom preclude a grasp of the meaning, value, and implications of both divine and human activity within the temporal sweep of finite existence. Qoheleth's concern is not merely ontological and anthropological; it is also epistemological.[7]

Axiology and Ethics

Qoheleth's ontological-anthropological and epistemological concerns lead to a consideration of axiological and ethical matters. Given human finitude, Qoheleth explores what is good for human beings. He betrays his axiological-ethical concern through his dynamic and varied use of the terms "good" and "rejoice," combined with economic language to assess the human predicament (e.g., "profit" and "toil" [1:3], "occupation/business" [1:13], "deficit" [1:15], "portion" [3:22], "wages" [4:9], "assets" [6:2], "accounting" [7:25]). Qoheleth evaluates human aspirations, activities, and circumstances through a term that resides within the conceptual realm of axiology: *hebel*, often translated "vanity" (1:2; see the discussion of *hebel* below).[8] And he identifies what is good for humans to do (3:12, 22; 5:18; 8:15). Qoheleth's axiological and ethical reflections are a natural corollary to his ontological-anthropological and epistemological observations.

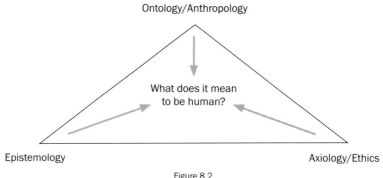

Figure 8.2

Qoheleth's Problem and the Philosophical Trinity

The interrelationship among ontology/anthropology, epistemology, and axiology/ethics across Ecclesiastes indicates that these concerns are not mutually exclusive. Qoheleth joins together what the history of Western philosophy and many readers of Ecclesiastes put asunder: the inseparable and indispensable union among ontology/anthropology *and* epistemology *and* axiology/ethics.[9] The members of this philosophical trinity provide unique frames of reference for exploring a central question posed by Qoheleth: What does it mean to be a creature in this world?

The Interpretive Problems in Ecclesiastes

Qoheleth's problem is multifaceted. The same is true of the interpretive problems in Ecclesiastes. These problems include matters of date and authorship, the structure of the book, Qoheleth's contradictions, and the meaning of the term *hebel*.

Date and Authorship

The date of Ecclesiastes's composition hangs on an understanding of its language, Qoheleth's thought, and the social climate of his observations. For most scholars, the language of the book, its resonances with aspects of Greek thought, and its resemblance to certain socioeconomic conditions suggest that Ecclesiastes was composed in either the Persian period (539–331 BC) or the Ptolemaic period (323–30 BC). Qoheleth's monetary language and concerns reflect a Persian background, while the bureaucratic hierarchy sketched in 5:8–9 reflects the Ptolemaic administrative system. For others, the book's features betray an exilic date of composition (596–538 BC).

While the precise date and context of Ecclesiastes remain open, explorations of its language and content indicate that the book does not stem from the Solomonic era. This conclusion informs proposals for the identity of Qoheleth, the first-person speaker within the book. Qoheleth may be Solomon, a king, a sage, a philosopher, a businessman, a fictional

The Date of Ecclesiastes

A Persian or Ptolemaic date for the composition of Ecclesiastes derives from numerous factors. In addition to many Aramaisms, the book includes a few Persian loanwords (i.e., "park" [*pardes*], 2:5; "decision" [*pitgam*], 8:11). Documents from a fifth-century Jewish community at Elephantine in Egypt clarify the economic language within and the social world of Ecclesiastes. Like Ecclesiastes, these documents include the language of "profit," "deficit," and "accounting."

The system of Persian royal land grants may serve as the backdrop of God's bestowal of gifts in Ecclesiastes 5:18–6:2. Other documents from the Ptolemaic period mirror the economic language of Ecclesiastes and Qoheleth's reflections on government bureaucracy and social oppression.

The nature of Qoheleth's thought also suggests a Ptolemaic setting for the composition of Ecclesiastes. His presumed skepticism and determinism are comparable to certain facets of Hellenistic philosophy.[b]

The Language and Date of Ecclesiastes

Focusing on the linguistic evidence for a late dating of Ecclesiastes, Daniel Fredericks argues that the words and grammatical features considered late either have antecedents in earlier texts or betray a particular Hebrew vernacular. According to Fredericks, Ecclesiastes was composed in the exilic period.[c]

Qoheleth as a Type of Christ

Among early Christian readers of Ecclesiastes, Jerome understood Qoheleth as a type of Christ. His understanding represents a stream of Christian interpretation. According to Jerome, Christ is Ecclesiastes: he is the teacher/preacher, and he is the head of the church, the *ekklesia*. This way of reading was developed by Gregory of Nyssa, who mapped Qoheleth's quest onto Christ's incarnation.[d]

construct, an orthodox saint, or an unorthodox sinner, among other options.[10] Regardless of how one construes Qoheleth's identity, his relationship to the author of Ecclesiastes remains hazy. The third-person voice of the prologue and epilogue (1:1–2; 12:9–14; cf. 7:27) distinguishes the book's frame from the first-person reflections of Qoheleth (1:12–12:8). Do these discrete voices represent different authors? Is Qoheleth the author of his first-person reflections? Or is a single author responsible for the book? That is, is the frame narrator the creator of Qoheleth's words as well as the composer of the prologue and epilogue?[11] As the history of reception reveals, whether Qoheleth's identity is constructed through the internal witness of Ecclesiastes or through external texts, his polysemous portrayal allows for different renderings.

Structure

The structure of Ecclesiastes also lacks clarity. The book does not follow a logical progression of thought and even defies modern conceptions of coherence. This does not mean that Ecclesiastes is a hodgepodge of random reflections; it contains at least four macrostructural features that orient one to the design of the whole. The first is the repetition of Qoheleth's basic conclusion: "Vanity of vanities, says Qoheleth, vanity of vanities! All is vanity" (1:2; cf. 12:8). This conclusion serves as an envelope around Qoheleth's observations; it frames his pursuit and informs his evaluation of various activities under the sun. The second structural feature is comparable to the first and concerns the placement of three poems within Qoheleth's exploration (1:4–11; 3:1–8; 12:1–7). Whereas Qoheleth opens his reflections with a poem pertaining to the place of human life in the context of cosmic time (1:4–11), he concludes them with a poem on the dissolution of human life in the context of eschatological time (12:1–7). These conceptions of time are mediated through the middle poem in 3:1–8, which situates human life within the cycles or seasons of present, divine time. The opening and closing poems create a literary framework for Qoheleth's reflections, and each poetic interlude makes a distinct contribution to Qoheleth's understanding of human life in the context of time. The third structural feature creates a measure of unity across Qoheleth's quest—namely, Qoheleth's use of the first-person voice. This autobiographical voice not only structures Qoheleth's mental and embodied discoveries; it also shapes the reader's engagement with the things Qoheleth has seen, perceived, and discovered.[12] Joy is among the things that Qoheleth has perceived, and his recurring call to joy constitutes the fourth structural feature of the book (2:24–26; 3:12–13, 22; 5:17–19; 7:14; 8:15; 9:7–10; 11:7–10). This call is woven throughout Qoheleth's observations, and it progresses from an impersonal recommendation to a personal stance that the reader is commanded to embrace.[13] If Qoheleth ventures anything like a resolution to the harsh realities of human finitude, it is found in the ethical stance of joy.

Figure 8.3. Life, death, time. *Vanitas* by Philippe de Champaigne (ca. 1671).

Contradictions

At minimum, these macrostructural features suggest that Ecclesiastes has at least a loose structure. Refrains, recurring calls, and the position of poetic pieces provide points of orientation that direct the reader's interpretation of Qoheleth's reflections. These hermeneutical points of orientation are necessary, for they help the reader navigate a distinctive characteristic of Qoheleth's thought: his contradictions.

Qoheleth's contradictions are real, not apparent. They reflect the contradictory perceptions, experiences, and realities of human being-in-the-world,[14] and they characterize the mode of Qoheleth's thought. Incongruities are integral to Qoheleth's exploration; the question is not whether Qoheleth's contradictions contribute to the meaning of Ecclesiastes, for the meaning of Ecclesiastes "resides precisely *in*" these contradictions.[15] The question is how a reader should interpret these contradictions.

The history of reception bears witness to many different approaches,[16] including different species of harmonization (b. Shabbat 30b), the attribution of contradictory opinions to different authors,[17] Qoheleth's psychological struggle between Israelite thought and autonomous Greek thought,[18] and claims that certain statements are unmarked quotations from another speaker, which Qoheleth cites to refute.[19] Some of these approaches try to neutralize Qoheleth's contradictions. Others attempt to furnish an interpretive framework for explaining them. The best approach is to receive Qoheleth's contradictions as genuine incongruities that humans perceive and experience. Human wisdom, for example, is both valuable (2:13; 7:11) and without value (2:14; 6:8). Both are true because both reflect the nature of human wisdom. Both, in other words, describe the sort of wisdom appropriate to finite creatures.

Hebel

Qoheleth's contradictions are indispensable for understanding the central evaluative term in Ecclesiastes: *hebel*.[20] This word refers to the phenomenon of breath or vapor (Ps. 144:4; Isa. 57:13). Many biblical texts leverage the physical qualities of this phenomenon to elicit notions of transience (Job 7:16; Ps. 62:10), uselessness (Deut. 32:21; Isa. 30:7; Jer. 16:19), or misapprehension (Ps. 39:6; Zech. 10:2).[21] These figural extensions of *hebel* construe things as ephemeral, insubstantial, opaque, or ambiguous. Ecclesiastes privileges this metaphorical sense of *hebel*. As Douglas Miller notes, *hebel* is a rich symbol, a pregnant image that produces a set of irreducible meanings.[22] This semantic reality has produced a variety of different proposals for the meaning of *hebel* in Ecclesiastes, ranging from "enigmatic," "transitory," and "illusory" to "futile," "absurd," and "meaningless."[23] The rendering of *hebel* reflects one's understanding of the nature of Qoheleth's thought and, more specifically, Qoheleth's "problem." If Qoheleth's problem is ontological or anthropological, then *hebel* may be understood as "transitory," "illusory," or "futile." If Qoheleth's problem is theological or cosmological, then *hebel* may mean "absurd" or "meaningless." If his problem is epistemological, then *hebel* may be translated as "enigmatic" or "mysterious." The meaning of *hebel* and the nature of Qoheleth's thought are intimately related to one another.

While *hebel* may convey different nuances in discrete contexts within Ecclesiastes, it is reasonable to assume that Qoheleth's use of the evaluative term aligns with his fundamental conclusion: "*Habel habalim!* All is *habel*" (Eccles. 1:2; 12:8). More than framing Qoheleth's quest, this conclusion frames one's interpretation of *hebel* across the book; it suggests that

Figure 8.4. Toiling under the sun. *The Sower* by Vincent van Gogh (1888).

all the things Qoheleth considers *hebel* are variations on or illustrations of this superlative exclamation. Ecclesiastes 1:3—"What profit belongs to a person in all his/her toil, which he/she toils under the sun?"—helps clarify the "all" in the superlative exclamation of 1:2. The expression "All is *hebel*" is interpreted as "all" human toil. This means that *hebel* does not refer to everyone or everything; it is restricted to human activities, experiences, and aspirations.[24] This explains why Qoheleth never uses *hebel* to describe God, God's activities, or God's world.[25] If these are not *hebel*, then it appears that the renderings "absurd" and "meaningless" miss the mark, for these translations intimate that Qoheleth casts judgment on God, God's world, or the nature of human life in relation to God. God is not Qoheleth's problem.

Humanity and epistemology, by contrast, remain significant problems for Qoheleth. The limits of finite existence preclude any potential profit in human pursuits. What makes these pursuits *hebel*, however, is not the epistemological limits of humans. Qoheleth does not cast judgment on human knowing per se; rather, he casts judgment on humanity's failure to embrace its place in the world and to live in light of the limited possibilities available to finite creatures. On this account, *hebel* issues a twofold judgment: (1) it evaluates human pursuits for profit as illusory, and (2) it evaluates human assumptions or aspirations concerning profit as delusions.[26] Like vapor, human pursuits and aspirations are outside of human control. These matters are opaque and illusory. They are perceptible yet fluctuating phenomena that elude human mastery by virtue of their unimaginable depth and immeasurable place in the context of divine and cosmic time.

Conclusion

Qoheleth seeks to answer a basic question: "What profit belongs to a person in all his/her toil, which he/she toils under the sun?" (1:3). Qoheleth also asks, "What does it mean to be a creature in this world?" He models finitude seeking understanding, and his pursuit of understanding traverses the realms of ontology/anthropology, epistemology, and axiology/ethics. The investigation below will explore these realms of Qoheleth's concern and develop the theological themes that mark each domain.

Christian Reading Questions

1. How is the wisdom of Ecclesiastes similar to and different from the wisdom of Proverbs and Job?
2. From a theological perspective, how is life *hebel*? How is life good?
3. How would you answer the question raised by the book of Ecclesiastes: What does it mean to be human?
4. Does anything in Ecclesiastes strike you as unorthodox? How does the book of Ecclesiastes function as Christian Scripture?

CHAPTER NINE

Theological Themes in Ecclesiastes

Q oheleth has a problem. This problem is multifaceted. It emerges through the interrelationship between God and humanity, the world and human pursuits. The convergence of these relationships raises questions about the meaning of human being and the meaningfulness of human life. Qoheleth addresses these problems and questions head-on. They will be treated here under the headings of ontology/anthropology, epistemology, and axiology/ethics.

Ontology/Anthropology

■ READ ECCLESIASTES 1:1–11; 5:13–6:12; 12:1–8 ■

Qoheleth's concern with ontology is seen in his observations about the natures of God, the world, and humanity, each of which informs his understanding of what it means to be a creature in this world.

God

On the surface, Qoheleth's depiction of God is grim.[1] Qoheleth refers to God with the generic designation *Elohim*; he never uses the personal, covenantal name of Israel's God, Yahweh. This impersonal way of speaking about God coincides with Qoheleth's seemingly cold reflections on God and God's activity. God is in heaven, far removed from humans on earth (5:2). From this transcendent position, God functions as the CEO of the cosmos, assigning humans a severe occupation with which to be occupied (1:13). Some are allotted the task of gathering and collecting resources for the benefit of others (2:26). Others are given everything desirable in life, with one exception: God has not enabled them to enjoy these things (6:2). God tests humans to show them that they are beasts (3:18). He implants a foreign entity into finite creatures: infinity (3:11). And God ensures that no one can straighten what he has made crooked (7:13; cf. 1:15). No one can contend with him (6:10).

This sketch of "Qoheleth's God" is distilled by Michael Fox, who argues that, for Qoheleth, "God runs the world like a distant monarch ruling a minor province. The ruler must be feared, not cherished. His subjects await his decisions nervously. He may expropriate one subject's property and give it to a favorite. Disobey him and he will harm you. Obey him and you'll be spared harm. Maybe. Renege on what you owe him and he'll punish you in kind. He offers little aid or assistance to his subjects."[2]

Qoheleth's God is both transcendent and immanent. He is the Creator who bestows gifts on his creatures. These gifts bear witness to his generosity, but they are also perceived as arbitrary (2:26; 6:2). God's providential acts reveal his involvement in and ordering of human life, but they are also mysterious (8:17). A comparable tension characterizes God's judgment. God is the sovereign Judge, the one to whom humans must give an account (cf. Heb. 4:13). Qoheleth contends that God will judge the righteous and the wicked (Eccles. 3:17). In fact, God will bring people into judgment for the ways of their heart and the sights of their eyes (11:9). This affirmation of God's judgment is a natural corollary of God's nature as the sovereign, omniscient Creator. Qoheleth clings to this basic theological conviction, but his observations and experience are unable to confirm it. Sinners are not punished immediately (8:12). The righteous perish prematurely, while the wicked prolong their days in evil (7:15). The righteous, the wise, and their works are in the hand of God, but humans cannot discern whether their moral character and actions bring divine favor or disapproval (9:1). God's providential acts of judgment are mysterious. Their nature and timing are unknown to humans, and these unknowns remind humans of God's independence.

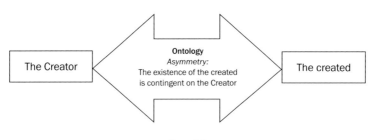

Figure 9.1

Figure 9.2. *The Creation of Woman* by Jens Adolf Jerichau (1915)

In his autobiographical reflections, Qoheleth paints a rich picture of the ontological implications of the Creator-creature distinction. This distinction creates a chasm between humanity and the divine that cannot be breached.[3] It also creates space for Qoheleth's account of God's transcendence and immanence, his knowability and unknowability, his attributes and the mysterious nature of his being and acts in human life.

The paradoxical relationship between these realities is also evident in Qoheleth's reflections on death. Qoheleth is preoccupied with death. It is a fundamental problem for Qoheleth, for it eliminates every opportunity for human profit in life. Death, however, is characteristic of creaturehood. To be a creature is to die. The recognition of this reality serves as the occasion for proclaiming the fundamental reality that God is the Creator. This fundamental reality is captured by Ephraim Radner, who writes, "To proclaim death, at least in its central aspect of our existence, is to return always to the form of our being as creatures. To announce our creaturehood is to proclaim God."[4] Qoheleth proclaims God by announcing his ontological otherness. God is transcendent, sovereign, and omnipotent. He is the Creator, Giver, and Judge, who orders, intervenes in, and evaluates human life.

Qoheleth's account of God may be "an uncomfortable theology,"[5] but the convictions that animate it also bring some measure of consolation.[6] While Qoheleth's affirmation of divine transcendence, sovereignty, and omnipotence is a source of creaturely discomfort, these attributes are also a reservoir of creaturely comfort. Both sentiments flow from Qoheleth's affirmation that God is the Creator (12:1). Just as God infused the first human with the life breath (Gen. 2:7), so also he gives and receives the life breath of all humans (Eccles. 12:7). God has made humans, and he has made them with a particular posture: upright or straight (7:29). Qoheleth privileges God's creation of humanity, but it is important to note that he also confesses that God is the one who makes everything (11:5). Qoheleth's reflections on God's work of creation are bound up with his observations regarding God's work of providence. God has made everything fitting in its time; he governs the seasons of human life (3:11). All that God does endures forever (3:14). His providential ordering of all things is perfect (3:14), including both good days and bad days (7:14).

Qoheleth's consideration of God's works of creation and providence causes discomfort because humans are contingent creatures. They are not the Creator.[7] This explains why humans cannot discern the work that God has done (3:14; 8:17). And it explains why God's providential acts are designed to elicit fear from his creatures (3:14). The uncomfortable nature of Qoheleth's theology is associated with the uncomfortable nature of his anthropology. Humans are dependent beings. God, by contrast, is independent. He is of himself and from himself. And yet God gives of himself and from himself in creation and providence.[8] His work of providence is mysterious, but it is not unintelligible. While Qoheleth acknowledges that no one can find out the work that God has done under the sun, he also realizes that what happens under the sun is the work of God (8:17). God reveals himself in human life. This revelation remains partial because humanity's ability to comprehend God's being and actions is partial. This revelation is mysterious because it is characterized by *"an unclassifiable superabundance"* that transcends the rational capacities of human beings.[9]

Qoheleth affirms the concept of divine aseity in his own idiom—that is, he affirms that God is of himself and from himself; he needs no one and nothing. This affirmation is surprising in light of Qoheleth's account of the ways in which God gives of himself and from himself. Among the verbs associated with God in Ecclesiastes, "giving" predominates, and God's giving produces comfort. According to Qoheleth, food, drink, and the enjoyment of labor are divine gifts from the hand of God (2:24; 3:13). God gives wisdom, knowledge, and joy to those who please him (2:26). He grants the days of one's life (5:18; 8:15; 9:9). He empowers people to enjoy the gifts of ordinary life and to accept their portion (5:19; cf. 6:2). God's immanent acts of giving are a suitable counterpoint to his transcendent rule. His gifts produce joy and consolation. His provision of a person's *portion* seeks to forestall the illusory pursuit of *profit*. When this provision of one's portion fails to forestall the pursuit of profit, humans experience an unusual gift from God: the severe business of comprehending that which happens in the world (1:13; 3:10). This task eludes human understanding; it is a terrible occupation with which to be occupied, a task that prevents humans from embracing their dependence on God and enjoying the generous hospitality of their divine host.

Creation

Qoheleth's account of God as Creator assumes a created world. While Qoheleth claims that God is the Maker of everything (11:5), he does not describe God's creation of the cosmos (cf. Job 28:25–27; 38:4–38; Prov. 3:19–20; 8:22–29). This does not mean that creation is insignificant. To the contrary, creation plays a formative role in Qoheleth's investigation, and the nature of creation informs Qoheleth's consideration of what it means to be human.

Creation frames Qoheleth's quest. Together, the poems in Ecclesiastes 1:4–11 and 12:1–7 form the context for his reflections (cf. 3:1–8). They move from human generations, human perception, and human memory within the cycles of cosmic time (1:4–11) to the dissipation and end of human life in eschatological time (12:1–7). Creation is the domain in which Qoheleth seeks a profit or payoff in human labor (1:3). The contribution of this domain to Qoheleth's inquiry may explain why the book opens with a poem on creation. This poem not only answers the fundamental question posed in 1:3, it also situates human life and human activity in a particular vision of the created world.

The vision of creation cast by the opening poem emerges from its juxta-position of the earth and its elements with human perception and human memory (1:4–7, 8–11). This structure captures the movement and logic of the poem. A comparable arrangement introduces the poem:

> A generation goes and a generation comes,
>> but / that is, the earth remains forever. (Eccles. 1:4)

The relationship between these poetic lines is ambiguous. The initial line foregrounds the reality of human mortality. Death makes its first appearance in the book. A human generation dies off, and another generation takes its place. This much is clear. What is unclear is how the succession of human generations relates to the earth. For some, "the earth" is a synecdoche for "humanity as a whole," not the physical earth:[10] "that is, the earth remains forever." This means that nothing changes in the world; it remains the same. A generation dies, another comes to take its place, and this succession recurs ad infinitum.[11] Others, by contrast, construe the lines as antithetical: "but the earth remains forever." Whereas human generations are transient, the physical earth remains constant.[12] This antithesis entails that the nature of the earth differs from the nature of human life. Human life is temporary and impermanent, but the earth is enduring and permanent.

The broader context of the poem is patient with both readings. The patterns that characterize the elements in creation may represent either monotonous cycles or permanent stability (1:5–7). And the polemical critique of humanity stands, regardless of the nature of the earth (1:8–11). What is at stake is whether creation is implicated with humanity in *hebel*. The semantics of the poem in general and its negative evaluation of humanity in particular suggest that the earth remains distinct from human life. In contrast to human life, creation is stable and irreplaceable; it serves as the necessary "ground and universal condition for all who come and go upon it."[13] The elements in creation are not marked by circularity; they are marked by constancy (1:5–7).[14] The constancy of creation is intertwined with the contingency of human life,[15] but creation does not share the contingency of human life. The permanence of creation is a foil for the contingent nature of humanity.[16] This explains how the permanence of the physical earth is relevant to humans.[17] Creation is constant; it remains stable in the face of change. The order of creation is recognizable, but humans are unable to harness creation's constancy, stability, and order to achieve profit. Humans cannot master contingency.[18] The human search for profit in creation is sabotaged from the start.

The ontology of creation differs from the ontology of human life, but the nature of this difference requires clarification. Because creation is created, it is contingent. What differentiates creation's contingency from

Table 1. Creation's Constancy and Contingency

Ecclesiastes 1:4–7	Genesis 8:22	Jeremiah 31:35–36
A generation goes and a generation comes, but the earth remains forever. What's more, the sun rises and the sun sets, and to its place longing, it rises there. Going to the south, and turning toward the north— round, round the wind goes, and upon its rounds the wind returns. All the streams flow to the sea, but the sea is not full. To the place from which the streams flow, there they flow again.	As long as all the days of the earth, seedtime and harvest, cold and heat, summer and winter, day and night, shall never cease.	Thus says Yahweh, who gives the sun for light of day, the order of the moon and the stars for light of night, who stirs the sea so that its waves roar— Yahweh of hosts is his name: If these orders were to cease from before me, the declaration of Yahweh, then also the seed of Israel would cease to be a nation before me forever.

Figure 9.3. *Death and Life* by Gustav Klimt (1910)

human contingency is God.[19] More specifically, the differentiation is due to covenant. The stability of creation and the constancy of its elements across the opening part of the first poem echo the promises of the cosmic covenant and their canonical construal. Table 1 compares Ecclesiastes 1:4–7, Genesis 8:22, and Jeremiah 31:35–36.

The stability, constancy, and order of creation are rooted in God's covenant commitment to creation and its orders. This covenant commitment distinguishes the ontology of creation from the ontology of human life; it renders creation as the stage on which human life and human history are performed. It also draws a distinction between "two types of temporal existence."[20] The earth remains irreplaceable, whereas human generations are replaced.

These types of temporal existence correspond with ancient Israel's dual conceptions of time. As Rolf Knierim notes, the Old Testament's theology of creation includes two types of time: cyclic, cosmic time and historical time. The former is "that structure of reality in which the same order of the cosmos keeps recurring in a never-ending pattern of successive cycles."[21] The latter is the linear structure of reality, according to which human life

Dust to Dust

Retrieving a medieval Jewish interpretation of Ecclesiastes 1:4, Nili Samet illuminates the relationship between the succession of human generations and the permanence of the earth. According to this tradition, each generation returns to the dust, and each new generation comes from the dust. The "unchangeable nature of the earth indicates that the coming and going of generations is cyclic. Humanity is being recycled rather than renewed."[a]

and events unfold chronologically. While cosmic time "coexists with historical time," it remains distinct.[22] Cosmic time constitutes the frame within which historical time operates. "In fact, this cosmic order exists for the earth, and the earth lives from it, just as the earth is part of it."[23] However, cosmic time does not need historical time. Cosmic time "is the indispensable presupposition and basis for human history. It can continue to exist without human history, but human history cannot exist without it."[24]

These conceptions of time inform a reading of Ecclesiastes 1:4–7. The distinction between cosmic time and historical time both reinforces and clarifies the ontological distinction between creation and humanity (1:4). Creation and cosmic time differ from humanity and historical time. A generation goes and the dust returns to the earth (1:4; 12:7), but the earth remains forever. The nature of creation teaches humans that they are contingent, and it intimates that contingent beings are unable to secure profit at the intersection of cosmic time and historical time.

Humanity

In view of the nature of God and the nature of creation, Qoheleth's concern with the nature of humanity comes into sharper focus. In different ways, both God and creation testify to the reality that humans are contingent creatures. To be human is to be created; it is to be dust enlivened by the divine life breath (12:7; cf. 11:5). To be human is to be mortal and ephemeral; it is to live amid change (9:3–5, 9). To be human is to be a temporal creature, to experience the conditions of life as both given and charged with future possibilities (3:11; 11:1–6).[25] To be human is to be morally accountable to the divine (11:9). To be human is to be a finite creature endowed with the infinite (3:11); it is to embrace these antithetical aspects of being, which enable the human pursuit and fear of God.[26] These are the ontological realities of creaturehood. According to Qoheleth, this is what it means to be human. To be human, quite simply, is to be dependent. Qoheleth bursts the bubble of human autonomy, exposing this conception of creaturehood as a delusion. Dependence is indicative of finitude; it is intrinsic to the goodness of human being. This entails that "vulnerability before God and others is fundamental to a Christian understanding of being human. . . . Everything about us points to our dependence on God, others, and the earth. We are creatures, and thus we are necessarily vulnerable."[27]

Qoheleth's account of the nature of humanity is both unsettling and exhilarating. It is unsettling because it lays bare human being as fragile and given, sustained by "borrowed breath."[28] It is exhilarating because it frees humans to embrace who they are by acknowledging whose they are (12:1, 7). Humans are not their own. They are neither the source of life nor the master of their own destiny. They are contingent, limited, vulnerable creatures. These conditions define the nature of humanity and describe what it means to be a creature in this world. They represent the conditions under which God considers humanity good, and they imply that the human pursuit of profit in life is a mirage, for it is not in keeping with the nature of humanity.

Epistemology

■ READ ECCLESIASTES 1:12–18; 3:1–15; 7:23–29 ■

Qoheleth's ontological-anthropological considerations are reinforced and extended through his musings on epistemology. His depiction of the nature of humanity informs his description of the nature of human knowing. Humans are finite creatures. This means that human knowledge is partial and limited. As with Qoheleth's account of ontology and anthropology, his reflections on the limits of human knowledge explore the epistemological implications of the Creator-creature distinction.[29]

This epistemological distinction provides a theological framework within which to understand Qoheleth's dynamic and disparate discourse on human wisdom. This discourse addresses several basic issues. Among them, the sources and limits of human wisdom and the nature of human memory are the most significant.

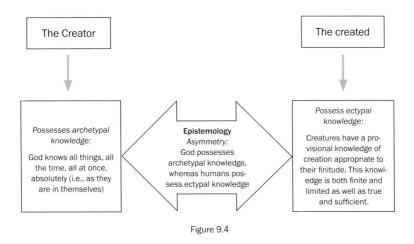

Figure 9.4

The Sources of Human Wisdom

Qoheleth's account of the sources of human wisdom is both traditional and novel. It is traditional insofar as Qoheleth affirms the witness of Proverbs. With Proverbs, Qoheleth contends that wisdom and its benefits are a divine gift (Eccles. 2:26; Prov. 2:5) and that wisdom is an inheritance passed on by one's predecessors (Eccles. 1:16; Prov. 4:1–9). This inheritance is memorialized in many of Qoheleth's observations. Wisdom is preferable to folly (Eccles. 2:13; Prov. 14:24). Despite appearances, those who fear God are better off than the wicked (Eccles. 8:12; Prov. 15:16; 23:17). The rebuke of the wise is better than the song of fools (Eccles. 7:5; Prov. 27:5). Wisdom offers security (Eccles. 7:12; Prov. 13:14; 14:3), and it is an instrument of power (Eccles. 7:19; 9:16, 18; Prov. 24:5). While Qoheleth never explicitly identifies the source of these representative evaluations, they reflect the advice of Proverbs and reinforce the axiomatic beliefs of biblical wisdom. For lack of a better term, they are traditional. But this is only half of the story. Qoheleth's quest for profit also introduces a novel source of wisdom: one's rational intellect.

Whereas Proverbs privileges hearing and casts the acquisition of wisdom as the gift of the other, Qoheleth privileges seeing and casts the acquisition of wisdom as the achievement of one's rational powers.[30] This achievement is conveyed through formulaic expressions that pervade Qoheleth's investigation: "I have seen" (1:14; 2:24; 3:10, 16, 22; 4:4, 15; 5:13, 18; 6:1; 7:15; 8:9, 10, 17; 9:13; 10:5, 7); "my heart/mind has seen" (1:16); "I myself turned to see" (2:12; cf. 7:25); "I set my heart/mind to examine" (9:1); "I know" (3:12, 14; 8:12); and "I found" (7:27, 29). These expressions of rational apprehension complement Qoheleth's instrumental rendering of wisdom.[31] He explores the world and assesses human activities *by* wisdom (1:13; 2:3, 21; 7:23). In Qoheleth's hands, wisdom is an "analytical tool" for clarifying knowledge.[32] Qoheleth investigates all that has happened in human life by means of wisdom (1:13; cf. 2:3). He tests things by wisdom (7:23). More specifically, Qoheleth employs wisdom to understand, to explore, and to seek wisdom (1:13, 17; 7:23, 25). This search for wisdom by means of wisdom yields some startling results. Qoheleth discovers that the investigation of all that has happened under the heavens is a severe business given to humans by God (1:13). He learns that an increase in wisdom increases vexation and pain (1:18). While he tested all things by wisdom to become wise, Qoheleth admits that wisdom eluded his grasp (7:23). In fact, his quest to understand wisdom and to perceive humanity's business on the earth culminated in the realization that humans cannot discern even an aspect of God's work (8:16–17).

Figure 9.5. *Vanitas Still Life with Self-Portrait* by Peter Claesz (ca. 1628)

Qoheleth goes where no sage has gone before. Relying on his rational intellect, he interprets his observations and experiences to reveal knowledge that is not dependent on the wisdom tradition.[33] And Qoheleth does what no other sage does. He conducts his investigation into the matter of human profit in life with an unusual conversation partner: his "heart/mind" (*leb*; "myself" in many English translations). Qoheleth personifies his *leb* "as an experiment partner distinct from himself."[34] He introduces it as a companion at the front end of his quest (1:13). He speaks with his *leb*, analyzing the findings of their exploration (1:16; 2:15; 3:17, 18). He makes his *leb* experience pleasure (2:1), and he initiates lines of inquiry with his *leb* (7:25). Both Qoheleth and his *leb* collaborate in the quest for profit, but they "do not always share experiences or draw similar conclusions (2:10, 20)."[35] This cooperative quest allows Qoheleth to experience and to examine some questionable activities of life, while retaining a hearing from his audience by recounting the "counter experiences" of his *leb*.[36] This shared investigation helps explain how Qoheleth can call human pursuits and activities both *hebel* and valuable. This collaborative venture also indicates that, even if Qoheleth exemplifies a form of autonomous epistemology through his reliance on the powers of rational intellect, his exploration is not devoid of interpersonal knowing. Qoheleth's "I-and-my-*leb*" partnership creates a strange yet collaborative context for coming to know things.

Whether Qoheleth grounds his discoveries in autonomous reflection (e.g., 2:11–15; 4:1, 4, 7; 5:18; 8:15) or in conversation with his *leb* (e.g., 1:13, 16–17; 2:1; 3:17–18; 7:25), these experiential discoveries constitute genuine knowledge. This knowledge is disturbing. If Michael Fox is right, it is disturbing because Qoheleth's discoveries attune one to the reality that "no human knowledge can lay claim to certainty. . . . Not only is there much that man cannot know (as all would agree), but even what one *does* know is in doubt."[37] Qoheleth's pessimism regarding the nature and extent of human knowing offers a painful corrective for finite creatures. The Creator-creature distinction implies that certainty eludes humans. By virtue of their creaturehood, humans possess limited, provisional knowledge: ectypal knowledge. This knowledge may be true and sufficient, but it is never certain. Certainty accompanies infallible, absolute knowledge, which is inappropriate to finite creatures. Confidence, however, is appropriate to human knowing. This is the best that humans can do. Qoheleth points readers in this direction. Esther Meek maps the terrain of proper confidence:

> Our creaturely situatedness is not a flaw or shortcoming, but rather what it is to be human. It is what locates us before God as creatures before Creator, but also quite specially as stewards, and in this respect reflective of him in our cultural engagement. This means that our efforts to know are fallible but also quite capable, *coram Deo* and in God's world, of leading us to truth. Our humanness serves as a beachhead within reality. Also, it is quite appropriate to attend well to what it is we are actually doing when we know . . . and to attend carefully to the world, in covenant love, to come to understanding. On the one hand, as contingent creatures, we may not exalt to ultimate epistemic status a bedrock of certainty or a surefire method; on the other hand, our rootedness affords confidence as we vector toward reality. Our creaturely rootedness—including our very selves—displays its characteristic glory as it remains ever revisable and transformable in light of subsequent insight.[38]

Meek guides readers between the Scylla of certainty and the Charybdis of skepticism. Among other things, creaturely knowing is situated, embodied, and enculturated.[39] It cannot "lay claim to certainty," but it can lay claim to confidence. Qoheleth models this form of finite knowing.[40] He neither pioneers an innovative approach to knowing nor publishes fresh discoveries. Instead, Qoheleth's wisdom provides a "clarity that enables him to 'see' better than others the reality of the human predicament." It cuts through assumptions "based on faulty perception and reasoning," offering clarification and correction concerning the nature of human knowing.[41]

The Limits of Human Wisdom

Qoheleth sees the human predicament for what it is: human knowing, like human being, is finite and limited. These epistemological limits are corroborated by the witness of both Proverbs and Job (e.g., Prov. 14:12; 16:1–2, 9; 30:2–4; Job 28; 42:2–3). However, Qoheleth not only affirms the limits of human knowledge; he defines their extent.[42] Humans forget the past (Eccles. 1:11; 2:16). They are unable to determine the future (3:22; 6:12; 7:14). And neither human working nor human wisdom can decipher the purpose and place of present activities within the broader sweep of God's work (3:1–11). Humans cannot interpret divine activity to achieve profit in life (8:17; 11:5). Qoheleth scrutinizes the limited scope of human wisdom within the broader context of time and in the face of God's providential activity—both of which clarify the limits of human wisdom and relativize the efficacy of human wisdom.

While Proverbs acknowledges the epistemological limits that accompany creaturehood, the resounding witness of the anthology is that wisdom is both desirable and efficacious. Qoheleth affirms the value of wisdom (Eccles. 2:13; 7:12, 19; 8:1), but given the epistemological limits of finite creatures, Qoheleth challenges and corrects a superficial understanding of wisdom's efficacy. According to Qoheleth, wisdom does not ensure success. Education leads to grief, not joy (1:17–18). The wise and the fool share the same fate: both die (2:14). The wise fade from memory (2:16; 9:15). Activities do not live up to expectations. "The race is not to the swift, nor the battle to the mighty, nor food to the wise, nor riches to the discerning, nor favor to the skillful" (9:11). Moral character and moral behavior do not necessarily yield reward; instead, righteous people experience the recompense of the wicked, and wicked people experience the reward of the righteous (8:14). Wisdom and hard work do not secure profit (2:1–11). Accordingly, the only sensible course of action is to perform moral acts without the expectation of reward (11:1–6). Qoheleth leverages the lack of correspondence between human actions and their expected consequences in the world to reveal the lack of correspondence between wisdom and success. In the context of Qoheleth's economic discourse, wisdom constitutes an "investment that guarantees no glorious return; its advantages are meager at best."[43] Wisdom is an advantage (7:12), but it is a limited one because human wisdom is limited.

The Nature of Human Memory

With the limits of human wisdom and wisdom's efficacy in mind, Qoheleth's account of the nature of human memory deserves brief comment. Qoheleth characterizes human memory as faulty and shortsighted. The

Figure 9.6. *Capricious of Memory* by Aharon April (2004)

wise are forgotten (2:19; 9:15), and people fail to remember the past (1:11). This generalization of human amnesia is illustrated through the apparent discovery of something new. Humans may claim to discover something new, but anything of meaning, value, and significance in human life is not new; it has always existed (1:10).[44] This reality may explain Qoheleth's remedy for faulty human memory—and that he has a remedy at all. Qoheleth did not offer a solution to the limits of human knowledge. He never entertains the notion that humans may transcend their epistemological limits; instead, he calls readers to embrace their limits. Nor does Qoheleth ever consider a solution for the inefficacy of wisdom; instead, he calls readers to lower their expectations for wisdom.[45] But Qoheleth offers a remedy for human memory.[46]

The treatment is twofold. The first is cognitive: "Remember your Creator in the days of your youth" (12:1). The second is embodied through rituals of remembrance: to eat, drink, and see good in toil—it is the gift of God (2:24–25; 3:12–13, 22; 5:18–20; 8:15; 9:7–9). These forms of treatment restore one's memory. They neither help one to perpetuate the memory of the wise nor allow one to recall the past. They perform a more basic function: attuning a person to what it means to be human. That is, they remind a person that to be human is to be created, sustained by a Creator. To be human is to be dependent, to eat, to drink, and to toil, rejoicing in God's gifts. Qoheleth's remedy for faulty human memory sensitizes one to the reality of humanity's nature and limits in the divine economy. This remedy contributes to Qoheleth's axiological-ethical considerations, specifically to his reflections on what is good for human beings.

Axiology/Ethics

READ ECCLESIASTES 2:1–16; 9:7–10; 11:1–10

Given the limitations of creaturehood, Qoheleth asks how a person should live. He explores the axiological-ethical implications of the

Creator-creature distinction. In accord with this distinction, Qoheleth allows God to be God. Although God's purposes and providential activities remain inscrutable, Qoheleth "simply accepts God on God's terms."[47] He acknowledges that God is the blesser and doer of good. More specifically, Qoheleth accepts God's gifts and relates to him in fear. These are the bricks and mortar of Qoheleth's ethical stance and the values that inform his evaluation of what is good for finite creatures.

Rejoicing in God's Gifts

If Qoheleth deems anything good for finite creatures, it is the enjoyment of the ordinary gifts that God bestows on humans throughout their lives. This evaluation of the good emerges out of Qoheleth's assessment of those things that are *hebel*. He devalues particular activities and pursuits to enhance the value of those activities and pursuits that are good. Enjoyment and work are among these goods, but these pursuits are also considered *hebel*. This is a classic example of Qoheleth's contradictions. Out of one side of his mouth, Qoheleth contends that the experience of pleasure is *hebel*; it accomplishes nothing (2:1–2). And after accomplishing great feats, Qoheleth confesses that these works are *hebel* (2:11). Qoheleth's quest only elaborates these assessments of pleasure and work: work is frustrating and painful (2:22–23; 5:16–17); the possessions gained through hard work are ephemeral (5:13–15); pleasure and the possessions that bring pleasure are deceptive (6:1–6); endless toil yields wealth but not satisfaction (4:8). However, enjoyment and work—though they be *hebel*—are also good, and out of the other side of his mouth, Qoheleth commends them (2:24; 3:12, 22; 5:18; 8:15). In fact, work and pleasure are the best life has to offer; there is nothing better for humanity (3:22). This explains why Qoheleth praises pleasure: there is nothing good for humans under the sun but to eat, drink,

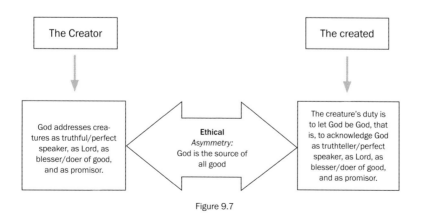

Figure 9.7

and take pleasure, for it will accompany them in their labor during the days of their life (8:15).

These commendations of pleasure and work sit in tension with Qoheleth's assessment of both as *hebel*. How should one negotiate this tension? As noted above, Qoheleth's contradictions are real. His contradictory evaluation of pleasure and work is real. Neither nullifies the other. What validates both assessments are the differing frames of reference through which Qoheleth evaluates pleasure and work. These differing frames of reference are established at the beginning of Qoheleth's quest:

> All that my eyes desired I did not keep from them;
> I did not withhold my heart/mind from any pleasure,
> because my heart/mind experienced pleasure from all my toil—
> and this was *my portion* from all my toil.
> But when I myself considered all the works that my hands had done
> and the toil that I toiled to do,
> Look!—the whole thing was *hebel* and a chasing of wind;
> there is no *profit* under the sun. (2:10–11)

When pleasure and work are viewed through the prism of "portion," they are good. They are partial yet real possessions that produce enjoyment (2:10). But when they are viewed through the prism of "profit," they fail to deliver the goods (2:11). According to Qoheleth, these pursuits are not enough. They do not provide an adequate payoff to meet the threshold of profit. They do not yield a sufficient advantage. In light of Qoheleth's search for profit in one's toil under the sun (1:3), pleasure and work are insufficient pursuits. They are *hebel*. But if one recalibrates the system of valuation and receives a portion in life, then pleasure and work are sufficient. They are good. Whereas humans may receive a portion from pleasure and toil, they are unable to secure a profit, for "there is no profit under the sun" (2:11).

The distinction between profit and portion explains Qoheleth's repeated commendation of food, drink, work, and pleasure. These activities are good because they are one's portion in life (2:10; 3:22; 5:18–19; 9:9). They do not operate under the expectation of profit. These activities are also good because they are "the gift from God" or "from the hand of God" (2:24; 3:13; 5:19; cf. 8:15; 9:7). As divine gifts and humanity's portion in life, food, drink, work, and pleasure are an antidote to *hebel*.[48] Eating and drinking are daily reminders of the giftedness of life. As Norman Wirzba observes, "Every time a creature eats, it participates in God's life-giving yet costly ways, ways that simultaneously affirm creation as a delectable gift, and as a

Figure 9.8. *The Romans in Their Decadence* by Thomas Couture (1847)

divinely ordered membership of interdependent need and suffering and help. Whenever people come to the table they demonstrate with the unmistakable evidence of their stomachs that they are not self-subsisting gods. They are finite and mortal creatures dependent on God's many good gifts."[49]

In other words, eating and drinking create "human self-understanding."[50] Work is a reminder of humanity's identity, vocation, and place in the divine economy (Gen. 1:26–28; 9:1–3, 7). The experience of pleasure or "seeing good" (Eccles. 2:3, 24; 3:13; 5:18) allows humans to see and to enjoy what God "sees" and enjoys—namely, the goodness of creation (Gen. 1:4, 10, 12, 18, 21, 25, 31).

According to Qoheleth, receiving and rejoicing in one's portion are what is good for finite creatures. These responses keep one human and cultivate contentment in the human situation. While some interpreters consider Qoheleth's commendations of food, drink, work, and pleasure as cynical resignations that confirm the dreadful plight of humanity, these recommendations need not be read as pessimistic concessions. Qoheleth does not endorse hedonism. He does not call readers to anesthetize themselves from the harsh realities of life and the inevitability of death by eating, drinking, and being merry. In fact, Qoheleth never calls readers to seek pleasure. Instead, he calls them to embrace what it means to be a finite human in this world by receiving good things "within the context of the possibilities and limits set by God."[51] Put simply, Qoheleth declares: "In reality, all is vanity. In truth, everything is a gift of God."[52]

Fearing God

The reception and enjoyment of one's portion are not the natural response of humans; it requires a particular posture: the fear of God (3:14; 5:7; 7:18; 8:12). This posture plays a formative role in Qoheleth's account of what is good for finite creatures. It is one of the few things that Qoheleth does not characterize as *hebel*. This posture also plays a pivotal role in Proverbs, Job, and Ecclesiastes, but each book has its own take on things. According to Proverbs, the fear of Yahweh is the "first principle" of wisdom (Prov. 1:7) and the "firstfruit" of wisdom's acquisition (2:1–5); it is instruction in wisdom (15:33) and a skilled practice embodied across one's life (31:10–31). According to Job, the fear of God is manifested in a form of life that turns away from evil (Job 1:1; 28:28); it is expressed through interpersonal, other-centered loyalty (6:14) as well as through lament, complaint, and protest oriented to God.

According to Qoheleth, the fear of God involves a recognition of human finitude; it emerges from a consciousness of one's nature and place in the cosmos in dependence on God.[53] The perspectival awareness of one's dependence on God engenders the fear of God. It accepts that no amount of human effort can discern God's doing (3:9, 14). Whatever God does endures forever; those who embrace their limits and the mystery of God's providential activity respond by fearing God—that is, by humbly receiving and living within the suitable seasons he has made (3:11, 14). The person who fears God acknowledges that God is in heaven and humans are on earth (5:2). Those who embrace their place in the cosmos not only watch their words in the context of worship; they also fear God by watching and listening *coram Deo* (5:7). More than this, those who fear God own up to the fact that they will go through life performing deeds that are wise and righteous, as well as foolish and wicked; they affirm the contradictory realities of life and embrace their creatureliness by refusing to overestimate moral character and human potential (7:15–18). The fear of God may not forestall premature death, but those who fear God are better off than the wicked (8:12).

Qoheleth's construal of the fear of God is bound up with his construal of the nature of humanity. Humans are finite, fragile, dependent creatures, and those who know what it means to be human fear God. They embrace their finitude, fragility, and dependence by acting humbly and prudently before the one to whom they must give an account. As Michael Legaspi rightly notes, "Wisdom follows

RECEPTION HISTORY

Enjoyment as Resignation

Among modern interpreters, Tremper Longman is representative of those who view Qoheleth's calls to enjoyment as resignations rather than affirmations. According to Longman, these calls to joy are limited to eating, drinking, and work, and they are far from enthusiastic. At best, they are calls to seize the day (carpe diem). On this account, Qoheleth says, "In the darkness of a life that has no ultimate meaning, enjoy the temporal pleasures that lighten the burden" (5:18–19).[b]

from this basic life-orientation—not as a body of knowledge capable of ordering or evaluating larger human aims and aspirations but rather as a way of conducting oneself . . . with intelligent respect for limits."[54] Qoheleth does not use the fear of God to denote terror and thus to elicit human paralysis before the divine.[55] Qoheleth uses the fear of God to describe "the normative mode of human existence"[56] that accepts human finitude, receives human life on its own terms, and acts in both obedience and reverent submission to God. Whereas Proverbs foregrounds the pedagogical necessity of the fear of Yahweh and Job privileges the embodied manifestation of the

fear of God, Qoheleth emphasizes the dependent posture and profound acceptance of limits associated with the fear of God.

The End of the Matter?

READ ECCLESIASTES 12:9–14

At minimum, Qoheleth's evaluation of what is good for finite creatures includes rejoicing in one's divinely bestowed portion and fearing God. But this is not the end of the matter. The end of the matter is delineated in the epilogue, where the author of Ecclesiastes declares,

> The end of the matter is that everything has been heard.
> Fear God and keep his commands,
>   for this is the whole of humanity,
> for every deed God will bring into judgment,
>   regarding everything hidden, whether good or evil. (12:13–14)

At face value, this climactic conclusion to Ecclesiastes is both familiar and unusual. It is familiar because it affirms the importance of fearing God and acknowledges the inevitable reality of God's judgment, both of which coincide with the witness of Qoheleth (3:14; 5:7; 7:18; 8:12; 11:9). But it is unusual because it fails to include Qoheleth's commendation of enjoyment and mentions obedience to God's commands, something that Qoheleth never says explicitly. While the final verses of Ecclesiastes present the end of the matter, this end sits in uneasy relationship with Qoheleth's conclusions. Is this an accurate summary of Qoheleth's quest? Does it reiterate yet reframe and extend Qoheleth's thought? Or does it undermine Qoheleth's pessimistic conclusions and baptize the book through an orthodox statement?

These questions cannot be answered in a hermeneutical vacuum, nor are they resolved through careful attention to the words in the epilogue, for the words can be interpreted in different ways. These differing interpretations are due to the ways in which Qoheleth and the author of the epilogue use the same words, and they are due to varying perspectives on the nature of Qoheleth's thought. If Qoheleth is a pessimist or a skeptic, then his call to fear God differs from the author's command in Ecclesiastes 12:13. Qoheleth prompts terror, but the author elicits reverential submission to God. If Qoheleth's thought is construed in more positive terms, however, then it appears that the author reiterates and reinforces Qoheleth's recommended posture of humble dependence on God. This reading may eliminate some tension between Qoheleth's conclusions and the author's summary, but it does not harmonize the voices of Qoheleth and the author. Although Qoheleth may allude to forms of behavior reminiscent of the ethical vision of the Torah,[57] he never instructs readers to keep God's commands (cf. 8:5). And while Qoheleth acknowledges the reality of divine judgment (11:9), that judgment concerns the matter of enjoyment in life, not accountability to God's commands against an eschatological horizon, where everything hidden is brought to light (12:14).[58]

The author of the epilogue takes his cue from Qoheleth. Just as Qoheleth refused to resolve every matter under the sun, so the author of the epilogue does not tie up the book in a nice, neat, interpretive bow. The sting of Qoheleth's painful wisdom continues to fester (cf. 12:11). Aspects of his thought are commended (12:13), but gaps remain. The final verses of Ecclesiastes do not contradict Qoheleth's testimony; they supplement it.[59] To rejoicing in one's divinely bestowed portion and fearing God, the book's

Making Sense of the Conclusion

Some interpreters find the frame narrator's conclusion in 12:13–14 to be at odds with Qoheleth's conclusions. In the epilogue, the narrator critiques Qoheleth, "warning his son of the dangers inherent in a writing like the one they just looked at together."[d] The frame narrator concludes the book with the central truths that one is to take away.

Among these truths, the call to keep God's commands feature prominently in rabbinic literature. The Talmud, for example, intimates that Ecclesiastes was deemed authoritative because "its beginning is words of Torah and its end is words of Torah" (b. Shabbat 30b).

In response to those who read 1:12–12:8 as an extended foil for the real message of the book in 12:13–14, Stuart Weeks offers a memorable observation: "If pious readers had found the preceding 239 verses disturbing and unorthodox, it seems unlikely either that their minds would really have been set at rest simply by a sudden reference to the Torah, slapped belatedly on to the end of the book like a smiley badge stuck to a bomb, or that whoever was responsible for those verses could have expected them to be."[e]

closing verses add obedience and accountability to God's commands. When read in the context of Ecclesiastes, this addition extends Qoheleth's conclusions. When read in the broader context of Scripture, this addition extends the conversation regarding the relationship between the so-called wisdom books and the Torah (cf. Sir. 1:11–30; 24:1–34).[60]

Conclusion

Proverbs exemplifies fear seeking understanding, and the book of Job typifies suffering seeking understanding. Qoheleth embodies finitude seeking understanding. The results of Qoheleth's exercise in finitude seeking understanding are difficult to digest. One's character and conduct do not secure certain consequences. Human wisdom is unable to ensure success; it is ill-equipped to determine the future and to discern the work of God. Human life and human activity are caught in a broad temporal context that humans neither understand nor control. Apart from the gift of ephemeral enjoyment, work and its products do not yield a reward. Whatever advantage they may have accrued is forfeited at death, and if this advantage is passed on to an heir, the expectation that it will be squandered trivializes the time and effort expended to amass it. Nothing is left to show for the effort. Even if something remained, humans would forget its source, for their memory is amnesiac. Qoheleth impresses on readers the extensive limitations of contingent creatures. This is not the product of negative thinking; it's a profound understanding of finitude, a realistic assessment of what it means to be human.

   This realistic assessment of the human situation exposes as fraudulent human aspirations and expectations that fail to account for the nature of creaturehood. It also helps people face reality. More specifically, it helps

CANONICAL CONNECTIONS

Ecclesiastes and Torah

Ecclesiastes 5:1–7 integrates and extends the Deuteronomic prescriptions regarding vows (Deut. 23:21–23). While intertextual affinities between Ecclesiastes and specific principles of the Torah would furnish a strong justification for the epilogue's call to keep God's commands, a general approach affirms the connection between Ecclesiastes and Torah. The ethical orientation of Ecclesiastes mirrors the ethical vision of Torah. The logic of the Torah's ethical vision is expressed through the Decalogue: love God and love your neighbor (Exod. 20:2–17; Deut. 5:6–21). These principles are developed and contextualized through the regulations of the covenant. They are also developed and contextualized in Ecclesiastes, where Qoheleth calls people to fear God and care for others (5:7; 4:1–12).

   In addition to the ethical orientation of the Torah and Ecclesiastes, Qoheleth's reflections bear a striking similarity to the motifs across the opening section of the Torah. As Thomas Krüger notes, like Genesis 1–11, Qoheleth affirms that God created the world good (Eccles. 3:11–15; cf. Gen. 1–2); God endowed humanity with a unique status in the cosmos (Eccles. 7:29; cf. Gen. 1:26–28); no one is free of sin (Eccles. 7:20, 29; 8:11; 9:3; cf. Gen. 6:5; 8:21); and death is the divine judgment on humanity (Eccles. 3:16–21; 9:1–3; 11:9–12:7; cf. Gen. 3:17–19; 6:3).[f]

THEOLOGICAL ISSUES

Finitude and Education

Dan Treier offers a brilliant sketch of the ways in which Ecclesiastes's vision of finitude informs a theology of education. Treier argues that embracing finitude frees one to perceive how God's strength is manifest in human weakness. More specifically, Treier concludes, "Christian educational efforts ought to pursue wisdom in realistic institutional contexts that provide communicative space for teachers and students to listen humbly and speak truthfully. As we learn to engage the limiting relational realms of human life with the hope of resurrection, we become less vulnerable to sleepless nights in pursuit of the money and status that almost inversely correlate with happiness. We also become less vulnerable to sleepless nights in despair over a world that we cannot substantially change."[9]

them face the reality of death and what it says about God and the nature of humanity. And it helps people taste and see the goodness and giftedness of human life lived in humble dependence on God.

Qoheleth offers Christian readers a rare gift. He does not allow them to escape the harsh realities of finitude by availing themselves of their eschatological inheritance. Instead, he moves his readers to embrace the realities of finitude and bask in "the glory of the finite."[61] Qoheleth does not allow readers to overestimate their work. Instead, he places human pursuits in God's providential ordering of all things, and he calls humans to double down on efforts that elude their calculation (9:10). From a human perspective, these efforts may be *hebel*. But from a theological perspective, labor in the Lord is not in vain (1 Cor. 15:58); its results are simply beyond human control. Qoheleth also refuses to allow readers to exaggerate the efficacy of their wisdom. While human wisdom is valuable, it remains limited and provisional; it cannot master life or the world. Qoheleth's vision of finite life is liberating, for it frees humans to enjoy their portion within their limits and without the expectation of any profit. 📖

Qoheleth's liberating vision of finite life has significant implications for the Christian life. Contrary to the ways in which some readers have (mis)appropriated early Christian readings of Ecclesiastes, the book envisions neither life before Christ nor life without Christ.[62] Ecclesiastes is not an extended evangelistic talk, designed to illuminate the vanity of earthly life and the surpassing joys of heavenly things. The book does not expose the irrationality of a secular worldview and replace it with a theological vision of life in relationship with God. Ecclesiastes casts a vision of earthly life. In so doing, it delivers a necessary wake-up call. Qoheleth's attention to human mortality orients life to its end, teaching humans to number their days so that they may gain a heart of wisdom (Ps. 90:12; cf. James 4:14). Qoheleth's recognition of God's gifts and commendation of enjoyment attune one to the goodness of God's creation and to the reality of human dependence. This assessment of human life cultivates remembrance and gratitude. It releases one to receive God's gifts as gifts, not as something one owns; and it ensures that one defines oneself as *creatura Dei* (i.e., a creature of God), not as *Homo faber* (i.e., self-made, man the maker).[63] If nothing else, Qoheleth awakens his audience to the nature of earthly life and its meaningfulness. He names the frustrations of human life in a fallen world (Eccles. 1:2; 12:8; cf. Gen. 3:17–19; Rom. 8:20) and invites humans to embrace their Creator. He identifies the illusory nature of work and its products, and he invites humans to accept their vocation and enjoy their lot. Like the broader biblical vision of life and faith, Qoheleth's vision of life and faith is not escapist.[64] With remarkable clarity, Qoheleth helps humans to see the hand they have been dealt. He does not allow one to fold; rather, he compels humans to play their hand, to use their chips accordingly, and to delight in the company, food, and drink that sustains all involved in the activity of human life.

In many ways, Qoheleth's quest in Ecclesiastes reflects the Christian pilgrimage.[65] Both involve frustration and joy. Both acknowledge human finitude and dependence on the divine. Both account for creaturely goods, and both negotiate nature and grace. These features may explain why Ecclesiastes is read during the Jewish observance of Sukkot (Feast of Tabernacles), when many memorialize Israel's wandering in the wilderness by eating in temporary structures, where they embody finitude and dependence on God's good gifts. These features may also explain why many Christians have read Ecclesiastes as a handbook on asceticism, as training to accept human limits. Life within these limits does not renounce the joys of the human endeavor. To the contrary, it places these joys in proper perspective and receives them with gratitude.

CANONICAL CONNECTIONS

Hebel in the New Testament

Qoheleth's conclusion that all is *hebel* resounds in certain New Testament texts, including Paul's reflections in Romans 8:

> I consider that the sufferings of this present time are not worth comparing with the glory about to be revealed to us. For the creation waits with eager longing for the revealing of the children of God; for the creation was subjected to *futility*, not of its own will but by the will of the one who subjected it, in hope that the creation itself will be set free from its bondage to decay and will obtain the freedom of the glory of the children of God. We know that the whole creation has been groaning in labor pains until now. (8:18–22 NRSV, emphasis added)

Whether the futility or frustration of creation is attributed to the fall in general or to humanity's misuse of creation in particular, humanity is implicated. This involvement results in death. James picks up on the metaphorical sense of *hebel* to describe human mortality: humans are a mist or vapor; they appear for a little while and then vanish (James 4:14).

CHAPTER TEN

Song of Songs

Desire Seeking Understanding

The Song of Songs is a lyric score that envisions and explores the mystery, pleasure, and power of love, as well as the dangers, delights, and doubts of desire. The Song assumes that human beings are lovers; they are desirers. Better, the Song acknowledges that "appetite or desire, not DNA, is the deepest principle of life."[1] If this is true, then the Song may represent the deepest book in Scripture. Its profound depth is demonstrated across the history of its reception. While short in length, the Song has commanded a disproportionate amount of attention.

While the Song's poetic forms and techniques are familiar, no interpretive approach has tamed its meaning and message. And while its subject matter is straightforward, its content is underdetermined: its authorship is anonymous; its structure is opaque; its characters are hazy; many of its images are unfamiliar; and the nature of its coherence is contested. These interpretive realities are difficult to navigate, but there is a more basic hermeneutical question: What *is* the Song of Songs? The answer to this question not only directs one's reading of the Song; it also determines the frame of reference through which the Song is read. If the Song is read as love poetry through the lens of our hypersexualized culture, it is "soft porn."[2] If the Song is read as lyric poetry in conversation with comparable ancient Near Eastern texts, it is a cultic marriage performance or a piece of entertainment.[3]

But if the Song is read as Christian Scripture, if it is construed in the context of the canon and with a sensitivity to its network of intertextual links, it is a work of theological imagination that yearns for what was, what ought to be, and what will be. It is a work that depicts

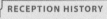

RECEPTION HISTORY

A Long History

The disproportionate amount of attention devoted to the Song is expressed by Marvin Pope, who writes: "A thorough survey of the history of interpretation of the Canticle would require the lifelong labors of teams of scholars."[a]

desire seeking understanding. More specifically, it is a work that refers to and moves seamlessly between two registers: the love between a man and a woman and the love between God and his people.[4]

These interpretive registers are discerned through the way in which the Song refers. Reference is the issue, not the specific sense of words or images. The referential character of language emerges through the connection between words (i.e., signs) and reality (i.e., signified). This connection creates the conditions for meaning, which is created by the interplay of words, their use, and their referents in particular contexts. When these aspects of semiotics and ordinary language philosophy are mapped onto Scripture and construed theologically, the interpretive registers of the Song become clearer. As canonical Scripture, the Song is revelation; its words are inspired and exist in "associative relationship with the whole of the Christian Bible, Old and New Testaments."[5] This means that the Song's words are more than historical words that refer to certain things. They are also words that refer to certain theological realities. 📖 👥

These theological realities are referred to and disclosed within the context of canonical Scripture. This theological account of the referential character of the Song's language indicates that "the distinction between Scripture's literal-historical sense and its theological sense is relative

Figure 10.1. *Song of Songs*, No. 14 by Egon Tschirch (1923)

LITERARY NOTES 📖

Lyric Poetry

Lyric poetry is a mode of poetic discourse that stands in contrast to drama, narrative, and epic. That is, lyric poetry is neither narrative nor dramatic. It manifests itself through the modes of song, prayer, and pronouncement; it is a vocal mode of discourse expressed through song; and it foregrounds the inner lives and emotions of its speakers.[b]

LITERARY NOTES 📖

The Song as Allegory

Among other things, reference explains why an allegorical reading of the Song predominated for most of its history of reception in Christian interpretation. This interpretive trajectory was set by patristic exegesis, which focused on reference, not merely on the meaning of words. The patristic attention to reference is exemplified in Augustine's discussion of words/signs and their reference in Scripture. In book 1 of *On Christian Teaching*, Augustine notes that a sheep is a sheep, but the sheep that Abraham sacrificed in the place of Isaac is more than a sheep. It is a sign that points beyond itself to the sacrifice of Christ. In the same way, a log is a log, but the piece of wood that Moses threw into the bitter waters of Marah to make them suitable to drink is more than a piece of wood. It points beyond itself to the cross of Christ.[c]

rather than absolute, and a separation between the two in terms of subject matter would be at odds with the inspired nature of the biblical text."[6]

A Divine-Human Love Song: Theological Reading

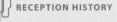 READ SONG OF SONGS 8:5–7

A theological account of scriptural language explains how the Song refers to both human love and divine-human love. The canon of Scripture clarifies these registers of reference, exerting a hermeneutical "pressure" on a Christian reading of the Song. In fact, the bookends of the canon create a pressure cooker for a twofold reading of the Song. The language and imagery of the Song evoke the opening chapters of Scripture (Gen. 1–3), and the final chapters of Scripture employ the language and imagery of the Song to portray the consummation of all things (Rev. 19–22). When read within the frame of the canon, the Song explores the love between a man and a woman (Gen. 1–3) and the love between the triune God and his people (Rev. 19–22). These readings are not mutually exclusive. They interpenetrate one another. Both explore the mystery of love. Both probe the mysterious union between a man and a woman and the mystery that is Christ's union with the church (Eph. 5:25–33).

The content of canonical Scripture also informs the realities to which the Song's language refers. The marriage metaphor, for example, punctuates the prophets (esp. Hosea; Ezek. 16), providing a conceptual lens through which to perceive the nature of God's relationship with his people. Jerusalem is both a city and a personified woman (Isa. 54:4–8; Jer. 3:19–20; Mic. 4:9–10), and God is love (1 John 4:8, 16). This connection between God and love contributes to the Song's interpretation as a reflection on divine-human love. God is not mentioned explicitly in the Song, but a veiled reference to the divine emerges in the poem's climax:

> For love is strong as Death,
> zeal as fierce as Sheol.
> Its flames are flames of fire,
> a raging flame.
> Many waters cannot quench love,
> nor rivers sweep it away. (Song 8:6b–7a)

When this description of love is heard in the context of the ancient world, it recalls the Northwest Semitic combat myth, which employs the formula "Death is strong." This formula recurs in Baal's confrontation with Mot ("Death"), and it is enshrined in Hebrew names in the Old Testament (Azmaveth, "Death is strong," e.g., 2 Sam. 23:31; Bethazmaveth, "House of Azmaveth," Neh. 7:28). The Old Testament also uses the word/name *mot* to leverage the conception of death as a personal, powerful force (e.g., Job 18:13; Ps. 18:4–5; Isa. 28:15; Hosea 13:14; Hab. 2:5). Song 8:6 deploys the "Death is strong" motif to characterize love. The remaining expressions in verses 6–7 play on the same idea, recalling descriptions of Yahweh as the victorious divine warrior to portray love: "zeal," "flames of fire," "a raging flame," "many waters," and "rivers."[7] Like love, Yahweh is "zealous" (Exod. 20:5; Deut. 4:24; 5:9), a God who is passionate about relationship with his people (Isa. 42:13; Zeph. 1:18; 3:8). As a

The Northwest Semitic Combat Myth

The Northwest Semitic combat myth is a story that features a conflict between a warrior god and one or more combatants, whether the sea god, his allies, or Death. With the help of historical linguistics, Aren Wilson-Wright identifies and explores three formulas that characterize the Northwest Semitic combat myth and illuminate its presence in Ugaritic texts, the Old Testament, the New Testament, and Jewish literature: "Leviathan, the twisting serpent, the fleeing serpent," "rebuke Sea," and "strong as Death."[f]

The Baal Myth

The Baal Myth played an important role in the thought of Semitic civilizations in the second millennium BC. Baal is depicted as a warrior god, who fights to secure a position of supremacy within the pantheon of deities, which is governed by the god El. To secure supremacy, Baal fights Mot ("Death"), the god of the underworld. The refrain across this battle is "Mot is strong; Baal is strong." While Baal is unable to defeat Mot, El's word forces Mot to submit to Baal, which leads to Baal's ascension to the throne.[g]

manifestation of his love, the divine warrior brandishes flames of fire and exercises control over both rivers and many waters (Ps. 29:7; Hab. 3:2–15). The terms and expressions used for love in Song 8:6–7 are used elsewhere for Yahweh. These comparative and intertextual links associate Yahweh with love. To be specific, the expression "'Love is as strong as death' equates Love with the divine warrior Yнwн, who is Death's primary opponent."[8]

This opposition to death and manifestation of love is anticipated in the Old Testament (Isa. 25:8) and is depicted in John's Apocalypse.[9] The river and the flood from the serpent's mouth fail to sweep away the woman (Rev. 12:15–16). Death and Hades are thrown into the lake of fire (20:14), setting the scene for the wedding of the Lamb and his bride (19:7; 21:9; cf. 22:17). As one of the earliest interpretations of the Song, the book of Revelation reuses the Northwest Semitic combat myth and the language and imagery of the Song to foreshadow the triune God's eschatological victory and consummate union with his people. 👣

Together with the nuptial metaphor in the prophets, this early canonical interpretation of the Song authorizes a divine-human interpretation

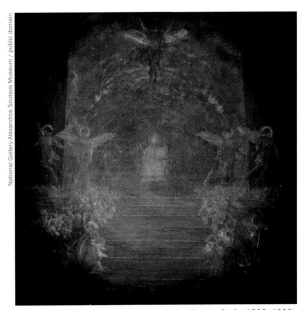

Figure 10.2. *Behold the Bridegroom Arriving* by Nikolaos Gyzēs (1899–1900)

of the poem. This form of reading is neither arbitrary nor dishonest;[10] it is the product of *analogia scripturae* (Scripture interprets Scripture). However, a divine-human interpretation of the Song neither abandons nor sublimates the literal-historical reference of the Song. This register remains. In fact, it is the instrument through which one is able to think through the Song so as to discern its theological subject matter. The Song *is* a song about human love. It *is* a song that probes and explores the desire, longing, pain, power, and mystery of human love. It *is* a song that embraces sexual discourse to describe the nature and direction of human desire. As Christian Scripture, the meaning potential of the Song of Songs is deep, and its depths are discovered through its registers of reference.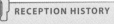

A Human Love Song: Literal-Historical Reading

■ READ SONG OF SONGS 1:2–17 ■

The Song's reference to divine-human love is perceived through its canonical position and intertextual associations, but its reference to the love between a man and a woman is evident in its association with ancient Near Eastern love poetry. This association not only reinforces the Song's literal-historical meaning; it also provides the context in which to understand the Song's literary nature. Many love poems in the ancient world resemble the love poems in the Song. These resemblances include similarities in style, imagery, and subject matter. Egyptian love songs, for example, cast a vision of love through the medium of dramatic presentation.[11] Personae are portrayed, and their emotions and experiences are explored through speech. The speeches of lovers include the language and imagery of vegetation, fruit, gardens, aphrodisiacs, and animals. And the motifs of longing, separation, sexual union, and lovesickness permeate Egyptian love songs. Consider the following example of independent songs:

> *(Boy)*
> The vegetation of the marsh is bewildering.
> [The mouth of] my sister is a lotus,
>   her breasts are mandragoras,
> [her] arms are [branches], . . .
> her head is the trap of "love-wood,"
>   and I—the goose!
> The cord is my . . . ,
>   [her ha]ir is the bait
>   in the trap to ensnare (me).

> *(Girl)*
> My heart is not yet done with your lovemaking,
>   my (little) wolf cub!
>   Your liquor is (your) lovemaking.
> I <will not> abandon it
>   until blows drive (me) away
>   to spend my days in the marshes,
> (until blows banish me)
> to the land of Syria with sticks and rods,
>   to the land of Nubia with palms,
>   to the highlands with switches,
>   to the lowlands with cudgels.
> I will not listen to their advice
>   to abandon the one I desire.[12]

If nothing else, ancient Near Eastern love poetry demystifies the literary nature of the Song; it situates Israel's love song in a broader conversation concerning human love and desire.

Comparative investigations of the Song orient the reader to its style, imagery, and themes. They also illuminate the Song's distinctiveness in its ancient Near Eastern environment. The differences between the Song and Egyptian love songs are sketched by Michael Fox,[13] who notes that these differences include matters of style, theme, and perceptions of love. Whereas Egyptian love songs are monologues, the Song is a dialogue.[14] The lovers in the former do not interact with one another, but the Song includes an intimate verbal exchange, which reflects on a consistent relationship, not different types of romantic relations. This dialogical nature of the Song reveals a fundamental difference in theme: across the Song, the lovers seek one another and invite one another to come away (1:4, 7; 2:10–13; 3:1–4,

6; 7:12–13; 8:14), motifs that are absent from Egyptian love songs. Love or desire is a prominent theme in both the Song and Egyptian love songs, but their conceptions of love differ. The "introspective description of love," characteristic of Egyptian love songs, is at odds with the "outward orientation" of love and the lovers in the Song.[15] The lovers in the Song exhibit their emotions rather than describe them internally. These differences indicate, at minimum, that the Song and Egyptian love songs view love differently. 📖📖

The Literary Coherence of the Song

■ READ SONG OF SONGS 2:7; 3:5; 8:4 ■

The dimensions of love develop across the Song through different voices, settings, and modes of discourse. This development, however, is not linear. Time does not unfold chronologically in the Song. While the voices are consistent and the landscapes are familiar, the Song does not display a narrative development.[16]

This does not mean that the Song is a haphazard collection of lyric poems. The poems betray signs of unity. The woman's voice predominates in the Song, while the woman, the man, and the daughters of Jerusalem represent the primary personae throughout the poems, creating continuity of characters. Variant forms of the adjuration refrain ("I adjure you . . ."; 2:7; 3:5; 8:4) and the expression of commitment ("I am my beloved's . . ."; 2:16; 6:3; 7:10) contribute to a homogeneous vision of love. The lovers depict one another's bodies through architectural and agricultural imagery, as well as with conventional conceptual metaphors (i.e., BODY AS LANDSCAPE, LOVE AS INTOXICATION, and THE OBJECT OF LOVE IS VALUABLE OBJECT).[17] The metaphor LOVE IS WAR is woven throughout the Song.[18] Imagery from the realms of family and the court infiltrate many of the poems.[19] These representative elements suggest that, despite its poetic diversity and dramatic shifts in speaker and setting, the Song may be read as a unified piece of lyric poetry. It is a literary exemplar of unity in diversity, a document that "has both disjunctive (centrifugal) and cohering (centripetal) sensibilities."[20]

LITERARY NOTES

Time in the Song

Chloe Sun observes that the poems in the Song do not unfold in a linear, chronological fashion. This is especially apparent in the language of chapters 4 and 8. As Sun notes, the expression "my bride" (4:8) suggests that the lovers are married, but the woman's wish to kiss her beloved in public without the threat of shame in the closing poem implies that they are unmarried (8:1).[j]

LITERARY NOTES

The Song as Drama

Some read the Song as a drama with a coherent plot, involving either two or three characters. This approach emerged in the nineteenth century. Those who perceive a two-character drama read the Song as a developing love affair between Solomon and the Shulammite.[k] Those who perceive a three-character drama read the Song as a love triangle, involving Solomon, a shepherd lover, and the Shulammite. On this reading, Solomon attempts to win the heart of the Shulammite, but she resists allurements of royalty and wealth, embracing the love of her shepherd lover.[l]

Solomon and the Song

■ READ SONG OF SONGS 3:6–11; 8:10–14 ■

The Song is a unified collection of lyric poetry, but it is important to note that the Song's unity is literary.[21] Its unity is not rooted in a coherent story or plot, nor is it located in Solomonic authorship (1:1). This raises the inevitable question: What is Solomon's relation to the Song of Songs? The king is mentioned in the title of the document (1:1) and referred to six times throughout (1:5; 3:7, 9, 11; 8:11, 12). Solomon, however, is never explicitly designated as a speaker. He is spoken about, and he is characterized in striking fashion, especially in Song 3:6–11 and 8:11–12. The strange scene in Song 3:6–11 follows the lovers' dialogue, pursuit of one another, and union (2:8–17; 3:1–5):

> Who/what is this coming up from the wilderness
>   like columns of smoke,
> perfumed with myrrh and frankincense,
>   from all the merchant's powders?
> Look! Solomon's litter!
>   Sixty warriors surround it
>   from the warriors of Israel,
> all of them holding the sword,
>   trained in warfare,
> each one with his sword at his side,
>   against terrors of the night.
> King Solomon made himself a
>   palanquin
>   from the wood of Lebanon.
> Its posts he made of silver,
>   its upholstery of gold,
> its seat of purple,
>   its interior inlaid with love
>   by the daughters of Jerusalem.
> Come out and look, daughters of Zion,
>   at King Solomon
> in the crown with which his mother
>   crowned him,
> on the day of his wedding,
>   on the day of his heart's joy.

Figure 10.3. *La Sulamite* by Odilon Redon (1897)

Speech gives way to sight. The opening question directs the daughters of Jerusalem to the spectacle emerging on the horizon: "Who is this coming up from the wilderness?" (3:6). As the spectacle comes into focus, a person fails to materialize. The reader is forced to double back and reinterpret the question: *What* is this coming up from the wilderness? It is Solomon's litter (3:7). This sight sets the stage for a description of a royal procession, culminating in Solomon's wedding day. An armed and experienced bodyguard surrounds the litter (3:7–8), and Solomon's palanquin includes posts of silver, upholstery of gold, and a seat of purple—its interior inlaid with love by the daughters of Jerusalem (3:10). These daughters are invited to look upon Solomon, donning a crown on his wedding day (3:11).

The contours of the procession are relatively clear, but this wedding scene borders on the bizarre. It attends to Solomon's litter, accompanied by sixty warriors of Israel. It offers a brief description of Solomon (3:11). It describes the work of the daughters of Jerusalem, who inlaid Solomon's palanquin with love. It admonishes the daughters of Zion to gaze at King Solomon, and it mentions Solomon's mother. But the most important woman is missing: the bride. Many assume the woman/bride is in Solomon's litter.[22] In the absence of a clear shift in speaker, however, it appears the woman continues her discourse from 2:8–3:5.[23] She is speaking. This suggests that if anyone is in the litter, it is Solomon. The entire scene is *about* Solomon. More specifically, it concerns the pomp and circumstance of Solomon's wedding day. The nuptial procession either ridicules Solomon's "egocentrism" or creates the symbolic atmosphere for the woman to imagine her beloved and their prospective wedding day in royal terms.[24] In both cases, Solomon is neither a speaker nor the beloved.

The same is true in the second text that mentions Solomon:

> Solomon had a vineyard in Baal-hamon;
>   he gave the vineyard to keepers,
>   each one would bring a thousand silver pieces for its fruit.
> My own vineyard is mine alone;
>   the thousand for you, Solomon,
>   and two hundred for the keepers of its fruit. (8:11–12)

Whether the man or the woman is designated as the speaker, the discourse draws a contrast between Solomon's vineyard and the speaker's vineyard. Solomon's vineyard is situated in Baal-hamon, an unknown locale that means "owner of wealth" or "lord of a multitude." The former designation corresponds with the description of Solomon's vineyard; its size requires keepers to tend it, and its choice produce is expensive (8:11). The latter designation corresponds with Solomon's harem (1 Kings 11:3). This metaphorical rendering of Solomon's vineyard is engendered by the speaker's vineyard, which belongs to him/her and remains at his/her

Figure 10.4. *Solomon Led to Idolatry by His Wives* by Raphael Sadeler I after Joos van Winghe (1589)

disposal (Song 8:12). If the man is speaking, he compares his vineyard (i.e., the woman) with Solomon's vineyard (i.e., the harem).[25] If the woman is speaking, she compares her vineyard (i.e., her body; cf. 1:6) with Solomon's vineyard (i.e., the harem).[26] While the meaning of the keepers and the economic distributions is unclear, the contrast between the vineyards remains: Solomon's vineyard is distinguished from the speaker's vineyard. The man's vineyard is worth more to him than the royal harem. The woman's vineyard is at her disposal, and her love is priceless (8:7). No matter how the vineyards are construed, Solomon is differentiated from the man and the woman.[27] He is neither a speaker nor the beloved.

Solomon's characterization in the Song may determine how to read the title of the book in Song 1:1. Often translated "the Song of Songs, which is Solomon's," the title compares to superscriptions in the book of Psalms. The addition of the relative pronoun "which" is unusual, but "Solomon's"—which represents *lishlomoh* in Hebrew—has the same interpretive difficulties as psalm superscriptions—namely, the inseparable preposition *le* on "Solomon" is ambiguous. Is the Song of Songs *of* Solomon, *to* Solomon, *for* Solomon, *belonging to* Solomon, or *concerning* Solomon?[28] The biblical biography of Solomon creates a case both for Solomonic authorship of the Song (1 Kings 4:32) and for the question of whether Solomon can serve as the normative voice of genuine love (11:1–13). An extrabiblical biography of Solomon creates an account that clarifies Solomon's relationship to the Song: he wrote it either in his youth (Canticles Rabbah 1:1) or as an act of repentance late in his life.[29] The internal witness of the Song, however, creates a different interpretive trajectory. Solomon, even on his wedding day, is surrounded by many women, but not his beloved bride (Song 3:6–11). The size and maintenance of his vineyard contrast sharply with the exclusivity and sole maintenance of the lover's vineyard (8:11–12). "Song of Songs" is the greatest song, but this sublime song does not seem to come from Solomon. At best, Solomon's relation to the Song is relatively positive. Like the Solomon of Ecclesiastes and Chronicles, he is a "constructed Solomon," who "both embodies the Solomonic ideal (3:6) and is better than the Solomonic reality (8:11–12)."[30] At worst, he is the Solomon of 1–2 Kings, who embodies lust, promiscuity, and polygamy, serving as a foil for genuine love. When read within the world of the Song, Solomon may be an imaginative construct. His wealth, glory, power, and appetite create the perfect storm for an imaginative exploration of what genuine love is. On this account, the Song of Songs mentions Solomon to create the ideal conditions through which to think about the nature, power, and mystery of genuine love.

While the Song tells readers little to nothing about its occasion, composition, and sociohistorical setting, it reveals much about love. Love is not an abstract concept in the Song; it is envisioned and expressed through speech.[31] This imaginative expression of love appeals to the senses, and it attends to several themes, which are explored in the next chapter.

Christian Reading Questions

1. The principle that Scripture interprets Scripture has long governed Christian biblical interpretation. What theological convictions are necessary to legitimize this approach? How can texts written by different human authors at different periods of time be used to interpret one another?

2. How do you know when a biblical text is interpreting another biblical text? What criteria, if any, would you suggest for determining cases in which Scripture interprets Scripture?

3. How would you describe the Song of Songs? What is it? How does it function as Christian Scripture?

4. How would you describe Solomon's relation to the Song?

CHAPTER ELEVEN

Theological Themes in Song of Songs

L ove is more than a feeling. Love is an embodied commitment. It is expressed through praise, and it sees one's beloved and the world in a particular way. The lyric discourse of Song of Songs helps readers perceive these aspects of love. The discussion that follows focuses on these aspects of love by attending to three prominent themes in the Song: the relationship between the lovers, the landscapes of love, and the nature of genuine love.

The Relationship between the Lovers

■ READ SONG OF SONGS 4:1–5; 5:10–16; 7:1–9 ■

Like love, the relationship between the lovers in the Song is complex. Their mutual love is expressed through a "poetics of relationality"[1]—that is, through a dialogue of seeking and finding, abandonment and return, yearning and union, desire and rejoicing, pain and praise. The lovers portray one another through the language of love, and each views the other through the prism of their love. But their perspectives differ. In the most general terms, the woman "tells others . . . what *love* does to her; the man speaks to the woman about what *she* does to him. . . . He is awestruck; she is lovesick."[2] These discrete perspectives, however, do not create different visions of love. The lovers' use of corresponding images to describe one another suggests they see one another in comparable ways.

The similarities between the lovers' description of the other's body, scent, sight, and taste are numerous. The woman wears her beloved as a sachet of myrrh between her breasts (1:13), and the man goes to her

Figure 11.1. *Song of Songs, Study H* by Egon Tschirch (1923)

mountains of myrrh (4:6). As an exotic garden filled with exquisite plants, the woman's body overwhelms the man's senses (4:12–15). She smells of frankincense and myrrh (4:14). Entering his garden, the man gathers his lover's myrrh, eats her honey, and drinks her wine (5:1). The woman compares herself to a lily (2:1); the man sees her as a lily among thorns (2:2) and grazes among the lilies—that is, lounges with his beloved (2:16; 4:5; 6:2–3). And his lips are like lilies (5:13). The man is as fragrant as henna blossoms (1:14), and the woman's garden smells of henna blossoms (4:13). Both lovers' eyes are likened to doves (1:15; 4:1; 5:12). The man's fruit is sweet to the woman's taste (2:3). Her garden is full of choice fruits (4:13), and she invites him to come to his garden and eat its choice fruits (4:16). The woman confesses that she is dark yet lovely (1:5); the man regards her form and mouth as lovely (2:14; 4:3; 6:4). In her opening expression of desire, the woman declares that the man's "love is better than wine" (1:2), and in his first extended speech, the man exclaims "how much better is your love than wine" (4:10). The woman depicts her lover as an apple tree, a place of shade and a source of sweet fruit (2:3). His apples refresh and nourish her (2:5); it is not surprising that her breath, in turn, smells of apples (7:8). The shared language and imagery between the lovers' bodies, senses, and desires illuminate their union and shared identity.[3]

The intermingling of the lovers' identities corresponds with the reciprocal nature of their speech. They not only come to one another; they also respond to one another in kind. The man yearns to hear his beloved's voice (2:14); she replies by affirming their love and inviting him to return to her: "Until the day breathes and the shadows flee, turn, my love, be like a gazelle, or a young stag on the cleft mountains" (2:17). In light of her invitation, the man answers, "Until the day breathes and the shadows flee, I myself will go to the mountain of myrrh and to the hill of frankincense" (4:6). More than echoing the woman's words, the man receives his lover's request and expresses his determination to go to the mountain: his beloved.[4]

The lovers also explore their mutual longing through the language and imagery of a fortified city.[5] The woman is as breathtaking as Tirzah and Jerusalem, the capitals of the Northern and Southern Kingdoms, respectively (6:4). Her neck is like the tower of David (4:4). She is a wall, and her breasts are like towers (8:10). The man is defeated by her beauty; she has stolen his heart (4:9). Her eyes overwhelm him (6:5), and her appearance evokes both terror and wonder (6:4). As an impenetrable city, the woman is immune to conquest, but she surrenders to her beloved. Against the siege of other suitors awaiting the woman's capitulation (8:8–9), she extends peace to her lover (8:10).[6] She does not negotiate the terms of surrender; rather, she freely succumbs to his love.

Although the man and the woman use similar images and comparable metaphors to articulate their union and probe the dynamics of their love, they do not see one another or perceive love in the same way. As noted above, their perspectives differ. These differences are especially apparent in their descriptive songs (4:1–5; 5:10–16; 6:4–7; 7:1–5), where the lovers create impressionistic portraits that blur the boundaries between the body, the natural world, and its material components. The man, for example, describes his lover through nature and military imagery:

> Look at you! You are beautiful, my darling!
>   Look at you! You are beautiful!
>   Your eyes are doves, from behind your veil.
> Your hair, like a flock of goats, moving down from Mount Gilead.
> Your teeth, like a flock of shorn ewes,
>   that ascend from the wash,
> all of them with its twin,
>   none among them is bereaved.
> Like a scarlet thread, your lips,
>   and your mouth is lovely.
> Like pieces of pomegranate, your cheek,
>   behind your veil.
> Your neck, like the tower of David,
>   built in layers,
> a thousand shields hung on it,
>   all the armor of warriors.
> Your two breasts, like two fawns,
>   twins of a gazelle,
>   feeding among the lilies. (4:1–5)

Moving from the eyes down to the breasts, the man describes his beloved as a paragon of beauty. Her eyes, hair, and teeth evoke the aesthetic delight of animals and their movements. Her cheek tastes like succulent fruit. Her neck is strong and intimidating, and her breasts, paradoxically, are grazing fawns. This is how the man *sees* his beloved. The beauty of her body and the beauty of the natural world blur in his enamored gaze.

Whereas the man describes his beloved through nature and military imagery, the woman conjures her lover through agricultural and metallurgical imagery. He speaks *to* her (i.e., "you"), but she speaks *about* him to the daughters of Jerusalem (i.e., "he").[7]

> My lover is dazzling and rudy,
>   distinguished among ten thousand.
> His head is gold, refined gold,
>   his locks, date panicles,
>   black as a raven.
> His eyes, like doves,
>   by springs of water,
> bathed in milk,
>   sitting upon brimming pools.
> His cheeks, like beds of spice,
>   pouring with perfumes.
> His lips, lilies,
>   dripping with myrrh.
> His hands, rods of gold,
>   set with Tarshish stones.
> His body, a bar of ivory,
>   covered with lapis lazuli.
> His legs, alabaster pillars,
>   set on gold pedestals.
> His appearance, like Lebanon,
>   choice as the cedars.
> His palate, sweet,
>   and all of him desirable.
> This is my lover; this is my friend,
>   O daughters of Jerusalem. (5:10–16)

LITERARY NOTES

A Grotesque Gaze?

Fiona Black sees something quite different through the man's gaze. Black's vision is mediated through the grotesque, which she employs as a heuristic guide for reading the Song's bodily imagery. *Grotesque* is a term coined in the Renaissance to describe a form of art that incorporates animal and human bodies. The concept of the grotesque and its artistic forms have developed in various ways, ranging from the playful to the dangerous. When the Song's descriptive poems of the woman are conflated and a fuller picture of her body is viewed through the concept of the grotesque, what emerges is "a creature who is ill-proportioned, odd-looking, and impossible." More specifically, Black concludes that the woman is "more like a biblical Barbie—though much less alluring—for she appears so ill-proportioned that she could not stand."[a]

Like the man's song, the woman's portrait of praise moves from the top down. Its language and imagery parallel the man's description of the woman in some respects, but the prominence of precious metals, minerals, and substances creates a different picture. If her body blurs with the beauty of the natural world, the radiance of his body makes his appearance noticeable. The language of gold, ivory, alabaster, and cedar signals the woman's appreciation of her lover's value, rendered in terms of his strength.[8] He is a source of protection and security. The woman's preferred imagery reveals her distinct perspective. When read in light of the man's song (4:1–5; cf. 6:4–7; 7:1–5), it appears that she focuses on "what he is to her," while he attends to what she looks like to him.[9]

These descriptive portraits of the woman and the man do not clarify their appearance. To the contrary, these imaginative portraits conceal more than they reveal. They show how the lovers see through what the lovers say. As Michael Fox observes concerning the nature of the descriptive songs, "A lover looks at his beloved and through the prism of her beauty sees an ever-present Arcady. In fact, the imagery shows us a world *created* by love, for it comes into being and is unified only through the lovers' vision of each other."[10] The lovers are united by love, which shapes and informs both their vision of one another and the world beyond.

While the Song neither clarifies the appearance of the lovers nor specifies their identity, it does explore their mutual desire and shared commitment. These aspects of their relationship are extended when the Song is placed in conversation with the broader canonical witness. As many have noted, the woman in the Song bears a strong resemblance to the women in Proverbs 1–9—namely, the strange woman, the wife, and Lady Wisdom.

The similarities between the woman in the Song and the strange woman are disturbing. Like the lips of the woman in the Song, the lips of the strange woman "drip honey" (Prov. 5:3; Song 4:11). In similar language as the Song, the strange woman invites the lad to an evening of erotic excess, where they will overindulge their sexual taste buds by drinking and lovemaking (Prov. 7:18; Song 1:2, 4; 4:10; 5:1; 7:13). To seduce the youth, the strange woman describes her bed in a manner comparable to the olfactory delights in the Song (Prov. 7:17; Song 1:16; 4:6, 14–15; 5:5). To capture her sexual prey, the strange woman kisses him (Prov. 7:13)—something unprecedented in the Old Testament[11]—while the woman in the Song longs for her lover's kiss (Song 1:2). When placed in canonical conversation, Proverbs and the Song use the same language of desire but in very different ways: the language of love, mutuality, and exclusive commitment within the Song is language that in Proverbs serves the interests of lust and infidelity.[12]

But this is only one side of the story. Proverbs also uses the language of love, mutuality, and exclusive commitment to direct one's desire to legitimate others. The instructional discourse in Proverbs 5, for example, counterbalances the danger of promiscuous sexual expression with the delights of marital sex. This delight is conceptualized through images of water from distinctive sources, each of which represents one's wife. Similar to the woman in the Song, the wife is depicted as a well of fresh or living water (Prov. 5:15–18; Song 4:15). And similar to the Song, drinking from her brings satisfaction and sexual enjoyment (cf. Song 8:2).[13] One's wife, however, is more than a well of satisfaction. Like the woman in the Song, she is also a "lovely hind" and a "graceful doe" (Prov. 5:19)—that is, beautiful, tender, and desirable (Song 4:5). This explains why the reader is invited to stray, overindulge, and lose oneself in the luxury of lovemaking with one's wife (Prov. 5:19; Song 5:1). As both an object of desire and one who can fulfill the man's desire, the wife is depicted as the woman in the Song—that is, as the source of sexual satisfaction and ecstasy.

Lady Wisdom is also a legitimate object of desire in Proverbs. With language similar to that of the Song, Lady Wisdom promises that those who seek her will find her (Prov. 8:17; Song 3:1–4; 5:6). That is, like the woman in the Song, she assures her lovers that she will not stand them up. Lady Wisdom promises reciprocal love, as affirmed by the woman in the Song: she loves those who love her (Prov. 8:17). But together with the seeking and finding motif, Lady Wisdom's promise of reciprocal love differs from the promise of the woman in the Song. The love of the woman in the Song is exclusive. Lady Wisdom's love, by contrast, is open to many lovers. The shared language and erotic dynamics between Proverbs 1–9 and the Song invite an intrabiblical conversation that opens the ways in which language from the Song's discourse of desire appears in Proverbs' discourse on sanctioned and unsanctioned objects of desire.

All this talk of desire necessitates a canonical account of the Song's contribution to the reversal of primeval desire. This contribution is staged in Song 7:10, where the woman reiterates and recasts earlier declarations of mutual commitment. Responding to the man's request to hear his beloved's voice, the woman announces, "My lover is mine, and I am his" (2:16). This assertion recurs in Song 6:3, where the woman transposes the clauses from her earlier declaration: "I am my lover's, and my lover is mine." Against the backdrop of her lover's desire for intimacy (7:8–9), the woman delivers an alteration to this refrain: "I am my lover's, and his desire is for me" (7:10). The expression of mutual commitment is extended to include the man's "desire" for his beloved. The term for "desire" is unique, appearing only two other times in the Old Testament: in Genesis 3:16 and 4:7. The latter text attributes "desire" to the personification of sin. Sin lurks at Cain's door; its "desire" is for Cain, and he must "rule over" it. The former text mentions "desire" in the context of the primeval curse on the woman. Her "desire" will be for her husband, and he will "rule over" her. Each text uses the term "desire" with the expression "rule over." This juxtaposition, combined with the literary contexts of Genesis 3:16 and 4:7, suggests that the desire in view is negative. It is a domineering form of desire. This is not the case in Song 7:10. The Song recasts the woman's desire for

Figure 11.2. *The Kiss* by Gustav Klimt (1908)

the man (Gen. 3:16) as the man's desire for the woman, and it withholds the language of rule. The desire mentioned in the curse on the woman is "reversed."[14] Better, when read in the context of the canon, this desire is "redeemed." As Phyllis Trible argues, "In Eden, the yearning of the woman for harmony with her man continued after disobedience. Yet the man did not reciprocate; instead, he ruled over her to destroy unity and pervert sexuality. Her desire became his dominion. But in the Song, male power vanishes. His desire becomes her delight. Another consequence of disobedience is thus redeemed through the recovery of mutuality in the garden of eroticism. Appropriately, the woman sings the lyrics of this grace: 'I am my lover's and for me is his desire.'"[15] Mutual commitment and belonging coalesce with mutual desire. This vision of love is not only Edenic; it is also nonutilitarian.[16]

The Song's nonutilitarian vision of the sexual relationship informs Paul's instructions concerning the nonutilitarian nature of the marital relationship. According to Paul, husbands and wives ought to love one another in the same way that they love their own bodies; that is, they ought to give their bodies willingly and mutually to one another as an expression of their love (1 Cor. 7:2–4; Eph. 5:22–33).[17] These instructions pertaining to the marital relationship develop the nonutilitarian conception of love in Genesis 2:23–24. A man leaves father and mother, and in union with his wife, they become one flesh. This union creates the conditions for the fulfillment of the cultural mandate (1:26–28). But in contrast to the emphasis of the cultural mandate, children are not mentioned at the end of Genesis 2.[18]

The union between the man and the woman is foregrounded. The man expresses his embodied ecstasy over the creation of the woman (2:23). The woman in Genesis does not speak; instead, her voice is heard across the Song.[19] The book of Genesis does not consider the erotic nature of the union in Genesis 2:23–24; instead, it is expressed across the Song of Songs. Within the context of the canon, the Song may be read as an explication of what is implicit and unaddressed in Genesis 2.

Like Genesis 2, the Song of Songs explores the ideal union of the man and the woman, not the reality. The sad realities of this relationship play out in different scenes sketched across the canon of Scripture (e.g., Num. 5:11–31; Deut. 22:22–29; 1 Sam. 18:17–27; 2 Sam. 3:13–16). These sad realities are fodder for the prophets' reflections on the state of Israel's relationship with God. Among the prophets, Isaiah (Isa. 50:1; 54:1–8; 62:4–5), Jeremiah (Jer. 2:1–3:13; 13:25–27), Ezekiel (Ezek. 16), and Hosea construe Yahweh's covenant relationship with his people in terms of marriage. Each prophet deploys the metaphor to describe the estrangement between Yahweh and his adulterous people.

Hosea performs a shocking sign act: he marries a woman of harlotry and has children of harlotry to capture Israel's betrayal and the rupture in her relationship with Yahweh (Hosea 1:2–2:1). As an estranged father and husband, Yahweh calls his people to remove their harlotries and their adulteries, lest he strip her naked (2:2–3). If she does not cease to publicly expose herself, Yahweh will be forced to expose her to public shame. Ezekiel paints a comparable portrait in Ezekiel 16, where he portrays Jerusalem as an abandoned infant whom Yahweh rescues, raises, and marries, adorning her with the trappings of royalty (Ezek. 16:3–14). But Jerusalem turns from Yahweh to other lovers (i.e., the nations), refuses payment for her love, and lavishes upon her lovers the gifts granted to her by Yahweh (16:15–34). In accord with the punishment for adultery, Yahweh intends to gather her lovers, who will strip her naked (16:35–39). These horrific depictions of the people's covenant infidelity offer a stark counterpoint to the love and relationship projected across the Song of Songs.

Prophetic texts also open a canonical conversation between the marriage metaphor and the Song of Songs. The language and imagery of stripping is reminiscent of the woman's search in Song 5:2–8, which culminates in the watchmen of the city beating and stripping her in public (5:7). The woman's pursuit of her beloved provides an appropriate counterpart to Yahweh's pursuit of his people. As Havilah Dharamraj notes, "If not for the Song of Songs, the Hebrew Bible would lack a woman whose tenacious pursuit of her separated beloved matches that of the husband in Hosea."[20] As a symbol of the people of God, the woman in the Song responds to the situation described in Hosea, declaring to Yahweh, "I am reciprocating your love."[21] The prophets deploy the marriage metaphor to foreground "God's side of the relationship,"[22] and the Song uses erotic language and imagery to foreground the people's response to the relationship.

Some find this canonical conversation between the prophets and the Song unsatisfying.[23] But this may not reflect ancient sensibilities. The prophets use gender categories to portray the nature of covenant infidelity. In its referential use of the marriage relationship, the Song emerges as a restorative text. Its imaginative discourse envisions both the healing of the relationship between man and woman (Gen. 3:16) and reconciliation between God and his people.[24] When read simultaneously through the prism of love *and* the story of Scripture, the Song invites one to "envision that the deep wounds that have plagued human existence almost from the beginning might yet be healed."[25]

The Landscapes of Love

■ READ SONG OF SONGS 3:1–5; 4:1–5:8 ■

The healing potential of the Song extends beyond its vision of human love and divine-human love; it also encompasses creation. The lovers in the Song see the world in particular ways, projecting a "poetic topography."[26] They create landscapes of love. These landscapes include different places and spaces—specifically, the city, the vineyard, and the garden, each of which deserves brief comment.

The City

The city is an ambivalent vista in the Song; it is the context for the union of the lovers as well as a barrier and a place of shame. These features of the city are evident in two parallel accounts, each of which is narrated by the woman (3:1–5; 5:2–8). The first blurs the boundaries between the woman's bed, the city and its streets, the mother's house, and the countryside to imagine a place of intimacy and union.

> Upon my bed nightly,
>   I have sought the one whom my being loves;
>   I have sought him, but I have not found him.
> I will arise now and go about the city,
>   in the streets and in the squares;
> I will seek the one whom my being loves;
>   I have sought him, but I have not found him.
> The watchmen found me,
>   those who go about the city,
>   "The one whom my being loves, have you seen him?"
> Scarcely had I left them
>   when I found the one whom my being loves.
> I took hold of him and would not let him go,
>   until I had brought him to my mother's house,
>   to the chamber of her who conceived me.
> I want you to swear, daughters of Jerusalem,
>   by the gazelles and does of the field,
> do not rouse or awaken love until it desires. (3:1–5)

The city is a place of seeking and finding. The movement from the woman's seeking and not finding to finding and seizing "the one whom her being loves" renders the city as a place of union that is hospitable to the lovers. The blending of the intimate and the public places suggests the city is a space of relational intimacy.[27]

This is not the case in the woman's second account, where her search for her lover takes a twisted turn (5:2–8). Following the beloved's knock at the door and invitation for the woman to grant him entry (5:2–4), she recalls,

> I myself rose to open to my lover,
>   and my hands dripped myrrh,
> my fingers, flowing myrrh,
>   on the handles of the bolt.
> I opened to my lover,
>   but my lover had turned and departed.
>   My being dissolved on account of him.

I sought him, but I did not find him,
    I called him, but he did not answer me.
The watchmen found me,
    those who go about the city;
they struck me, they wounded me,
    they took my shawl from me,
    the watchmen of the walls.
I want you to swear, daughters of Jerusalem,
    if you find my lover, what will you tell him?
That I am faint with love. (5:5–8)

As in 3:1–5, the city is a place of seeking here. But while 3:1–5 merges private and public places to recount the reunion of the lovers, 5:5–8 is full of barriers that impede the lovers' union. Doors and "watchmen of the walls" create obstacles, and the absence of the beloved prevents the woman from finding him. The account culminates with a battered, lovesick woman. Far from representing a hospitable space of union and intimacy, 5:5–8 portrays the city as a place of boundaries, restrictions, and danger.[28]

These parallel accounts construe the city in different ways. While the term "city" is restricted to these accounts in the Song, cities litter the landscape of the lyric poem. Among these cities, Jerusalem may be the most significant (1:5; 2:7; 3:5, 10; 5:8, 16; 6:4; 8:4). The use of Jerusalem in the Song indicates that the city is not only a place but also a person. Features of the woman's body resemble architectural features of Jerusalem (4:4). Her beauty is likened to Jerusalem (6:4), and she is depicted as an impenetrable city (8:8–10). The language and imagery of the city are mapped onto the body of the woman. The relationship between the woman and the city recalls the metaphorical concept CITY IS A WOMAN, which pervades the witness of the Old Testament, especially with reference to Jerusalem. Jerusalem is personified as a wife (Hosea 2:19–20; Ezek. 16), a nursing mother (Isa. 54:1–8; 66:7–14), a daughter (Isa. 1:8; 52:2; Jer. 14:17; Mic. 1:13), a woman in labor (Jer. 4:31), an injured person (Jer. 14:17), and one who laments (Joel 1:8). Jerusalem is a woman, and the woman of the Song may be understood as a representation of Jerusalem. In fact, the woman's characterization as a "Shulammite" gestures toward this connection (Song 6:13); the place and people behind this designation are unknown, but the name resembles the ancient name of Jerusalem: Shalem (Gen. 14:18).[29] The identification of the woman as Jerusalem reinforces and extends the canonical relationship between the marriage metaphor in the Prophets and the woman of the Song. As a symbol of Jerusalem, the woman embodies an essential characteristic of Jerusalem: shalom, peace.[30] She is a place of milk and honey (Song 4:11), and her connection to the land signals the restoration of city, people, and countryside.[31]

The Vineyard

The vineyard in the Song is a liminal space and a source of erotic delight. Like the city, it is a place and a person. As a place, the vineyard is a human creation (cf. Gen. 9:20), requiring cultivation and care (Song 1:6). Its vines blossom in season, signaling the opportune time for love (2:13). This cultivated space is neither public nor private; it is somewhere between these two realms. It is a communal space, "a place of wider male-female interaction."[32] This place of wider interaction is exemplified in Song 2:10–15, where the foxes enter the vineyards, endangering their vines and posing a threat to their fruit. The brief description of this intrusion appears to merge an actual place with the lovers' bodies; the foxes represent suitors, who enter the communal space of the vineyard, threatening the relationship between the lovers. This merger between place and person is also reflected at the frame of the Song. The woman's brothers oversee the vineyards (1:6), and the woman is a vineyard (1:6; 8:12). These representative texts indicate that the vineyard is a place that is open to others, a figure for the lovers' bodies, and a symbol of the woman's agency and independence.[33]

How does the vineyard contribute to the Song's vision of love? In addition to providing a liminal space that incorporates openness to others with the bodies of the lovers, the fruit of the vineyard plays a formative role in the Song's vision of love. Wine funds the Song's discourse on erotic desire.[34] It captures the taste of the lover's kisses (1:2); its delight serves as the basis of comparison for the ecstasy of the lover's love (4:10); it is consumed by the lover in his beloved's garden (5:1). Drinking is evocative of love in the Song. Accordingly, intoxication is an appropriate figure for erotic indulgence. This may explain why the vineyard, wine, and drinking provide the context for the only invitation to the reader or audience of the Song (5:1): "Eat, friends, drink, and be drunk with love."

The vineyard serves as a landscape within the Song's exploration of love, but viewed within the broader landscape of Scripture, it also appears to represent the people of God. Just as the vineyard is a symbol for the woman (1:6; 8:12), so also the vineyard is a figure for Israel. According to Isaiah, Israel is the vineyard of Yahweh, and Judah is his pleasant plant (Isa. 5:7; 27:2–4). In Psalm 80, Israel is a vine that Yahweh uprooted in Egypt and planted in the land of Canaan (Ps. 80:8–9), where it blossomed and flourished. More than depicting the people of God as a vineyard or a vine, both Isaiah 5 and Psalm 80 move from promise to tragedy. Although Yahweh cleared the ground and planted Israel in the land, enabling her to germinate and encompass Canaan, the divine vinedresser no longer watches over the

vine he once transplanted with great care
(80:8–11). The walls that protected it are in
disrepair. Those who pass by pluck its fruit.
The scavengers of the field feed on its produce (80:12–13). Isaiah's song of the vineyard
follows a similar pattern. The "beloved"
had a vineyard on a fertile hill. This beloved
weeded the field, hoed the soil, removed the
stones, planted the choicest vines, built a
tower, and constructed a wine vat in anticipation of the harvest (Isa. 5:1–2). The harvest
season arrived, but rather than producing
good grapes, the vineyard produced stink
fruit. The fate of this vineyard echoes the
fate experienced by the poet of Psalm 80, for
Yahweh announces he will remove its hedge,
break down its wall, allow it to be consumed
with thorns, and prevent rain from falling on
its soil (Isa. 5:5–6). These lyrical allegories

Figure 11.3. *Lovers Vineyard* by Marianne von Werefkin (1915)

of Israel offer a counterpoint to the vineyard in the Song. The allegories
depict Israel scorning God's love and care, but the Song envisions a love
that is wanted and welcomed. Isaiah's song casts Yahweh as the singer, but
the Song of Songs casts the woman as the singer. The Song's vision of what
love ought to be responds to these allegories and their vision of love gone
awry.[35]

The Garden

Together with the city and the vineyard, the garden in the Song represents the nature and delight of love. This landscape is also both a place and
a person. It is an enclosed space that represents the place of love. Beds of
spices as well as flora and fauna are found in the garden (6:2). The place,
however, is not the focus of attention in the Song; it furnishes concepts
and imagery for describing a person—namely, the woman. She is a locked
garden and a sealed spring (4:12). Her body smells of exotic fragrances,
and she tastes like choice fruits (4:13–14). She satisfies like a well of fresh
water (4:15) and offers honey for food and milk and wine for drink (5:1).
The man is captivated by her, looking at the blossoms, the vine, and the
pomegranates (6:11). These descriptions portray the woman as paradise,
the source of delight, who epitomizes the perfect unity between the man
and the land.[36]

Figure 11.4. *Earthly Paradise* by Pierre Bonnard (ca. 1916–20)

The garden imagery within the Song is evocative of the garden of Eden. Some regard the parallels between these gardens as overstated,[37] but others consider the links essential to a canonical account of love. As in Eden, the man and the woman inhabit the garden. They are naked but not ashamed. Like Eden, water, trees, and plants populate the Song's garden. Eden is the home of every tree that is pleasing to the sight and good for food (Gen. 2:9); the garden in the Song is the place of cedars and cypresses (Song 1:17), as well as apples (2:5), figs (2:13), and pomegranates (4:3; 6:7).[38] Eden is inhabited by every beast of the field and every bird of the air (Gen. 2:19); the garden in the Song is occupied by a flock of goats (Song 4:1; 6:5), lions and leopards (4:8), the raven (5:11), the gazelle (2:9, 17; 4:5; 7:3; 8:14), and the dove (1:15; 4:1; 5:12; 6:9).[39] In Eden the man praises the woman (Gen. 2:23), but the woman praises and pursues her beloved in the Song. God's withdrawal from the scene following the creation of the woman in Eden (Gen. 2:22–25) explains his absence in the Song's garden of erotic love.[40] The imagery of the garden in the Song corresponds to the imagery in the account of the garden of Eden, with the garden in the Song specifying, extending, and modifying aspects of Genesis 2:5–25.

Whether or not Genesis 2–3 provides "the hermeneutical key" to unlock the garden of love in the Song,[41] the primeval garden complements and supplements the Song's vision of "paradise" (i.e., Eden). This vision affirms the goodness of creation; it welcomes others into the celebration of love (Song 1:5; 2:7; 3:5; 5:8, 16; 8:4),[42] it acknowledges the presence of anger and abuse (1:6; 5:7), and it countenances forces inimical to love (8:6–7).[43] But it also ventures a return to the garden, where "eroticism becomes worship in the context of grace."[44] When read together with Genesis 2–3, the Song's vision of the garden stocks the theological imagination with the resources necessary to consider the restoration of erotic love and, by implication, the consummation of love between the triune God and his people (Rev. 21:1–4; 22:17).

The Nature of Genuine Love

■ READ SONG OF SONGS 7:10–8:4 ■

The Song of Songs is about love, but as noted earlier, this love is not abstract.[45] It involves all the senses: how one sees, smells, hears, tastes, and touches their beloved. This sensory exposition of love differs dramatically from contemporary conceptions. How? It is not about the self; it is about the other. It is not about compatibility; it is about commitment: "I am my lover's, and my lover is mine" (2:16; 6:3; cf. 7:10). It is not inclusive; it is exclusive. Readers of the Song debate whether the couple's relationship is marital or premarital; regardless, the nature of genuine love is the point and the pivot of the Song's lyric discourse.

This discourse explores the dynamics of genuine love through the motifs of seeking and finding, absence and presence, yearning and satisfaction, rousing and awakening. The woman seeks the "one whom her being loves" (3:1–4). His absence fuels her desire. When she is unable to find him, part of her "being" goes missing (5:6). She experiences a loss of self that is only regained in relationship with her beloved.[46] Love longs for the other, causing one's guts to churn (5:4). Love is given to the other (7:11–12); it conquers the other (4:9; 6:5). Love yearns for satisfaction, but the Song implies that its desire is not fulfilled. Just as the Song opens with yearning, so also it closes with yearning (1:2; 8:14).[47] Love is alive and active across the Song; it burns, yet it is never quenched. 📜

The Song's account of the overwhelming power of love builds across a repeated refrain and culminates in its description of love (8:6–7). The refrain operates under the assumption that love is powerful: "I want you to swear, daughters of Jerusalem, . . . do not rouse or awaken love until it desires" (2:7; 3:5; 8:4). While this refrain may be a request for privacy,[48] it appears to serve as a warning against stirring love before the time is right.[49] Love is personified as a passion with its own proclivities. Love will awaken when it pleases. It is not a passion to be trifled with; it is as strong as death, and it is a raging flame that cannot be extinguished (8:6–7). The Song does not attempt to master love; rather, it seeks to forestall the untimely awakening of this potent power through "cautionary instruction."[50] This instruction is invaluable. As the lovers in the Song demonstrate, desire is "an utter, thrilling *loss of control*, a giving over to the sensation of want, a foregrounding of that exquisite, aching sense of yearning, while *everything* else

CANONICAL CONNECTIONS 📜

Love with All Your Being

The repetition of the unusual expression "the one whom my being loves" leads Ellen Davis to suggest that it is an echo of a well-known text, Deuteronomy 6:5: "You shall love Yahweh your God with all your heart/mind, and with all your *being*, and with all your strength" (cf. Mark 12:28–30). Davis contends that the "repeated echo of the weightiest verse in the Old Testament confirms—in my judgment, beyond reasonable doubt—that at one level of the poet's meaning, the one who is loved and sought after so intently is God."[d]

blurs, falling to the wayside."[51] Like death, love brings an end to autonomy and a loss of the self.[52] In so doing, it opens one to the love of the other.

The ultimate Other is the triune God, the one who is love and whose love is stronger than death. Death is no contest to the triune God's indestructible love. Nothing can separate the Christian from the love of God in Christ Jesus (Rom. 8:37–39). As noted above, if the expression "Love is as strong as death" draws upon the Northwest Semitic combat myth to equate love with Yahweh as the divine warrior,[53] then the power of love in the Song reflects the power of God's love for his people. In theological terms, the power of love in the Song contributes to an understanding of divine impassibility.

Unfortunately, this divine attribute has fallen out of favor in modern theology, especially in the wake of the horrors of the Holocaust. How can a person claim that God is immune to emotional change in general and suffering in particular?[54] How can someone serve a God who is apparently aloof, apathetic, and impersonal? The Christian tradition has employed the language of impassibility (*apatheia*) to mark off appropriate parameters for speaking about God. That is, it has used a negative term to create a clear distinction between who God is and who God is not. Contrary to modern perceptions, the classical construal of impassibility does not concern God's psychological or emotional life; it concerns God's being, who God is. God is impervious to any external compulsion. He is unaffected by any external influence and "incapable of experiencing shifting emotions within himself."[55] This does not mean that God is aloof. Quite the opposite, impassibility creates "a condition of radical attachment."[56] Divine love is not a reaction; love is a person who exceeds every human conception of love and makes every human act possible by his love. God is love, and God's love is an inherent attribute of his being, as well as an inextinguishable passion for his people. God is not a disinterested watchman; he loves his people with an indestructible vehemence, "with an *impassible yet fervent, vigorous, genuine, indissoluble love.*"[57]

This powerful love reflects the love portrayed in Song 8:6–7. The irresistible power of this divine love is evident in the love between the man and the woman in the Song. The dangers of this power are sounded in the Song's instructional refrain (2:7; 3:5; 8:4). The Song's climactic description of love orients one to an understanding of divine love. Its imaginative depiction of human love imitates and

THEOLOGICAL ISSUES

Divine Impassibility

The conviction that God is impassible seems to sit in uneasy relationship with biblical texts that refer to God's sorrow, repentance, change of mind, or emotional turmoil. From a theological perspective, these types of texts employ analogical language. That is, they use human concepts to describe divine effects in the economy of salvation in a manner intelligible to human beings. This language describes God in creaturely terms, not God as he is in himself. A failure to maintain a distinction between God as he reveals himself in history (i.e., the economic Trinity) and God as he is in himself (i.e., the immanent Trinity) not only opens the door to divine mutability; it also creates a framework in which God's nature and being are exhaustively revealed through his immanent acts in history. God, on this account, is revealed fully in the immanent realm of history. The immanent Trinity is collapsed into the economic Trinity, and the distinction between Creator and creatures is dissolved.

embodies the fierce devotion and beautiful mutuality of triune love, a love experienced by those united to the divine family. This triune love is manifested in the relationship between human lovers, and it opens one to love and to receive the love of others.

Conclusion

The Song of Songs stages a performance of desire seeking understanding. This lyric performance moves seamlessly between two registers: the love between a man and a woman and the love between God and his people.[58] These registers of reference intermingle, filling out the nature and dynamics of love. Together they create a profound vision of love that is at odds with the shallow modern conceptions of love. According to the Song, love is not a "secondhand emotion" or some "sweet old-fashioned notion."[59] Love is fundamental to human being. And love is much more than an emotion; it is marked by mutuality rather than dominance, commitment rather than compatibility, resolute constancy rather than flaky feelings, appreciation and praise rather than humiliation and condemnation, and passion for the other rather than self-centered lust. Love is a mysterious gift rather than a commodity for trade. In a world of Me Too, high rates of divorce, and internet pornography, among other things, this vision of love is unusual.

The same is true of the Song. Its attention to love and sexual desire seems out of place in Scripture, but its contribution is invaluable. On one level, the Song affirms the goodness of embodied sexuality. Sexuality and sexual expression are gifts. The Song's vision of love, however, is much broader than sexual intimacy; it cannot be reduced to sex, even "safe sex," whatever that means. The Song embraces a love expressed in passionate praise, unrestrained indulgence, mutual enjoyment, and belonging. Love, desire, and passion—the stuff that drives human beings—find a place in the Song's celebration of human life. This celebration imagines a restoration of the effects of the fall—that is, a reconciliation between man and woman, humanity and the earth, and humanity and God.[60]

This conclusion sets the stage for another level of the Song's contribution to the witness of Scripture—namely, the ways in which it probes the love between the triune God and his people, whether the church in general or the Christian in particular. The intrabiblical conversation that emerges from the literary texture of the Song is striking. The theological construal of the Song, however, is not limited to its associative links with other texts in the canon of Scripture; it is also expressed through the Song's language of sexual desire. As Sarah Coakley argues, sexual desire is "the 'precious clue' woven into our created being reminding us of our rootedness in God."[61] The Song is a distinctive witness to this clue, reminding us of "the divine 'unity,' 'alliance,' and 'commingling' that we seek."[62] When sung in the church, the Song directs this search, nurturing desire for the triune God and "closer union with Christ."[63] As with its vision of human sexual intimacy, the Song refuses to romanticize or sentimentalize divine-human love. Its refrain shows a clear awareness of love's power and the dangers associated with rousing love before it desires. This is the most explicit instruction offered by the Song. Whether this instruction is read in the context of male-female or divine-human relations, Ellen Davis's advice is refreshing, for it steers clear of a reductionistic reading of the Song. Reflecting on the theological and practical significance of the refrain, she writes:

> "Do not stir up or awaken love until it is ready!" Our secular society gives the contrary advice, urging every unattached (or unsatisfied) person to be on the lookout for sexual love and offering countless tips on how to kindle its flame. In reaction, the church worries about how to contain the worse effects of raging passion. Virtually every modern church, whether liberal or conservative, is centrally occupied with "sexuality issues": infidelity, pederasty, harassment, the legitimacy of homosexual relations and premarital sex. The church needs to be concerned with these matters. But would not our spiritual vision be clearer, and our proclamation of the gospel be more persuasive, if we gave more attention to the bedrock ethical issue to which the woman's words directs us: How do we make our souls ready for love? How does the passion of love enter into character and become stabilized as a habitual disposition of loving? What can the church do to foster the soul-work that "let[s] love be genuine" (Rom. 12:9)? Imagine what a change would occur in the household of God if those questions were established at the heart of our common life, and all of us—youths and adults, single and married, seekers after human love partners and seekers after God—were committed to finding answers and living them out together.[64]

Admittedly, Davis's counsel is dated; the contemporary church's sexuality concerns include additional matters. But her point and her questions remain. The "sexuality issues" confronting the church are significant, and these issues must be addressed with biblical clarity, theological conviction, and personal charity. In addition to this important work, what can the church do to prepare all its people, regardless of their circumstances, to prepare for love, receive this love, and filter this love through a "habitual disposition of loving"? What can the church do to disciple all its people in a vision and practice of Christian sexuality that is nourished by faith, directed by hope, and governed by love?

Psalms

Praise Seeking Understanding

Elie Wiesel endured the horrors of Auschwitz and Buchenwald. He saw countless atrocities, including the death of his father.[1] Among the many gifts Wiesel bestowed on humanity in the aftermath of the Holocaust, a collection of essays provides a peek into the astonishing tenacity of a praying life.[2] How could one pray in Auschwitz or Buchenwald? Why would one pray amid such an existence? Wiesel ventures an answer to these sorts of questions: "It is indeed possible to live or at least to exist without hope, perhaps even without truth, but not without prayer; for prayer, as an urgent movement inward and outward, is a way toward life."[3]

The poems within Psalms model this way toward life. Their manifest diversity bears witness to the ways in which prayer propels the life of faith in all its variety. The psalmists' expressive movement inward and outward conveys their absolute dependence on the author of life. As the one who gives and sustains life, God receives the prayers and praises of everything that has breath (150:6). This orientation toward life and the author of life implies that humans are more than *Homo sapiens*; they are *Homo quaerens*, creatures who ask and ask.[4] Psalms stages this asking *coram Deo*. The psalmists' varying questions, pleas, and prayers depict the life of faith as jubilant and fraught, as safe and unsettling, as promising and painful. Singing the lyrics of Psalms' poetic performance of the life of faith, a person is caught up in the harmony of "praise seeking understanding."[5]

Reading Individual Psalms

The Covenantal Context of the Psalms

Understanding is hard won in the book of Psalms. One could make a strong case that Psalms envisions a life of "pain seeking understanding."[6]

Psalms and the Moral Self

Psalms' portrayal of a person's ability to think, choose, and act in accord with the divine will creates a dynamic vision of the moral self. Several psalms indicate that humans can make choices that are compatible with the divine will (18:20–24; 26:1–5). That is, humans possess the moral ability to choose and to act rightly. This vision of the moral self is exemplified through the book's depiction of the righteous (37:30; 112:1–10; 125:3). Other psalms assume humans are deeply flawed creatures who are unable to think, choose, and act rightly. On this account, humans do not possess the moral ability to live in accord with the divine will, because their faculties are incapacitated by sin (51:5; 53:1–3; 130:3; 143:2). They suffer from congenital sinfulness (14:3). These perspectives on the moral self in Psalms are not mutually exclusive. The Psalter assumes that humans sin, but their moral ability may be rehabilitated through relationship with Yahweh and knowledge of his will.[a]

According to the Psalter, understanding surfaces in human experience at the intersection of knowledge of God and knowledge of self.[7] Psalms' understanding of the moral self in relation to God is profound. This is not surprising, for the Psalter may be the most introspective book in all of Scripture.[8] Its introspection, however, does not serve as the occasion for what moderns call "expressive individualism." Instead, the psalms map the dynamics of relational expressivism. They explore the realism of a life lived before the face and under the sovereign reign of the triune God. In so doing, they not only portray all the movements of the human soul; they also offer a rich description of how one lives in and maintains covenant relationship with God.

Covenant is the underlying premise of the poems in Psalms; it is the relational framework within which the poems live and move and have their being. Within this framework, the psalmists offer praise to the one who is worthy of praise (18:3). They express gratitude for God's specific, concrete intervention in human life (30:2–3, 11–12), and they question God's covenant fidelity (44:23–24). They ask for forgiveness (51:1–2) and cry out for help (60:11). They recommend certain judgments (109:6–20), exhibit trust in God's generous care (Ps. 27), and celebrate God's sovereign reign (Ps. 97). And they remember God's mighty acts in history (Ps. 105). The psalmists stand on the promise at the essence of covenant relationship with God: "I will be your God, and you will be my people" (Exod. 6:7; Lev. 26:12; Jer. 7:23; 11:4; 30:22; 31:33; Ezek. 36:28). This stance pervades the prayers in the Psalter, where the psalmists employ the expressions "*my* God" (e.g., Pss. 3:7; 7:1, 3; 13:3; 18:6; 22:1–2; 30:2), "*my* Lord" (16:2; 35:23), "*my* king" (5:2; 68:24; 74:12), "*my* shepherd" (23:1), "*my* helper" (54:4), "*my* strength," "*my* rock," "*my* fortress," "*my* deliverer," "*my* shield," and "*my* stronghold" (18:1–2; cf. 31:3–4; 59:9, 17; 62:6; 71:3). The use of the first-person pronoun "my" is more than a minor syntactical detail. This little word carries the weight of the psalmists' covenant relationship with God.

The Genre of Individual Psalms: The Form-Critical Approach

Covenant may be the relational context within which to read, meditate on, and perform the psalms, but the book is hospitable to other forms

Figure 12.1. *David Praising God* by unknown artist (1810)

of reading. Hermann Gunkel's form-critical approach means that most modern interpreters focus on the discrete genres within Psalms, classifying the poems according to their poetic structure, literary characteristics, and mood.[9] This way of reading creates the conditions for discerning family resemblance among poems, distinctive features of various poems, and the literary categories within which the psalms participate. While Gunkel identified a handful of poetic genres, others have refined and extended his generic types, classifying and exploring psalms under the headings of laments, hymns, and psalms of thanksgiving, as well as royal psalms, wisdom psalms, torah psalms, and psalms of remembrance. This approach to the individual poems in the Psalter is helpful, provided that one sees genres as porous or fluid, not hermetically sealed categories.[10] A psalm may have characteristics of different types of lyric poetry. The combination of these elements reveals the creativity, literary texture, and aesthetic delight of the psalms.

The Liturgical Setting of Individual Psalms: The Cult-Functional Approach

Gunkel's form-critical approach reached beyond shared characteristics and structural features endemic in certain genres to include their settings in life (*Sitz im Leben*). This aspect of the form-critical project found new life in Sigmund Mowinckel's exploration of the psalms. Most interpreters in the history of reception argued or assumed that the psalms functioned in the context of liturgical worship. Mowinckel focused on this liturgical setting, transforming Gunkel's form-critical approach to the Psalter into a "*cult-functional*" approach.[11] Although Mowinckel acknowledged that the Psalter contains some noncultic psalms,[12] in light of the broader witness of the Old Testament and the testimony of the psalms, he argued that the poems were composed for and used in formal worship. He situated individual poems in specific festivals and rituals. The psalms, on this account, are "real cult psalms, made for cultic use."[13] For example, the Feast of Tabernacles and its connection with both the harvest and the new year festival serve as the liturgical occasion for the reenactment of Yahweh's enthronement as King. This enthronement includes the acclamation of Yahweh's kingship, the dramatic procession of the ark, the consecration of the temple, and the renewal of the Davidic covenant.[14] This enthronement festival is said to be the setting for almost forty psalms. While some prefer a rural setting for the psalms and others attenuate Mowinckel's totalizing reading of the psalms in the cult,[15] most interpreters recognize the intimate connection between the psalms and worship.

The Movement, Function, and Imagery of the Psalms

The forms and liturgical settings of the psalms provide a necessary context for interpretive developments in the Psalms' movement, function, and imagery. Claus Westermann perceived a movement from plea to praise and then thanksgiving, where the lament is resolved and praise culminates in the fulfillment of a vow expressing the psalmist's gratitude for Yahweh's intervention.[16] This movement coincides with Walter Brueggemann's functional approach to the Psalms. Channeling Paul Ricoeur's reflections on the dynamic movement of human life (see the sidebar "Ricoeur on the Text and the Human Self"), Brueggemann identifies the "sequence of orientation-disorientation-reorientation" as a useful guide for understanding the function of the psalms.[17] The psalms situate the reader in one of these positions: in praise, where human life in relation to God and others is marked by orientation; in lament or distress, where human life in relation to God and others is disorientated; and in thanksgiving, where human life in relation to God and others is reconstituted through a new coherence.[18] The psalms not only

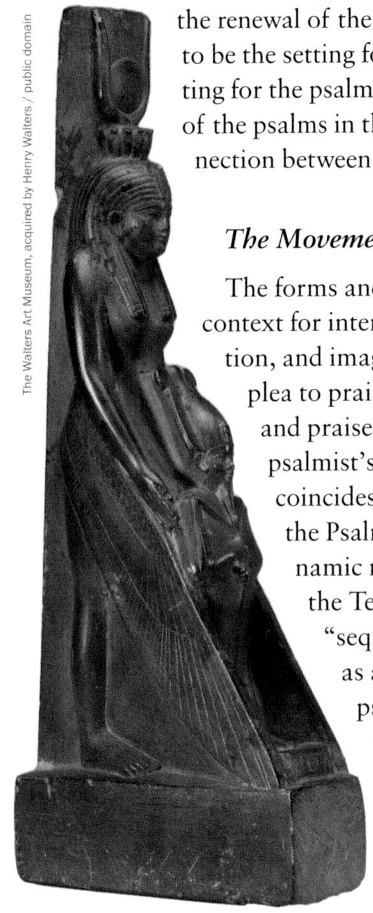

Figure 12.2. Statue of Isis protecting Osiris

situate the reader in one of these positions; they also provide the means for negotiating these positions and moving to a new—or renewed—place in the life of faith. This movement is neither simple nor cyclical, but it is enriched by an appreciation of the imagery and symbolic world of the psalms. William Brown constructs a sturdy bridge between the iconography of the ancient world and the imaginative metaphors in the psalms,[19] and many have crossed this bridge, focusing on metaphors or metaphorical networks in the psalms, as well as the ways in which iconographic representation informs a reading of the imagery in the psalms.[20]

This type of reading requires both imagination and historical sensitivity. Unfortunately, in the modern context, imagination and historical awareness are strange bedfellows, but both are necessary for a responsible, deep reading of the book of Psalms.

Reading the Psalms as a Coherent Collection

The covenantal-relational context of the psalms, the genre of the poems, their liturgical setting, and their movement, function, and imagery offer invaluable insight regarding how to read individual psalms. But what about the structure of Psalms as a whole? Is there any rhyme or reason for the architecture of the anthology? Is the book a random assemblage of lyric poetry or a deliberately crafted collection of prayers and instructions? The history of the Psalter's reception makes the answer to these questions clear: the book of Psalms has a deliberate design, which shapes its message and informs a reading of individual psalms. An influential book by Gerald Wilson regarding the canonical shape and shaping of Psalms changed the entire landscape of psalmic studies,[21] such that an interpreter must attend not only to the genre, setting, and function of individual psalms but also to the ways in which they fit within and contribute to the message of Psalms as a whole.

PHILOSOPHICAL ISSUES

Ricoeur on the Text and the Human Self

If anything binds together the work of Paul Ricoeur, it is the interrelationship between texts and the human self. The meaning of texts is bound up with the meaningfulness of human life. One comes to know oneself in front of a work. As Ricoeur argues concerning the understanding and appropriation of a text,

Ultimately, what I appropriate is a proposed world. The latter is not *behind* the text, as a hidden intention would be, but *in front of* it, as that which the work unfolds, discovers, reveals. Henceforth to understand is *to understand oneself in front of the text*. It is not a question of imposing upon the text our finite capacity of understanding, but of exposing ourselves to the text and receiving an enlarged self, which would be the proposed existence corresponding in the most suitable way to the world proposed.[b]

This understanding of the interrelationship between texts and the human self informs Ricoeur's poetics of faith. The language of Scripture reorients the reader by first disorienting the reader.[c]

HISTORICAL MATTERS

Ancient Iconography and Psalms

A sensitivity to ancient Near Eastern iconography adds a visual and historical focus to the imagery in Psalms. For example, Psalms often depicts Yahweh as a bird, covering his people in the shadow of his wings (17:8; 36:7; 57:1; 61:4; 63:7; 91:4). This metaphor is concretized in images across the ancient world that depict deities sheltering others under their wings.[d]

The Five Books of Psalms

The book of Psalms is divided into five books.

Book 1: Psalms 1–41
Book 2: Psalms 42–72
Book 3: Psalms 73–89
Book 4: Psalms 90–106
Book 5: Psalms 107–150

Wilson drew on the nature and the organization of ancient Near Eastern hymnic collections to identify explicit and implicit signs of editorial activity in the book of Psalms (i.e., its "shape"). These signs inform his description of the editorial purpose of the book's organization (i.e., its "shaping"). Among the signs of editorial activity, the division of Psalms into five books (Pss. 1–41; 42–72; 73–89; 90–106; 107–50), the presence of a doxology at the conclusion of each book, the placement of Psalms 1–2 and Psalms 146–50 at the frame of the anthology, the assemblage of psalms attributed to a particular author within specific books, and the positioning of royal psalms at the seams of certain books may be the most significant.

The fivefold division of Psalms reflects purposeful arrangement. This division mirrors the division of the Pentateuch, and it also invites the reading of Psalms in conversation with the rest of Scripture. Just as the second section of the Hebrew Bible (the Prophets) opens with Yahweh's command to Joshua to meditate on the Torah day and night (Josh. 1:8), so also the third section of the Hebrew Bible (the Writings) opens with a depiction of the blessed person, who delights in the Torah and meditates on it day and night (Ps. 1:2). The doxologies at the conclusion of each book of Psalms are not editorial appendages. They are "integral parts" of the concluding psalms.[22] When received within the shape of the anthology, they signal that the life of faith is always oriented toward praise. The same is true of the Psalter as a whole. Psalms 1 and 2 serve as a formal introduction to the anthology. Framed by "blessed" formulas (1:1; 2:12), these psalms provide a "pair of hermeneutical spectacles" through which to read Psalms.[23] They sketch a form of life marked by obedience under the reign of Yahweh and his king. They also alert the reader to the Torah-like, instructional nature of the psalms, as well as to the reality that the life of faith is lived in view of the sovereign rule of Yahweh. This vision explains the conclusion of Psalms, a sequence of psalms framed by the imperative "Hallelujah"—"Praise Yahweh!"—and the climactic call for everything that has breath to praise Yahweh (146:1, 10; 147:1, 20; 148:1, 14; 149:1, 9; 150:1–6).

In addition to the Psalter's fivefold division, the doxological conclusion to each book, and the frame of the anthology, Wilson identified authorial attributions as an organizing principle in books 1–3 and thematic groupings in certain portions of Psalms. But Wilson's most influential observation concerns the positioning of the royal psalms at the seams of books 1–3. These psalms recall the story of the Davidic monarchy and set the stage for the appropriate response to its demise. Together, the royal psalms give the book of Psalms a storied character.[24] Psalm 2 describes the coronation of the Davidic king and Yahweh's protection of his anointed amid the raging of the nations. At the close of book 1, Psalm 41 reinforces the assurance of Yahweh's protection of his king. At the close of book 2, Psalm 72 marks the passing of royal rule to Solomon, asks Yahweh to enable the king to govern in justice and righteousness, and concludes with the editorial remark that the prayers of David have ended (72:20). Since Solomon failed to embody the vision of royal rule in Psalm 72, it is not surprising that book 3 ends with the apparent failure of Yahweh to preserve the Davidic monarchy; Psalm 89 foregrounds the Davidic covenant and its promises. The psalmist appeals to Yahweh's loyal faithfulness, calling him to remember his promises to David and restore the dynasty. Book 4 then offers an unexpected

Figure 12.3. *David with a Lute* by Zoltán Joó (2012)

response. Standing at the "editorial 'center'" of Psalms,[25] it provides an answer to the absence of a Davidic king by reasserting Yahweh's kingship, emphasizing the fact that Yahweh has always been and will always be a refuge for his people, and announcing a blessing on all who trust in him.[26] Book 5 elaborates, cultivating dependence on and trust in Yahweh alone.[27] The entire book concludes on a definite note: "YHWH is *eternal* king, only *he* is ultimately worthy of trust. Human 'princes' will wither and fade like the grass, but the steadfast love of YHWH endures forever."[28]

The story Wilson narrated through the seams of books 1–3 and the theological themes of books 4–5 has garnered widespread agreement. Wilson has modified aspects of this metanarrative,[29] and others have adjusted its contours.[30] Walter Brueggemann, for example, identifies Psalm 73 as the theological and canonical "center" of Psalms.[31] As the introduction to book 3, it plays a paradigmatic role in the Psalter's movement from obedience (Ps. 1) to praise (Ps. 150) by distilling and reenacting the argument brewing between

CANONICAL CONNECTIONS

Psalm 2 and the New Testament

Psalm 2 plays an important role in the rest of the canon. By staging the ascension of the Davidic king to the throne, it celebrates Yahweh's covenant commitment to the Davidic dynasty (2 Sam. 7:5–16). The psalm's description of the nations and peoples that oppose the Lord's anointed provides the pattern for the opposition that Herod, Pilate, the gentiles, and the Jews have toward Jesus (Ps. 2:1–2; Acts 4:25–27). The declaration "You are my son" marks the coronation of the Davidic king (Ps. 2:7) and signals the beginning of Jesus's extended coronation as king, which commences at his baptism (Mark 1:11; Luke 3:22; cf. Gen. 22:2, 12, 16; Matt. 3:17; Acts 13:32–33). More than this, the writer to the Hebrews uses the declaration "You are my son" to illuminate Jesus's sonship and unique relationship with the Father and to reveal the eternal generation of the only begotten Son (Heb. 1:5).

Psalm 1 and Psalm 150: the poem moves from an affirmation of God's loving faithfulness to doubt regarding that loving faithfulness, then to the ultimate embrace of it in confidence.[32] On this account, Psalms is not necessarily a "story" of the establishment and downfall of the Davidic dynasty, which lays the foundation for the reaffirmation of Yahweh's reign; instead, the book maps a journey from obedience to praise by way of the crisis and resolution of Yahweh's loving faithfulness.[33] David Mitchell builds on Wilson's work but shifts the anthology's horizon away from a chronology of the Davidic monarchy to a vision of eschatological events,[34] while James Mays focuses on the place and contribution of the torah psalms to the message of the book.[35] Far from undermining Wilson's canonical reading of Psalms, these alternative accounts of the book's shape and message illuminate different ways in which the anthology may be construed. Each bears witness to the fact that Psalms is a deliberately crafted anthology of lyric poetry.

This assumption has not only resulted in different canonical readings of Psalms; it has generated close investigations of specific books, smaller groups of psalms, and themes woven throughout the anthology. Studies devoted to the message of book 3, the structure of and relationship between Psalms 93–100, and the anti-imperialist agenda of book 5 represent explorations of how coherence at the macrolevel of the Psalter has attuned readers to micro-level coherence within the anthology.[36] These analyses are complemented by thematic investigations. The motifs of Yahweh as refuge, Yahweh's loving faithfulness, and kingship are just a few examples of the Psalter's theological interests.[37] Whether read from a compositional or a thematic perspective, the conviction that Psalms is a coherent anthology with a purposeful shape supports a multileveled reading that considers individual psalms and their settings, their relationship with poems that share a family resemblance, and their place within the book as a whole.

This multileveled way of reading is the hermeneutical ideal. The broad sketch of interpretive approaches to Psalms narrated above opened with Gunkel and his work in the twentieth century. The Psalter, of course, captured the attention of the people of God well before this time.[38] In light of the focus of this volume, historicist considerations of the date of the psalms and the nature of their superscriptions are passed off to other works.[39] Christian interpretation of Psalms will govern the discussion that follows. As Christian approaches to and interpretations of Psalms demonstrate, perhaps there is nothing new under the sun.

RECEPTION HISTORY

Psalms in the Dead Sea Scrolls

Among the texts recovered from Qumran, thirty-six fragments bear witness to Psalms. This is the largest representation of any single biblical book at Qumran. Some manuscripts contain psalms only from books 1–3, while others contain psalms only from books 4–5. Still others contain unknown or noncanonical psalms (e.g., Ps. 151, see LXX). These manuscripts from Qumran are invaluable. They inform text-critical investigations of certain psalms. They offer a window into the canonical development and editing of Psalms. Commentaries on particular psalms illuminate their reception and function within a particular community in the Second Temple period, providing a context for their interpretation in the New Testament.[e]

Figure 12.4. The Great Psalms Scroll

Christian Readings of the Psalms

Christian readings of the psalms are diverse—like the book itself. Three representative readers from the early church will serve as the focus of attention here: Athanasius, Gregory of Nyssa, and Augustine. Athanasius's *Letter to Marcellinus* provides a window into the ways in which Christians conceptualized, read, and used the psalms. Gregory of Nyssa's *Treatise on the Inscriptions of the Psalms* exemplifies a canonical reading of Psalms oriented toward a particular end. Augustine's *Expositions of the Psalms* is a treasure of theological readings of Psalms. While Gregory's work has been less influential in the history of reception, Athanasius's letter was so significant that it was used as the introduction to Psalms in the Greek manuscript Codex Alexandrinus.[40] Augustine's theological approach to the psalms was so influential that it governed Western Christian readings of the book for more than a thousand years.[41] These early interpreters not only model different ways of reading the Psalter as Christian Scripture; they also help us understand modern approaches to the book.

> **HISTORICAL MATTERS**
>
> **Codex Alexandrinus**
>
> Dated to the fifth century AD, Codex Alexandrinus is one of the earliest manuscripts that includes both the Old and New Testaments.

Athanasius: The Psalms as Prayers for Christians

Athanasius's interpretation of the Psalms in his *Letter to Marcellinus* is wide ranging. The letter does not have the form-critical sophistication of Gunkel and his followers, but it does demonstrate a sensitivity to different types of psalms and, more importantly, the circumstances within which they may be sung.[42] With many early Christian interpreters, Athanasius operates under the assumption that Scripture is useful (2 Tim. 3:16).[43] The usefulness of individual psalms extends well beyond their prophetic witness to the incarnation, suffering, death, resurrection, and ascension of the Son; it also includes their (trans)formative nature.

> **CANONICAL CONNECTIONS**
>
> **Jesus and the Psalms**
>
> The New Testament uses a handful of psalms to describe the person, suffering, death, resurrection, and exaltation of the Son. Several of these psalms are discussed in this chapter and the next. Others deserve a brief mention here. Psalm 16, Psalm 110, and Psalm 118 play an important role in the witness of the New Testament. Psalm 16 bears witness to the resurrection of the Son (Ps. 16:10; Acts 2:26–31; 13:35). Psalm 110 speaks of Jesus's divine nature and royal status (Ps. 110:1; Matt. 22:44; Mark 12:36; Luke 20:42–43; Acts 2:34–35). Psalm 118 provides the grammar for describing the anticipated deliverance, rejection, and exaltation of the Son (Ps. 118:22–23; Matt. 21:42; Mark 12:10–11; Luke 20:17; Acts 4:11; cf. Ps. 118:25–26; Matt. 21:9; 23:39; Mark 11:9; Luke 19:38; John 12:13; Eph. 2:20–22; 1 Pet. 2:4–8).

Athanasius on Psalms

Reflecting on the scriptural uniqueness of Psalms, Athanasius writes:

> The Book of Psalms thus has a certain grace of its own, and a distinctive exactitude of expression. For in addition to the other things in which it enjoys an affinity and fellowship with the other books, it possesses, beyond that, this marvel of its own—namely, that it contains even the emotions of each soul, and it has the changes and rectifications of these delineated and regulated in itself. Therefore anyone who wishes boundlessly to receive and understand from it, so as to mold himself, it is written there.[f]

HISTORICAL MATTERS

Hellenistic Music

Music was part of the Hellenistic liberal arts curriculum. The mathematical structure of music served as a lens through which to discern the rational nature and order of reality. More specifically, the mathematical character, rational design, and harmony of music provided a pattern for human life. Early Christian readers leveraged this conception of music in their understanding of the psalms. Like music, the psalms restored and attuned humans and human life in harmony with their Creator.[g]

PHILOSOPHICAL ISSUES

The *Logos*

Logos is a Greek term denoting "word" or "reason." Its significance emerged in early Western philosophical thought. According to the pre-Socratic philosopher Heraclitus, the *logos* is the principle underlying the change or flux within the world, endowing the cosmos with order and intelligibility. And for Plato, the *logos* is the ordering principle of all reality. The Gospel of John adopts and recasts this term, identifying Jesus Christ as the *logos* (John 1:1–14).

Athanasius's description of the psalms as useful resembles Brueggemann's functional typology, but Athanasius casts things in a different frame of reference. Filtering the language of Hellenistic philosophical schools through a Christian perspective, Athanasius attends to the ways in which the psalms are a "mold" or "model" on and through which to form or conform the self.[44] Reframing Hellenistic music theory, Athanasius identifies the ways in which the psalms attune the self in harmony with creation in general and the Logos in particular.[45]

The form of individual psalms provides a model on which the reader might form themselves. But the psalms offer more than a pattern for readers; they also provide a mirror. Athanasius argues,

> It seems to me that these words become like a mirror to the person singing them, so that he might perceive himself and the emotions of his soul, and thus affected, he might recite them. . . . And so, on the whole, each psalm is both spoken and composed by the Spirit so that in these same words, as was said earlier, the stirrings of our souls might be grasped, and all of them be said as concerning us, and the same issue from us as our own words, for a remembrance of the emotions in us, and a chastening of our life.[46]

In addition to embracing humanity's embodied and emotional creatureliness, the psalms serve as a "corrective lens," illuminating what has become obscured and disfigured through sin.[47] They are a mirror, but no ordinary mirror. They do not necessarily show readers their own faces; they give the reader a face.[48] In so doing, the psalms provide a pattern on which humans may amend their lives in harmony with God, with others, and with the created world. They map "the perfect image for the souls' course of life."[49] Their words create spiritual harmony in the soul.[50]

Gregory of Nyssa: The Psalms as a Guide to Spiritual Ascent

While Athanasius sketched the form and function of individual psalms, Gregory of Nyssa described the form and function of the anthology throughout the first part of his *Treatise on the Inscriptions of the Psalms*. According to Gregory, the shape of Psalms shapes a life of virtue, leading one on a journey toward blessedness. This form of reading is similar to functional and canonical approaches to Psalms. Westermann perceived a movement in the book from plea to praise and thanksgiving; Brueggemann saw a dialectical movement from orientation to disorientation, then to reorientation; Wilson read an unfolding story in Psalms. Gregory identified a progressive program of spiritual development across the book.

The book's boundaries mark the order (*taxis*) and goal (*telos*) of this program. Blessedness is both the entryway and the destination of Psalms (Pss. 1, 150),[51] and the pathway to blessedness is charted across the fivefold division of Psalms. As the entryway to spiritual ascent, Psalm 1 describes two ways of life, guiding one to the good and to the avoidance of evil.[52] At the threshold of book 2, Psalm 42 cultivates a desire for the good. The virtuous person thirsts for more intimate union with God, just as the deer longs for springs of water.[53] This longing is honed through the introduction to book 3 (Ps. 73), where spiritual discernment enables the virtuous person to discriminate between good and evil, to see the hope that transcends physical appearances, and to declare that apart from God, nothing on earth is desirable (73:25).[54] When the virtuous person reaches the lofty height of book 4 (Ps. 90), like Moses, they become a teacher of the Law and an intercessor for those in need.[55] At the summit of the book (Ps. 150), one finds the fulfillment of human salvation, summed up in the expression "Praise the Lord!" (150:1).[56] The fivefold division of Psalms, the doxology at the end of each book, and the psalms at the seams of the books all serve as clues for Gregory. They reveal a program of ascent, guiding one to the goal of divine blessedness.

Augustine: Reading the Psalms in Union with Christ

Augustine's approach to Psalms was to harness certain theological resources to exemplify Christian interpretation of the psalms. With Athanasius, Gregory, and other Christian interpreters, Augustine viewed the psalms as a means of healing and as an instrument through which the Christian is attuned to life with the triune God. Augustine's *Expositions of the Psalms* not only reinforces these uses of the psalms; it provides a theological lens through which to read them. This theological lens is forged through the concept of *totus Christus* (the "whole Christ").

This concept is grounded in representative biblical texts. Among them, the most significant may be the parable of the sheep and the goats (Matt. 25:31–46), Saul's encounter with the ascended Christ on the road to Damascus (Acts 9:1–19), and Paul's discourse on the unity of the body (1 Cor. 12:12–31). In different ways, each of these texts explores the intimate, inseparable union between Christ and his people. When one of Christ's people is hungry, thirsty, marginalized, naked, sick, or imprisoned, then Christ is hungry, thirsty, marginalized, naked, sick, or imprisoned (Matt. 25:34–40). When Saul is confronted by the ascended Lord, Jesus asks him, "Why do you persecute *me*?" (Acts 9:4). When Paul describes the nature of the church, he envisions many parts that form one body of Christ; if one part suffers, then every part of the body suffers with it (1 Cor. 12:12, 24, 26–27).

Totus Christus funds a theological approach to Psalms. This approach, however, is by no means monolithic. The ecclesial and christological resources of *totus Christus* help the reader to perceive different things in different types of psalms. *Totus Christus*, for example, allows one to negotiate the variegated content of the psalms. Those psalms that speak of distress, suffering, and deliverance from the realm of the dead are construed as Christ's prayers in his passion and redemptive victory. Psalms that express sin, guilt, and divine abandonment are perceived as either the church's words to Christ or Christ's words prayed on behalf of his people. Because the Christian is part of the body and the church is the body united to its head, Christ remains present in this form of reading. Michael Cameron captures the exegetical and theological logic of *totus Christus* when he writes, "The logic of this exegesis is that the individual Christian prays *within* the church's voice, just as the church prays *within* the voice of Christ. The different voices of the body and the head speak in unison (*simul*) with Christ's voice, but the church and its members speak *through him*."[57] When read through the lens of *totus Christus*, the psalms invite individual Christians and the church to read themselves into the poems as the speaking voice. They speak, but they speak with Christ and through Christ. They speak or pray, and Christ, by implication, speaks or prays in the Christian and the church as its head.

THEOLOGICAL ISSUES

Augustine on Psalms

In his helpful introduction to Augustine's *Expositions*, Michael Fiedrowicz catalogs five different forms of reading the psalms that exemplify Augustine's concept of the "whole Christ." Through the lens of *totus Christus*, the psalms may be read (1) as a word to Christ (*vox ad Christum*); (2) as a word about Christ (*vox de Christo*); (3) as a word spoken by Christ himself (*vox Christi*); (4) as a word about the church (*vox de ecclesia*); and (5) as a word spoken by the church (*vox ecclesiae*).[i] Each of these forms of reading understands the psalms as prophetic poems that probe the mystery of Christ and his relationship to the church.

What does this mean? It means that Christ speaks in every psalm, and the Christian as well as the church speaks in every psalm. Christ prays for his people, and the church prays to the triune God, united to Christ. This dynamic characterizes Augustine's reading of the psalms. Psalm 3, for example, presents the words of Christ, reflecting his betrayal by Judas, his abandonment by his disciples, and his passion;

Figure 12.5. *The Parable of the Sheep and the Goats*, reproduction of sixth-century Byzantine mosaic

and Psalm 3 represents the prayer of the persecuted church united to its head.[58] Psalm 30 expresses the lament, the fear, and the trust of Christ and his church through a unified voice.[59] The cry of dereliction in Psalm 22:1 assumes the union between Christ and the church: "We were in him," Augustine writes, "when he cried out, *My God, my God, why have you forsaken me?* for in the psalm which opens with those words the next phrase speaks of *the tale of my sins.* . . . What sins could there be in him?

THEOLOGICAL ISSUES

Christ Speaking in Psalms

Like other Christian interpreters, Augustine identifies places in the psalms where only Christ speaks. This represents prosopological exegesis, according to which the interpreter assigns a nontrivial speaker or addressee to an ambiguous voice or agent to make sense of the text. When a reader encounters a psalm where a speaker or actor is ambiguous, the New Testament invites the interpreter to identify these ambiguous figures. Jesus, for example, quotes Psalm 110:1 and invites his audience to assign an appropriate persona to the psalm's ambiguous

"my Lord": "Yahweh says to my Lord, sit at my right hand, until I make your enemies a footstool for your feet" (Matt. 22:43; Mark 12:36). If the Messiah is the son of David, then how can David call this figure Lord? Who is this Lord? The writer to the Hebrews also employs prosopological exegesis. The author quotes Psalm 2:7 (Heb. 1:5a), 2 Samuel 7:14 (Heb. 1:5b), Psalm 45:6–7 (Heb. 1:8–9), Psalm 110:1 (Heb. 1:13), and Psalm 40:6–8 (Heb. 10:5–7), assigning appropriate speakers and addresses to the persons of the Trinity.[j]

RECEPTION HISTORY

Convocation and Psalms

The unison of Christ's voice, the church's voice, and the Christian's voice in the voice of the psalmists is comparable to Wendell Berry's concept of convocation. Convocation is a rich concept that captures the reality of a person's membership within a community and the process by which a person understands themselves as members of a community. On Berry's own admission, convocation is a concept that he derives from Paul's description of the church as the body of Christ (1 Cor. 12). As the body of Christ, the people of God are members of one another. "Convocation" captures this membership within

a community; it "is both a fact and a process: it describes the fact of our membership as well as the process by which we come to inhabit our roles within this membership."[k] The process of this membership is mediated by a convocation, where the voices of the past are brought to life to sustain the members of the community. Poetry plays an important role in this process. Berry notes that "any poem worth the name is the product of a convocation. It exists, literally, by recalling past voices into presence."[l] Augustine's theological reading of the psalms bears the marks of this recollection.

Jesus and Psalm 22

Jesus's use of Psalm 22:1 on the cross not only captures his experience of divine wrath; it also signals
the importance of the entire psalm for his passion,
resurrection, and ascension. Jesus experiences deri-
sion and mocking (22:6–7; Matt. 27:39–44), the taunt
of divine deliverance (Ps. 22:8; Matt. 27:43–44), the
gaze of wicked observers (Ps. 22:16; Luke 23:35), the
piercing of his hands and feet (Ps. 22:16; John 19:37),
and the division of his garments by lot (Ps. 22:18;
Matt. 27:35). Just as the psalmist's lament led to the
expectation of universal joy at his deliverance (Ps.
22:22–31), so also Jesus's lament is answered in the
resurrection and ascension, which precipitates a cry
of praise across the nations. Jesus's use of Psalm 22:1
and the striking parallels between his passion and
the metaphorical language of the psalm suggest the
entire poem plays out in his death, descent, resurrection, and ascension.

None whatever, but our old nature was crucified
together with him, that our sinful body might
be destroyed, and that we might be slaves to sin
no more."[60]

The inseparable union between Christ and his
church underwrites the concept of *totus Christus*
and guides Augustine's theological reading of the
psalms. The breadth and depth of this theological
concept is capable of adapting to the breadth and
depth of the psalms. It explores the psalms within
the covenantal context of union with Christ. It leverages Christ's incarnation and redemptive work
to direct the church's reading of Psalms, and it
directs this reading along a clear path. Augustine
maps the contours of this path in his reading of
Psalm 140:

> If then he [Christ] is the head and we [the church] are the members, one
> single individual is speaking. Whether the head speaks or the members speak,
> the one Christ speaks. . . . This is how we should hear Christ speaking. Yet
> each one of us should at the same time hear his or her own voice, since we
> are all organically parts of Christ's body. Sometimes he will speak words that
> none of us can recognize as our own, for they belong only to the head, but
> even then Christ does not divorce himself from our words and withdraw into
> his own, nor does he go so far away as not to return from his own words to
> ours.[61]

This account of *totus Christus* explains why Augustine found the psalms
as a source of healing. *Totus Christus* allowed both the Christian and the
church to understand the life of faith and the implications of Christ's redemptive work in conversation with the psalms. This theological form of
reading helps Christians and the church understand Christ's share in their
pain, as well as the work of Christ that overcomes all sin and pain.[62]

Conclusion

These brief sketches of Christian readings of Psalms are representative of
different theological approaches to the anthology. Many metaphors deployed by Christian readers provide insight into the nature and function of
the psalms. In addition to a mirror, a means of attunement, and a source of

healing, the Psalter is characterized in a variety of ways across the history of its reception in the Christian community. In view of humanity's distaste for virtue, Basil the Great surmises that the Holy Spirit "mixed sweetness of melody with doctrine so that inadvertently we would absorb the benefit of the words through gentleness and ease of hearing, just as clever physicians frequently smear the cup with honey when giving the fastidious some rather bitter medicine to drink."[63] Ambrose describes the psalms as "a communal gymnasium of souls" and "a treasury of memories."[64] Chrysostom contends that the psalms "cleanse the soul."[65] Luther sees the Psalter as "a little Bible."[66] Calvin calls the Psalter "An Anatomy of All Parts of the Soul."[67] Gerhard von Rad treats Psalms under "Israel's answer" to Yahweh.[68] And John Witvliet observes that the Psalter provides "the deep grammar" for Christian prayer.[69]

These metaphorical descriptions of Psalms indicate that the anthology expresses "a *lived theology*," to use Rolf and Karl Jacobson's words.[70] This theology, like the book of Psalms itself, is rich and multifaceted, and it is performed within the covenantal framework of life in relation to God. The covenantal context of Psalms entails that the poems operate under a constellation of convictions that govern the way in which life is perceived. That is, the poems assume a particular theological worldview. At minimum, this worldview is founded on God's uniqueness and sovereignty, as well as his relational goodness.[71] These pillars of the book's worldview will occupy the discussion of theological themes in the next chapter.

Christian Reading Questions

1. Luther described the book of Psalms as "a little Bible." Is this an accurate description? How do the themes within the Psalms align with the major themes elsewhere in Scripture? Are any major themes that contribute to the message of Scripture missing from the Psalms?

2. Rolf and Karl Jacobson characterize the book of Psalms as "a lived theology." What is the content of this lived theology? Does Psalms exclude anything from its theological vision of life?

3. How would you evaluate the representative Christian readings of the psalms (i.e., Athanasius, Gregory, and Augustine)? How are these similar to and different from other readings of the psalms (i.e., form-critical, cult-functional, functional approaches)?

4. How do the psalms function as Christian Scripture?

CHAPTER THIRTEEN

Theological Themes in Psalms

The history of reception bears witness to the reality that the psalms have been sung, read, and used in different ways. Far from representing a liability, these multifaceted readings of the psalms reflect the multifaceted nature of the life of faith. Regardless of one's interpretive approach, the psalms operate within the context of covenantal communion with God. This context guides any reading of the psalms, and it is based on two theological themes: the character of God and the nature of the life of faith.

The Character of God

> READ PSALMS 18, 46, 93

Who is the God with whom the psalmists have to do and whose face they long to see? God is known by the psalmists. God receives the prayers of the psalmists, and his character is revealed through the praises, pleas, and testimonies of the psalmists. The diverse voices of the psalms merge into a harmonious song of God's character. The melodies of this harmonious song provide revelation through relationship. This revelation creates a theo-logic, showing who God is in himself as well as who God is in relationship.

God in Himself

The Psalter testifies to who God is in himself—that is, to who God is in his essence. For many, talk about God in himself is abstract and speculative, an unfortunate hangover from the Christian appropriation of aspects of Hellenistic philosophy. But for the psalmists, this sort of talk is invaluable, for God's essence informs their understanding of God's attributes. The psalmists consider God's essence through different forms of lyric discourse. They raise rhetorical questions, which praise God for his uniqueness: Who is God except Yahweh (18:31)? O God, who is like you (71:19)? What god is as great as God (77:13)? Who in the skies can be compared with Yahweh (89:6)? Who is like Yahweh among the divine beings (89:6)? O Yahweh, God of hosts, who is as mighty as you (89:8)? The answer to these questions is "no one." The psalmists celebrate God's incomparable nature. He is ontologically unique. He exists on a different level of being, in a class of his own, above all gods (95:3; 96:4; 135:5). His greatness is unsearchable (145:3). No one or nothing compares with him (40:5).

God's utter uniqueness explains the psalmists' descriptions of God's incomparable nature. In contrast to everything created, God is independent or self-subsistent. He is the living God (42:2), who exists forever (90:2; 119:89). His counsel and power do not derive from another (33:11; 62:11). He is the source of every good thing, the fount of life, and the wellspring of light (36:9). He does not change (102:26–27), and he cannot be measured by finite time because he is eternal, from everlasting to everlasting (90:2; 93:2). A thousand years in God's sight are like a watch in the night (90:4). These depictions of God's incomparable nature also indicate that God needs no one and nothing. This is one of the paradoxes of the psalms: God is self-subsistent, yet he works in creation and on behalf of his people for his glory and praise. The psalmists render to God the glory and praise due to his name, yet they give God nothing, for he is not in need of anything. Far from depicting a static, remote deity, these paradoxes reveal a God of grace and goodness; from his fullness, God gives himself freely and lovingly in covenant relationship, in providence, and in the salvation of his people.

Despite God's incomparable nature, the psalmists use names and analogical language to portray God's character. God is named by a multitude of names in Psalms. Some are familiar, like Yahweh, Most High, God of

---

THEOLOGICAL ISSUES

Greek Philosophy and Christian Reading

Many have criticized early Christian readers for uncritically integrating aspects of Greek philosophy into their reading of Scripture and construction of doctrine. As the argument goes, by integrating these aspects of Greek philosophy, early Christian readers exchanged the historical character and content of Scripture for philosophical reflection on abstract concepts, such as divine aseity, immutability, impassibility, and simplicity. Metaphysical accounts of the character and identity of God were considered Greek philosophy in theological dress.

Among others, Michael Allen and Craig Carter have pushed back on this perception of uncritical embrace of Greek philosophy by early Christian readers. More than demonstrating that early Christian readers were sensitive to the narrative logic and historical content of Scripture, they show how these Christian readers recast certain tenets of Greek philosophy within a Christian theological framework. This theological framework rejects the materialism, mechanism, and nominalism of modernity, privileging the supernatural, miracles, providence, and inspiration, all under a thick theological metaphysic.[a]

Jacob, my strength, my rock, and my redeemer. Others betray the psalmists' intimate relationship with God, such as my refuge (61:3), God of my right (4:1), my light (27:1), my hope (71:5), and keeper (121:5). More than any other book in the canon of Scripture, Psalms designates God with many names. This rich diversity of divine names gestures toward the attributes indicative of God's essence and his relationship with his creatures. As Herman Bavinck observes,

> The name of God in Scripture does not describe God as he exists within himself but God in his revelation and multiple relations to his creatures. . . . What God reveals of himself is expressed and conveyed in specific names. To his creatures he grants the privilege of naming and addressing him on the basis of, and in keeping with, his revelation. The *one* name of God, which is inclusive of his entire revelation both in nature and in grace, is divisible for us in a great many names. Only in that way do we obtain a full view of the riches of his revelation and the profound meaning of his name.[1]

God's many names in the Psalter not only reveal the profound depths of his essence; they also specify his attributes and who he is in relationship.

God in Relationship

The self-subsistence, immutability, and eternity of God's incomparable being in Psalms do not inhibit his relationship with his people. To the contrary, they create the conditions for relationship with his people. God is of himself and from himself, but he gives of himself in creation, in his providential ordering of all things, and in covenant relationship with his people (Pss. 104, 105). The psalmists draw confidence from divine immutability, addressing God through the epithet "rock" (19:14; 31:3; 62:2, 7). Like a rock, God does not change; he is reliable. The psalmists find hope in God's eternity. While God exists outside of finite time, he intervenes within finite time and remains present within every second of time (139:7). The psalmists bear witness to the security and comfort brought by God's transcendence and immanence. God sits enthroned on high (113:5; cf. 93:4; 97:9; 115:3), and from this transcendent position, he looks down (14:2; 53:2; 80:14; 102:19). His transcendence, however, is not an obstacle to his immanence. As the psalmists testify, God is a father to the fatherless, a defender of widows (68:5), a refuge (7:1; 9:9; 73:28), and a dwelling place (90:1). His eyes and ears are attentive to the righteous (34:15). He is close to the brokenhearted (34:18). He looks upon the lowly (138:6) and hears the needy (69:33). He is near to any and all who call upon him (145:18).

THEOLOGICAL ISSUES

Divine Immutability

The doctrine of divine immutability affirms that God does not change. In contrast to created beings, God is not contingent on his becoming. He is absolute being or actuality.

Figure 13.1. God looking down from his throne. Vault fresco in the Church of St-Léon de Westmount, Montreal, Canada

God as Creator

The logic of God's transcendence and immanence corresponds with the logic of God's relationship with creation. The divide between Creator and creation is clear in Psalms (33:6–9; 89:47–48), but this divide does not prevent the Creator from attending to the works of his fingers. The world and all who live in it belong to Yahweh (24:1). He knits together each human in the womb (139:13); he endows humanity with a unique status, dignity, and vocation within the economy of creation (8:5–8; 95:6). He preserves creation in his generous providence and provides for each creature (104:10–18). God's commitment to creation is given particular expression in Psalm 104:19–23, where the psalmist declares,

> He made the moon for appointed times;
>   the sun knows its time for setting.
> You make darkness, and it is night;
>   all the animals of the forest come creeping out.
> The young lions roar for their prey,
>   seeking their food from God.
> The sun rises, and they withdraw.
>   They lie down in their dens.
> Humans go out to their work,
>   to their labor until the evening.

The rhythm of creation attests to God's generous governance of the cosmos. He sustains all things. Humans are the object of his attention. He knows that they are dust, and he has compassion on those who fear him (103:13–18).

God as King

Although God is separate from creation, the psalmists use a range of images and concepts from creation to describe God's character and attributes. The natural implication of God as Creator is that God is King. This metaphor plays an indispensable role in the book's vision of reality. The confession of Yahweh's kingship and the declaration "Yahweh reigns" are part of what James Mays calls "a vision of reality that is the theological center of the Psalter. . . . The psalmic understanding of the people of God, the city of God, the king of God and the law of God depends on its validity and implications. The psalmic functions of praise, prayer and instruction are responses to it."[2] These sweeping observations suggest that Yahweh's sovereign reign orients and orders all of life. It places the entire spectrum of human life with all its ups and downs under the rule of Yahweh. It classifies the king of God and the people of God as subjects of Yahweh, and it identifies Yahweh's revealed instruction as the authoritative guide for the life of his people.

Yahweh's kingship serves as a central metaphorical concept through which the psalmists see the world, and it opens the door for other metaphors. If God is the absolute sovereign, it is not surprising that the psalmists describe him as shepherd (23:1), judge (7:11), warrior (78:65), shield (28:7), redeemer (19:14), deliverer (18:2), portion (73:26), and father (89:26), to name just a few. These metaphors explore God's benevolence, justice and righteousness, zeal, protection, salvation, provision, compassion, and discipline. The imagery awakens the imagination, inviting one to discern the deep dimensions of God's character and nature in relationship. They force a person to come to terms with *how* God is like these images and concepts from the natural world. In so doing, they initiate the process of contemplation, discernment, and synthesis to create new ways of understanding God.[3] 📜

CANONICAL CONNECTIONS 📜

God as Shepherd

The metaphor of God as shepherd plays an important role throughout Scripture, especially the Old Testament (Gen. 48:15; 49:24; Pss. 23:1; 28:9; 77:20; 78:52; 80:1; Isa. 40:11; Ezek. 34:11–31). As a shepherd, God protects and provides for his sheep, guiding them along a life of flourishing. He stands in sharp contrast to the shepherds/leaders of Israel, who use their position and power to brutalize the flock and to satisfy their own desires (Ezek. 34:1–10). The metaphor GOD IS A SHEPHERD and its contrast with self-interested human shepherds/leaders creates the context for Jesus's declaration "I am the *good* shepherd" (John 10:11, 14).

The God of Loving Faithfulness

The images across the Psalter mediate God's character and nature in relation to both creation and his people. While God's kingship is a central metaphor in the book's vision of reality, Yahweh's "loving faithfulness" (*hesed*) is central to Psalms' vision of the way in which God exists in relationship.[4] This defining attribute of God pervades Psalms; more than half of the occurrences of the term in the Old Testament are found in Psalms. Why? Yahweh's loving faithfulness captures his relational goodness. This explains the familiar refrain "for he is good, for his loving faithfulness endures forever" (106:1; 107:1; 118:1, 29; 136:1; cf. 1 Chron. 16:34; 2 Chron. 5:13; 7:3; Ezra 3:11). The interrelationship between God's goodness and loving faithfulness seems to derive from Exodus 33–34, where Yahweh offers the most extensive description of his character in the Old Testament. After the golden calf incident, Moses asks to see Yahweh's "glory" (Exod. 33:18). Yahweh accepts Moses's request, affirming that he will cause all his "goodness" (33:19) to pass before him. When Yahweh descends in the cloud and stands with Moses, he proclaims his "name" (34:5):

> Yahweh, Yahweh,
>> a God compassionate and gracious,
>> slow to anger and abounding in loving faithfulness [*hesed*] and truth,
>> keeping loving faithfulness [*hesed*] to thousands,
>> forgiving iniquity and transgression and sin,
>> but not leaving the guilty unpunished,
>> visiting the iniquity of the parents upon the children,
>> to the third and fourth generation. (34:6–7)

According to the logic of Exodus 33–34, God's goodness is inextricably linked to his loving faithfulness (*hesed*). Psalms uses this link to explore the relational goodness of the God of loving faithfulness.

This link is also evident through the psalmists' use of Exodus 34:6–7. In Psalm 86, the threat of a violent gang prompts an appeal for God's mercy as expressed in Exodus 34:6: "But you, O Lord, are a God compassionate and gracious, slow to anger and abounding in loving faithfulness and truth" (Ps. 86:15). God's relational goodness to Moses and his people provides the occasion for claiming God's relational goodness in the psalmist's own experience in Psalm 103, which is cast in terms of Exodus 34:6: "Yahweh is compassionate and gracious, slow to anger and abounding in loving faithfulness" (Ps. 103:8). In praising God *the* King (145:1), the psalmist extols Yahweh's attributes, developing his "abundant goodness" (145:7) with the help of Exodus 34:6: "Gracious and compassionate is Yahweh, slow to anger and great of loving faithfulness. Yahweh is good to all, and his compassions are over all his works" (Ps. 145:8–9). What is noteworthy about these uses of Exodus 34 is which of God's attributes they highlight: Yahweh's punishment of the guilty is not mentioned; his compassion, grace, patience, and loving faithfulness are foregrounded. This is not surprising, for these attributes distill who God is in relationship with his people.

God's relational goodness and loving faithfulness define the nature of his sovereign rule and the way he relates to his people in Psalms. These theological concepts orient one to who God is in relationship, and so they also orient one to the nature of the life of faith.

The Nature of the Life of Faith

▓ READ PSALMS 19, 23, 30, 51, 100, 109 ▓

The Psalter's vision of the life of faith rings true to reality. This vision is capacious; it includes praise and pain, joy and despondence, confidence and doubt, dancing and weeping, confession and confusion. These expressions mark the experiences of the life of faith, and they characterize the tone of the different types of poems in Psalms. These different types of psalms reveal God's relational goodness and loving faithfulness across the different seasons of the life of faith.[5]

Hymns

The hymns in the Psalter praise Yahweh for his character and for his work in creation and history on behalf of his people. These psalms are catechetical, concerned with the fundamental elements of faith. They celebrate Yahweh's creation of all things by his word (33:6, 9; 148:5–6), through his wisdom (104:24–26), and as a manifestation of his loving faithfulness

(136:4–9). They rehearse Yahweh's mighty acts in history: his covenant with Abraham, his redemption of his people from Egypt, his presence at Sinai, his provision for and protection of his people in the wilderness, his gift of the land of Canaan, and his restoration of the people after the exile (Pss. 68; 105; 107; 136:10–26).

The psalmists do not praise God in the abstract. They specify God's attributes and his work in creation and history, providing concrete reasons for praise. The closest Psalms gets to abstract praise is Psalm 150. By this point in the journey through the Psalter, however, the reader is fully aware of Yahweh's nature and works. Praise drives the life of faith across Psalms. The book is entitled "praises." Each of its five books ends with praise (41:13; 72:19; 89:52; 106:48; 150:6), and the entire book culminates in a crescendo of praise (Pss. 146–50). Praise names and extols God's character and the incalculable manifestations of his loving faithfulness. It is a primal form of speech that orients the life of faith. In fact, it represents humanity's "most characteristic mode of existence: praising and not praising stand over against one another like life and death."[6]

Laments

The life of faith, of course, is not always rosy. It involves suffering, despair, sin, and oppression. The Psalter embraces these realities of the life of faith; lament is the most prominent type of psalm in the book, and notes of distress sound across the other types of psalms as well.[7] Whether the source of distress is personal sin, external enemies, or God himself, the laments identify and describe troubles intrinsic to the life of faith. These troubles haunt the psalmists. The scheming of the wicked and the onslaught of enemies cause emotional anguish and physical disintegration (6:6–7; 13:2; 18:4; 22:14–15; 55:4–5). As powerful embodiments of evil, the wicked are depicted as ferocious beasts, skilled trappers, and tyrannical oppressors that pursue, catch, afflict, and kill the psalmists and vulnerable members of the community (10:2, 8–9; 35:17; 37:14; 109:16; 140:5; 141:9). The psalmists' sin produces brittle bones, festering lesions, and burning loins (32:3–4; 38:5, 7); it kindles anxiety, sorrow, guilt, and groaning (6:2–3; 31:9–10; 38:4, 8; 51:8). It brings about public humiliation and social abandonment (31:11; 38:11). Regardless of the source of trouble, the psalmists lament their situation and implore God to intervene. Within the context of covenant relationship, the psalmists appeal to God's loving faithfulness. They make their problem God's problem. They challenge God's relational goodness and call on him to demonstrate the reality of his reign in their situation.

When read within this covenantal context, lament is "a learned skill," not a form of whining.[8] It is a faithful expression of pain to the only one who is faithful and capable of transforming the psalmists' situations. While most laments move from pain to praise, Psalm 88 is the exception that proves the rule;[9] it ends in darkness, suggesting that the life of faith is messy. The darkness may linger. This possibility uncovers a paradox at the heart of Psalms' laments: these laments both question God's loving faithfulness and cling to it as the very basis of their hope (25:6–7; 44:26; 109:26).[10]

Thanksgiving and Trust

This hope, rooted in God's loving faithfulness, is the predominant testimony across the psalms of thanksgiving. These psalms look back on a season or situation of distress (30:1–2, 6–9; 118:5, 10–13). They recall the lament (30:9–10; 118:5), but they bear witness to God's specific intervention in the psalmists' predicaments (30:3, 11–12; 118:5, 13, 21, 23). As powerful witnesses to God's response to lament, the psalms of thanksgiving reveal God's relational goodness through the concrete demonstration of his loving faithfulness. They testify to a God who hears and answers the prayers of his people, and so they strengthen hope in the life of faith. 📖

A comparable dynamic is manifest in the psalms of trust. Fear characterizes the life of faith, but when facing danger (23:4–5; 46:2, 6), the psalmists counter their fears with vivid images and metaphors redolent of God's loving faithfulness: God is a shepherd (23:1), a host (23:5), and a fortress (46:1). The psalmists use these metaphors not only to express trust but also

LITERARY NOTES

Types of Psalms

Under the influence of form criticism, scholars have classified the psalms into different literary forms based on their tone or mood, characteristic features, and function. The following are the primary types of psalms and their distinctive characteristics:

1. Hymns or psalms of praise: These poems are marked by their exuberant acclamation of God. They tend to move from a call to praise to a reason for praise (e.g., Ps. 100).

2. Laments: These poems focus on the source(s) of trouble (i.e., God, enemies, the psalmist's or community's sin) and cry out to God for intervention. They consist of a lament or complaint and a petition. What's more, they tend to include an affirmation of trust and conclude with a vow to praise God (e.g., Ps. 22).

3. Psalms of thanksgiving: These psalms look back on a situation of distress and thank God for his specific intervention in the psalmist's or community's life (e.g., Ps. 30).

4. Psalms of trust: These poems mention a vague source of trouble (e.g., "the valley of deep darkness" [23:4]), which serves as an occasion for declaring or reaffirming trust in God. The psalms of trust tend to include vivid images or metaphors for God that capture his trustworthiness—such as that of a shepherd or refuge (e.g., Pss. 23, 46).

5. Royal psalms: These psalms focus on either the human king or the divine King, attending to the nature of their reign and its implications (e.g., Pss. 72, 93).

6. Wisdom psalms: These psalms are lectures or lessons, not prayers. They include character types, sayings, and themes characteristic of the wisdom literature (e.g., Ps. 37).

7. Torah psalms: These psalms focus on God's word or instruction and its implications for the shape of human life (e.g., Ps. 119).

Figure 13.2. *The Good Shepherd* mosaic (fifth century AD) in Mausoleum Galla Placidia, Italy

to ground their trust in God's relational goodness. They foster confidence in God's faithfulness and attest to his trustworthiness in the life of faith.

Instruction

The different types of psalms reflect different seasons of the life of faith. Whatever the season, Psalms affirms that the life of faith is never lived in isolation. It is not only experienced in covenant relationship with God; it is also directed by God's gracious instruction. The didactic poems in the Psalter align the life of faith in relationship with God, others, and the created world. The vision of life portrayed through Psalm 37's proverbs, for example, rhetorically reinforces the psalm's instructional refrain: do not fret because of the prosperity of the wicked (37:1, 7; cf. 37:8). The juxtaposition of creation and God's instructions in Psalm 19 intimates that a life ordered in accord with God's instruction is a life ordered in accord with the grain of creation. This ordering of life under God's trustworthy instruction is developed through the form and content of Psalm 119.[11] The poem is cast in the form of an alphabetic acrostic; it moves from *aleph* to *tav* or from A to Z. Each stanza contains eight lines, and each line includes one of eight synonymous terms used throughout the poem for God's instruction. The symmetry of the poem reflects the symmetry of a life directed by God's revealed will. Its structure corresponds with its content. Taken together, the structure and content of Psalm

119 indicate that God's revealed will is sufficient and trustworthy for the life of faith; it nurtures covenant relationship with God and offers stability.

Prayed Ethics

The didactic poems in Psalms are a microcosm of the function of the anthology as a whole. If Psalm 1 directs a reading of the book, then the psalms are torah;[12] they offer instruction in the life of faith. This instruction is far reaching. It includes instruction about God and the self. It provides a grammar for discourse with God, offering instruction in prayer. And Psalms presents ethical instruction; following Gordon Wenham, we might say that the book sketches a "prayed ethics."[13] Like Proverbs, Job, and Ecclesiastes, the Psalter profiles virtue and vice through prototypical character types. But it does more than this. The use of the psalms in liturgical song or recitation involves the singer or reciter in a distinctive way. Reflecting on the ethics of liturgy, Wenham notes, "It makes a stronger claim on the believer than either law, wisdom, or story, which are simply subject to passive reception: one can listen to a proverb or a story and then take it or leave it, but if you pray ethically, you commit yourself to a path of action."[14]

Singing or reciting the psalms commits one to a path of action or to a particular form of belief. The question is, How? The ethical implications of singing or reciting the psalms necessitates a crash course on speech-act theory. Speech-act theory operates under the assumption that language is functional. That is, words perform actions; one does something through what one says.[15] While words perform different types of actions, speech-act theory maps the performative nature of language through three categories: locutions, illocutions, and perlocutions. A locution is the act *of* saying something, an illocution is the act *in* saying something, and the perlocution is the act *by* saying something.[16] For example, if I say to my daughter, "I will pick you up at 5:00 p.m.," I make a locutionary statement. I say something. But I do more than this; this locutionary statement also performs an illocutionary act. *In* saying this, I make a promise: I commit myself to picking my daughter up at 5:00 p.m. This commitment produces a perlocutionary effect. *By* promising that I will pick my daughter up at 5:00 p.m., she expects that I will pick her up at 5:00 p.m. She takes me at my word.

How does speech-act theory contribute to prayed ethics? If one sings or recites Psalm 51, one commits oneself to the locutions and illocutions of the psalm (see table 2). 📖

LITERARY NOTES

Speech-Act Theory

J. L. Austin identifies five different types of illocutionary acts: verdictives, exercitives, commissives, behabitives, and expositives. Because these types are vague, Austin's student John Searle clarifies and refines the categories under the following headings: assertives (stating or representing something), directives (getting someone to do something), commissives (committing to something), expressives (the expression of thoughts or feelings), and declarations (bringing about what one has said).[b]

As a lament, Psalm 51 includes particular locutions and illocutions, which seek to move God to hear the speaker's confession, forgive the speaker's sins, and restore the speaker in covenant relationship with God (see table 2). *By* singing or reciting this psalm, one performs certain acts. Other types of psalms incorporate different types of speech acts. Hymns, for example, foreground expressives, specifically the act of praise (146:1–2; 147:1). Many laments and psalms of thanksgiving contain commissives in the form of oaths or vows, promises to perform some act in response to God's intervention (22:25; 66:13). The imprecatory psalms involve performative declarations—that is, passing sentence on someone (109:6–19). While different types of psalms consist of different types of speech acts, every psalm contains locutions that perform illocutionary acts and elicit perlocutionary effects. Singing or reciting the psalms, therefore, involves a person in discrete ways. Most generally, singing or reciting a psalm commits a person to specific beliefs and acts:[17] "Praying the psalms is a performative . . . act: saying these solemn words to God alters one's relationship in a way that mere listening does not."[18]

The Imprecatory Psalms

Wenham's account of "prayed ethics" attunes one to the ethical implications of the psalms' use in private prayer, corporate song, or communal recitation. This ethical perspective enlivens the use of the psalms, sensitizing us to their personal and practical consequences, but it also raises questions. Among them is, Is it appropriate for Christians to pray *all* the psalms—and

Table 2. Speech Acts in Psalm 51

Psalm 51	Locution	Illocution
51:1	Have mercy upon me, O God, according to your loving faithfulness; according to the greatness of your compassion, blot out my transgressions.	*Directives:* requests/commands for mercy and cleansing
51:3–4	For I myself know my transgressions, and my sin is before me continually. Against you, you alone, I have sinned, and I have done what is evil in your eyes. Because you are righteous in your speaking, you are pure in your judging.	*Assertives:* a representation of the state of affairs, which includes self-awareness of personal sin against God and belief claims regarding God's just judgment
51:15	O Lord, open my lips, and my mouth will declare your praise.	*Directive:* a request for God's help *Commissive:* a promise to declare God's praise
51:17	The sacrifices of God are a broken spirit; a broken and crushed heart, O God, you will not despise.	*Assertive:* a theological claim, stating what God deems as an acceptable response to personal sin

most notably, the imprecatory psalms? Jesus calls his disciples to love their enemies and to pray for those who persecute them (Matt. 5:44). While the imprecatory psalms *are* prayers for those who persecute us, they are deeply uncomfortable prayers, for they appear to demonstrate hatred toward our enemies. The psalmists ask God to execute vengeance against their enemies by blotting out their names from the earth, making their children beggars, and using human agents to bash the heads of their babies against rocks (Pss. 109:10, 15; 137:8–9). Can Christians pray these prayers?

Many people answer this question by psychoanalyzing the psalmists, probing their internal motives to determine whether their verbal desires are appropriate. While this line of inquiry may serve as a helpful mirror for one's own prayers, it is impossible to discern the motives of the psalmists through the text. They remain hidden. The psalmists' desire for divine vengeance, however, is clear. And this expression of vengeance *is* fitting for Christians. How? Following Walter Brueggemann, it is important to note that the psalmists' expressions of vengeance are verbal.[19] They do not act on their violent wishes; rather, they submit them to God's sovereign rule and providential care.[20] The psalmists serve as prosecuting attorneys, recommending forms of punishment that align with either the principle of *lex talionis* or the regulations of the covenant.

The verbal form of the psalmists' requests for vengeance not only differentiates them from physical acts; it is also a profound act of faith. It affirms that vengeance belongs not to humans but to God (Deut. 32:35; Ps. 94:1; Rom. 12:19). The verbal submission of one's desire for God's just judgment is a manifestation of trust. The psalmists embrace the reality that Yahweh probes human hearts and minds, perceiving the secrets of the heart (Pss. 7:9; 44:21). They refuse to hide these secret desires from the one who knows all secrets. Instead, they trust God with them. They hand them over to him. The expectation is not that Yahweh will do whatever the psalmists say. The expectation is that Yahweh will hear and act in his own timing, in his own way, and in accord with his own purposes.

When viewed through this frame of reference, the imprecatory psalms may be read, sung, or recited as honest expressions of pain and candid demands that God demonstrate who he is: a God of justice and righteousness (33:5; 97:2). Anyone who has ever prayed the Lord's Prayer calls for God to manifest his justice and righteousness through the veiled imprecation "Your kingdom come, your will be done, on earth as it is in heaven" (Matt. 6:10 NIV). Many do not flinch at the implication of reality signaled through that line of prayer, the consummation of God's heavenly kingdom on earth, which will seal the eschatological fate of the righteous and the wicked. This suggests that Christian aversion to calls for divine vengeance in Psalms may hinge on their eschatological horizon. In contrast to the developed eschatological vision traced across the New Testament, the psalmists knew of no recourse to divine judgment after death (cf. Dan. 12:1–2). This heightened their perception of the necessity of divine judgment in the present world. More than this, it cultivated a deeper understanding of God's justice and righteousness. This sort of understanding of God's justice is lost on many Christians, who dispense with any need to pray for God to demonstrate that he is a God of justice. They betray a lack of urgency, content to wait for the eschaton, when God will make all things right. If the Psalter serves as a mirror, perhaps the imprecatory psalms help Christians to see their impoverished view of God's justice. If nothing else, the imprecatory psalms help Christians see and deal in a faithful fashion with the natural desire for vengeance and for an end to all forms of injustice.

As Athanasius wrote to Marcellinus, the psalms allow people to comprehend "the emotions of the soul" and "to possess the image deriving from the words."[21] These emotions encompass the life of faith, and the image deriving from the words is the image of the life of faith. This image is forged in covenant relationship with God. It is formed through praise, lament, thanksgiving, and persistent trust, and it is directed by God's gracious instruction. It is nourished through a sensitivity to the ethical function of the psalms, and it possesses a vibrant language with which to work out the lived tension between God's justice and the experience of violence. Psalms maps the highways and byways of the life of faith; it is both the atlas and the guide. This is captured by Athanasius, who declares:

> For I believe that the whole of human existence, both the dispositions of the soul and the movements of the thoughts, have been measured out and encompassed in those very words of the Psalter. And nothing beyond these is found among men. For whether there was necessity of repentance or confession, or tribulation and trial befell us, or someone was persecuted, or, being plotted against, he was protected, or if, moreover, someone has become deeply

sorrowful and disturbed and he suffers something of the sort that is described in the things just mentioned, and he either attends to himself as one who is advancing, being set free from his foe, or he wants to sing praises and give thanks to the Lord—*for any such eventuality he has instruction in the divine Psalms*. Let him therefore select the things said in them about each of these circumstances, and reciting what has been written as concerning him, and being affected by the writings, lift them up to the Lord.[22]

Conclusion

The Psalter casts a vision of praise seeking understanding that emerges at the intersection of knowledge of God and knowledge of self. This relational context not only engenders understanding in and through lived experience; it also creates the conditions for the union of a person's "stated theology" and "functional theology"—that is, the interrelation between what a person believes and how a person's life manifests a particular understanding of the world.[23]

The Psalter's stated theology is clear. God is incomparable, in a class of his own. He is eternal and immutable. He cannot be measured by finite time, and his being is not subject to his becoming. Instead, his nature is manifest through his coming into finite time, specifically through his preservation of all things, his providential ordering of all things, and his gracious intervention in the lives of his people. The God of heaven is attentive to the lowly. As Creator and King, he is the absolute sovereign, who exercises beneficent rule and relational goodness through his loving faithfulness. The God who needs no one and nothing freely gives from his fullness in covenant relationship with his people.

The Psalter's stated theology is the necessary context for the performance of its functional theology. This stated theology is not a catalog of theological beliefs to which one offers intellectual assent. Rather, these theological beliefs inform an understanding of reality and form the life of faith. They place any and every form of speech in covenant relationship with God. Nothing is out of bounds. Praise and thanksgiving are pleasing forms of prayer. The same is true of forms of discourse that strike many as inappropriate in conversation with God. According to the witness of Psalms, challenges to God's relational goodness and loving faithfulness are welcomed. Pleas for help are grounded on the belief that God is "my helper" (54:4). Cries of grief, outrage, and vengeance in the experience of horrendous evil not only model faithful feelings before the face of human atrocities; they also call Yahweh to account for the contradiction of evil in a world governed by a just and righteous God.[24] Far from representing some primitive ethic, these vernaculars of prayer illuminate the intimate relationship between the book's stated theology and its functional theology. The prayers of the psalmists surface in real life, lived in relationship with a God who is known. In so doing, they illustrate the Christian maxim *Lex orandi, lex credendi*, "The pattern (or rule) of prayer [is] the pattern of belief."[25] A life of communion with God directs what is believed about God, and what is believed about God directs a life of communion with him.

Sociologists and psychologists say belief in the triune God and a life of communion with the Father, the Son, and the Holy Spirit are on the wane. Twenty years ago, Christian Smith and Melinda Lundquist Denton concluded that "Moralistic Therapeutic Deism" was the dominant religion of American teenagers. Its tenets included a particular vision of relationship with God: "God does not need to be particularly involved in one's life except when God is needed to resolve a problem."[26]

Figure 13.3. Stained glass window based on Psalm 148 by Walter Crane and J. S. Sparrow (1896)

Things have changed in twenty years, but not for the better. Fewer young people affiliate with a religion. More young people have never attended a religious service.[27] By 2016, more than one out of four young people declared that they never prayed.[28] When members of the so-called iGeneration do pray, their prayers reflect the old creed of Moralistic Therapeutic Deism. "I've stopped praying just to thank God," wrote Tiara, age 17. "I only pray when I need something or when someone else needs something. . . . To be honest, I kind of just forget to pray until a bad situation arises and I want to change it."[29] In light of this climate, the grammar, emotions, and movements of Psalms' relational expressivism seem irrelevant.

Individual Christians and the body of Christ will take exception to this idea. The Psalter continues to serve as a perpetual fountain that irrigates the life of faith in general and personal prayer and communal song in particular. Nonetheless, the case for the irrelevance of some psalms remains, even if implicit within the Christian community. As noted above, the lament is the most prominent type of poem in Psalms, but its language and expression, especially corporately, are missing from many of the church's songs and prayers. The consequences of this are devastating. The absence of lament not only reinforces the American Christian facade, the weekly affirmation that everyone and everything is "good"; it also leads to an anemic and disingenuous vision of the life of faith, one that cannot account for the realities of being-in-the-world. The poems of the Psalter are attuned to the realities of human life in the world and before the face of God. They are honest. They name these harsh realities, and the psalmists believe unashamedly in a God who intervenes in them. Failure to lament is a failure to affirm God's personal intervention in personal lives and situations. It is a form of functional atheism that refuses to wrestle with God's relational goodness and loving faithfulness. This refusal prevents the book's laments from providing the church and the world with that for which they long—namely, hope.[30]

The Psalter sustains the hope of God's people. Its poems nourish the life of faith and stock the theological imagination of the faithful in their earthly pilgrimage. The psalms are an invaluable resource. They diagnose human life before the face of God. Their words offer a way for humans to remedy relationship with God. Their language and imagery convert and order human affections for God. As one of the most introspective books in the canon of Scripture, the Psalter not only informs the life of faith, but it also shapes and strengthens the life of faith.

Glossary

act-consequence connection   A principle that assumes individual acts or deeds are organically connected to certain consequences. *See also* retribution principle.

admonition   A command or warning that prescribes or proscribes certain forms of behavior.

aesthetics   A branch of philosophy that attends to the principles of beauty and taste. *See also* axiology.

allegorical reading   A form of interpretation in which the words of the text are symbols that refer to spiritual realities.

angelology   The study of semidivine, angelic beings.

anthropology   A broad area of research that studies human cultures and societies, as well as the biological and physiological features of human beings.

aphorism   *See* proverb.

Aramaism   A case in which features characteristic of Aramaic are reflected in the vocabulary and grammar of the Hebrew or Greek text.

archetypal knowledge   Absolute knowledge of all things, which belongs to God alone.

asceticism   The practice of abstaining from all forms of indulgence to cultivate control over one's passions.

autonomy   The idea that an agent is self-governing and independent— that is, acting in accord with their own laws.

axiology   The study of value and those things that are considered valuable; it includes ethics and aesthetics.

canonical Scripture   The authoritative texts that Christians consider as set apart and distinct. In Protestant Christianity, "canonical Scripture" refers to the sixty-six books of the Old and New Testaments, which constitute the unique means through which God establishes and maintains covenant relationship with his people.

character-consequence connection   A principle that assumes rewards and punishments are meted out to certain character types: the righteous are rewarded, while the wicked are punished. Whereas the act-consequence connection assumes rewards or punishments are dispensed in response to specific acts, the character-consequence connection assumes that rewards or punishments are distributed to certain character types. *See also* retribution principle.

contingent   When applied to beings, "contingent" conveys dependence on someone or something other than oneself/itself for existence.

coram Deo   A Latin expression that expresses a life lived before the face or in the presence of God.

covenant   An agreement between two parties that establishes relationship and identifies the obligations that govern that relationship.

divine aseity   Located in the doctrine of God, divine aseity affirms the triune God's self-existence and self-sufficiency: God is of himself and from himself.

divine council   The heavenly court, consisting of the heavenly host; for Israelites, Yahweh presided over this host.

divine immutability   The theological conviction that God does not change but rather remains the same.

divine impassibility   The theological conviction concerning God's being that God's will is determined within himself rather than influenced or affected by something outside of himself.

divine simplicity   The theological conviction that God is absolute, without parts or division.

dramatic irony   A literary technique in which the reader knows something that the characters in a narrative do not.

economic Trinity   A theological expression that refers to God's self-revelation in history—that is, in the economy of salvation.

ectypal knowledge   Limited, provisional knowledge appropriate to finite creatures.

empiricism   The philosophical theory that all knowledge is derived from sensory experience.

encomium   A speech that praises someone or something; it is comparable to a eulogy.

epigram A terse and witty poem that evokes a sense of surprise and then clarifies the astonishing situation in an unexpected way.

epistemology A branch of philosophy that attends to the sources, substance, and justification of knowledge; it seeks to provide an account of what can be known and how it may be known.

eschatology The study of the end of all things.

eternal generation of the Son The belief that the Second Person of the Trinity came forth from the Father to be the Son in eternity, sharing the one, same, undivided essence as the Father; the Nicene Creed affirms this belief.

ethics A branch of philosophy that focuses on the moral principles that inform a person's behavior. *See also* axiology.

faith A relational and volitional disposition of trust in the triune God and his promises.

finitude A state or condition defined by limits.

form criticism An approach to biblical literature that seeks to identify the literary forms of different texts and the original life settings in which these forms emerged.

Hebrew Bible An expression used by Jewish people and scholars for the collection of authoritative texts that Christians typically call the Old Testament. The Hebrew Bible consists of three sections: the Torah (i.e., the Pentateuch), the Prophets (i.e., the Former Prophets or "historical books" and the Latter Prophets), and the Writings (i.e., Psalms, Job, Ruth, Song of Songs, Ecclesiastes, Lamentations, Esther, Daniel, Ezra, Nehemiah, and Chronicles).

Hellenism Greek culture, language, and thought, which spread across the world under the campaign of Alexander the Great.

hypostasis A discrete, individual agent or being, as opposed to an attribute or idea.

immanent Trinity A theological expression that refers to God's eternal being.

inclusio A literary device that creates a frame or envelope through the use of repeated words or expressions.

intertextuality A case in which one text intentionally or unintentionally draws on another through citation, allusion, or echo.

lex talionis A principle of just retribution, according to which a punishment corresponds with an offense in both kind and degree.

LXX An abbreviation for the Septuagint, a catch-all term for the Greek version of the Old Testament. The abbreviation derives from tradition, according to which seventy scholars (or seventy-two, six from each of the twelve tribes) translated the Hebrew Pentateuch into Greek in Alexandria.

lyric poetry   A mode of poetic discourse expressed through song; it foregrounds the inner lives and emotions of its speakers and contrasts with drama, narrative, and epic.

memento mori   The practice of remembering that humans must die, which motivates a sober life before the face of God. See also *coram Deo*.

merism   A literary device that combines two opposites or extremes to convey a sense of the whole (e.g., "the heavens and the earth" can be used to mean everything in existence).

metaphysics   A branch of philosophy that considers the nature of reality and things beyond the physical world; ontology and cosmology are offshoots of metaphysics.

MT   The Masoretic Text, the traditional Hebrew text of the Hebrew Bible / Old Testament.

ontology   A branch of philosophy that considers the nature of being; it is a part of metaphysics, which explores first principles and things beyond the physical world, like time and space.

orthodoxy   True and authorized belief.

orthopraxy   True and authorized living that flows from correct and authorized belief.

Persian period   The period marked by Persian rule across the ancient Near East, spanning from Cyrus II to Darius III (ca. 539–331 BC).

prosopological exegesis   An interpretive technique in which the reader assigns a nontrivial speaker or addressee to an ambiguous voice or agent in a text to clarify its meaning.

proverb   A short, pithy saying that communicates a traditional and traditioned truth.

providence   A doctrine of the triune God's care for, guidance of, and rule over all things. The doctrine includes God's preservation and governance, as well as an account of concurrence (i.e., how divine and human agency coexist).

Ptolemaic period   The period marked by the rule of the Ptolemies in Egypt during the Hellenistic period (ca. 323–30 BC).

Qumran   A region near the Dead Sea where the Dead Sea Scrolls were discovered. These scrolls consist of a variety of different types of texts, including copies of or commentaries on scriptural texts and texts produced for use in the sectarian community that inhabited Qumran in the first and second centuries BC.

reception history   A mode of investigation that considers how biblical texts have been received, interpreted, and used in various genres and media, ranging from commentaries and homilies to art and music.

retribution principle   A principle that assumes good people prosper and the evil suffer; it is another designation for the act-consequence connection, and it is comparable to the character-consequence connection.

Second Temple period   The period from the building to the destruction of the second temple in Jerusalem (ca. 515 BC to AD 70).

semiotics   The study of signs and symbols in language, their use, and the way they convey meaning.

soliloquy   A speech that expresses one's thoughts, whether alone or in the presence of others.

Sukkoth   A Hebrew term for the Feast of Tabernacles, which was celebrated in the autumn to mark the harvest. The people celebrated this feast by living in temporary shelters to commemorate the wilderness wanderings.

synecdoche   A figure of speech in which a part of something is used to signify the whole (e.g., "soul" for one's whole being).

text criticism   The study of the versions of ancient texts that seeks to establish the most reliable reading of the text.

torah   A Hebrew term that means "instruction"; it also is used as a designation for the Pentateuch (Torah).

triune God   An expression for God that captures a central component of the doctrine of God—namely, that God exists as one God in three persons: Father, Son, and Holy Spirit.

Unitarianism   The belief that God is one person, not three.

Notes

The endnotes for each chapter appear first, followed by the notes to the sidebars for that chapter.

Chapter 1 Introduction to Wisdom Literature and Psalms

1. Anselm of Canterbury, *Proslogion*, in *The Major Works*, trans. M. J. Charlesworth, ed. Brian Davies and G. R. Evans (New York: Oxford University Press, 1998), 87.

2. For an excellent theological account of the ontology of the biblical text and the reader in the interpretive enterprise, see Darren Sarisky, *Reading the Bible Theologically* (Cambridge: Cambridge University Press, 2019), esp. 141–365.

3. Kevin J. Vanhoozer, "Holy Scripture," in *Christian Dogmatics: Reformed Theology for the Church Catholic*, ed. Michael Allen and Scott R. Swain (Grand Rapids: Baker Academic, 2016), 30–56, esp. 44.

4. Christopher R. Seitz, *The Character of Christian Scripture: The Significance of a Two-Testament Bible*, Studies in Theological Interpretation (Grand Rapids: Baker Academic, 2011), 22, 128; Don Collett, "Reading Forward: The Old Testament and Retrospective Stance," *Pro Ecclesia* 24 (2015): 178–96.

5. The following discussion of poetry is adapted from Christopher B. Ansberry, *Proverbs*, Zondervan Exegetical Commentary on the Old Testament (Grand Rapids: Zondervan Academic, forthcoming). Copyright© 2024 by Christopher Ansberry. Used by permission of HarperCollins Christian Publishing. www.harpercollinschristian.com.

6. Jill Peláez Baumgaertner, "'Silver Catching Midday Sun': Poetry and the Beauty of God," in *The Beauty of God: Theology and the Arts*, ed. Daniel J. Treier, Mark Husbands, and Roger Lundin (Downers Grove, IL: IVP Academic, 2007), 147.

7. Baumgaertner, "'Silver Catching Midday Sun,'" 147.

8. Nicholas Wolterstorff, *Art in Action: Toward a Christian Aesthetic* (1980; repr., Carlisle, UK: Solway, 1997), 3–11, 78–79.

9. Wolterstorff, *Art in Action*, 4–5.

10. Wolterstorff, *Art in Action*, 3–18; Craig G. Bartholomew and Ryan P. O'Dowd, *Old Testament Wisdom Literature: A Theological Introduction* (Downers Grove, IL: IVP Academic, 2011), 50–55.

11. Sir Philip Sydney, "The Defence of Poesy (c. 1580; printed 1595)," in *"The Defence of Poesy" and Selected Renaissance Literary Criticism*, ed. Gavin Alexander (New York: Penguin, 2004), 13.

12. Wolterstorff, *Art in Action*, 122; Bartholomew and O'Dowd, *Old Testament Wisdom Literature*, 55–56.

13. Wolterstorff, *Art in Action*, 123–44; Bartholomew and O'Dowd, *Old Testament Wisdom Literature*, 56.

14. Luis Alonso Schökel, *A Manual of Hebrew Poetics*, Subsidia Biblica 11 (1988; repr., Rome: Editrice Pontificio Istituto Biblico, 2000), 104.

15. Ellen F. Davis, *Proverbs, Ecclesiastes, and the Song of Songs*, Westminster Bible Companion (Louisville: Westminster John Knox, 2000), 19.

16. William P. Brown, *Seeing the Psalms: A Theology of Metaphor* (Louisville: Westminster John Knox, 2002), 9.

17. Flannery O'Connor, "The Nature and Aim of Fiction," in *Mystery and Manners*, ed. Sally Fitzgerald and Robert Fitzgerald (New York: Farrar, Straus & Giroux, 1969), 75.

18. For discussion of the distinctiveness of the wisdom literature, see James L. Crenshaw, *Old Testament Wisdom: An Introduction*, 3rd ed. (Louisville: Westminster John Knox, 2010), 1–40.

19. Will Kynes, "The Nineteenth-Century Beginnings of 'Wisdom Literature', and Its Twenty-First-Century End?," in *Perspectives on Israelite Wisdom: Proceedings of the Oxford Old Testament Seminar*, ed. John Jarick, Library of Hebrew Bible / Old Testament Studies 618 (London: Bloomsbury T&T Clark, 2016), 83–108; Kynes, *An Obituary for "Wisdom Literature": The Birth, Death, and Intertextual Reintegration of a Biblical Corpus* (Oxford: Oxford University Press, 2019), esp. 82–104.

20. Will Kynes, "The Modern Scholarly Wisdom Tradition and the Threat of Pan-Sapientialism: A Case Report," in *Was There a Wisdom Tradition? New Prospects in Israelite Wisdom Studies*, Ancient Israel and Its Literature 23 (Atlanta: SBL Press, 2015), 11–38; Kynes, *Obituary for "Wisdom Literature."*

21. Mark R. Sneed, ed., *Was There a Wisdom Tradition?*; Katharine Dell and Will Kynes, eds., *Reading Job Intertextually*, Library of Hebrew Bible / Old Testament Studies 574 (London: Bloomsbury T&T Clark, 2013); Dell and Kynes, eds., *Reading Ecclesiastes Intertextually*, Library of Hebrew Bible / Old Testament Studies 587 (London: Bloomsbury T&T Clark, 2016); Dell and Kynes, eds., *Reading Proverbs Intertextually*, Library of Hebrew Bible / Old Testament Studies 629 (London: Bloomsbury T&T Clark, 2019).

22. Hartmut Gese, *Lehre und Wirklichkeit in der alten Weisheit: Studien zu den Sprüchen Salomos und dem Buche Hiob* (Tübingen: Mohr, 1958), 2; James L. Crenshaw, "Prolegomenon," in *Studies in Ancient Israelite Wisdom*, ed. James L. Crenshaw, Library of Biblical Studies (New York: Ktav, 1976), 1.

Chapter 1 Sidebar Notes

a. Immanuel Kant, *Critique of the Power of Judgment*, trans. Paul Guyer and Eric Matthews (Cambridge: Cambridge University Press, 2000), 191–207; Roger Scruton, *Beauty: A Very Short Introduction* (Oxford: Oxford University Press, 2011), 23–26.

b. Will Kynes, *An Obituary for "Wisdom Literature": The Birth, Death, and Intertextual Reintegration of a Biblical Corpus* (Oxford: Oxford University Press, 2019), 60–104.

Chapter 2 Proverbs

1. Peter T. H. Hatton, *Contradiction in the Book of Proverbs: The Deep Waters of Counsel* (Burlington, VT: Ashgate, 2008), 47–170.

2. For the reading sketched here, see Ronald L. Giese Jr., "'Iron Sharpens Iron' as a Negative Image: Challenging the Common Interpretation of Proverbs 27:17," *Journal of Biblical Literature* 135 (2016): 61–76.

3. Eva Mroczek, *The Literary Imagination in Jewish Antiquity* (New York: Oxford University Press, 2016), 51–85.

4. Gerhard von Rad, *Wisdom in Israel*, trans. James D. Martin (Harrisburg, PA: Trinity Press International, 1972), 24; Anne W. Stewart, *Poetic Ethics in Proverbs: Wisdom Literature and the Shaping of the Moral Self* (Cambridge: Cambridge University Press, 2016), 29–69.

5. For this reading of the collections in Proverbs, see William P. Brown, "The Pedagogy of Proverbs 10:1–31:9," in *Character and Scripture: Moral Formation, Community, and*

Biblical Interpretation, ed. William P. Brown (Grand Rapids: Eerdmans, 2002), 150–82; Christopher B. Ansberry, *Be Wise, My Son, and Make My Heart Glad: An Exploration of the Courtly Nature of the Book of Proverbs*, Beihefte zur Zeitschrift für die alttestamentliche Wissenschaft 422 (Berlin: de Gruyter, 2011).

6. Brown, "Pedagogy of Proverbs 10:1–31:9," 174–75.

7. Christine Roy Yoder, "Forming 'Fearers of Yahweh': Repetition and Contradiction as Pedagogy in Proverbs," in *Seeking Out the Wisdom of the Ancients: Essays Offered to Honor Michael V. Fox on the Occasion of His Sixty-Fifth Birthday*, ed. Ronald L. Troxel, Kelvin G. Friebel, and Dennis R. Magary (Winona Lake, IN: Eisenbrauns, 2005), 167–83.

8. This expression is taken from William P. Brown, *Wisdom's Wonder: Character, Creation, and Crisis in the Bible's Wisdom Literature* (Grand Rapids: Eerdmans, 2014), 24.

Chapter 2 Sidebar Notes

a. For a recent discussion of these texts, see Nili Shupak, "The Instruction of Amenemope and Proverbs 22:17–24:22 from the Perspective of Contemporary Research," in *Seeking Out the Wisdom of the Ancients: Essays Offered to Michael V. Fox on the Occasion of His Sixty-Fifth Birthday*, ed. Ronald L. Troxel, Kelvin G. Friebel, and Dennis R. Magary (Winona Lake, IN: Eisenbrauns, 2005), 203–20.

b. Saint Basil the Great, *On Christian Doctrine and Practice*, trans. Mark DelCogliano, Popular Patristics Series 47 (Yonkers, NY: St. Vladimir's Seminary Press, 2013), 39–78.

Chapter 3 Theological Themes in Proverbs (1)

1. Aristotle, *Posterior Analytics* 2.13.

2. Michael V. Fox, "The Epistemology of the Book of Proverbs," *Journal of Biblical Literature* 126 (2007): 684.

3. Esther Lightcap Meek, *Loving to Know: Introducing Covenant Epistemology* (Eugene, OR: Cascade Books, 2011); Dru Johnson, *Biblical Knowing: A Scriptural Epistemology of Error* (Eugene, OR: Cascade Books, 2013).

4. My translation here—particularly "There is this"—draws on Agustinus Gianto, "On יֵשׁ of Reflection in the Book of Proverbs," in *"When the Morning Stars Sang": Essays in Honor of Choon Leong Seow on the Occasion of His Sixty-Fifth Birthday*, ed. Scott C. Jones and Christine Roy Yoder, Beihefte zur Zeitschrift für die alttestamentliche Wissenschaft 500 (Berlin: de Gruyter, 2018), 157–62.

5. M. Beth Szlos, "Body Parts as Metaphor and the Value of a Cognitive Approach: A Study of the Female Figures in Proverbs via Metaphor," in *Metaphor in the Hebrew Bible*, ed. P. van Hecke, Bibliotheca Ephemeridum Theologicarum Lovaniensium 187 (Leuven: Leuven University Press, 2005), 185–95.

6. Greg Schmidt Goering, "Attentive Ears and Forward-Looking Eyes: Disciplining the Senses and Forming the Self in the Book of Proverbs," *Journal of Jewish Studies* 66 (2015): 242–64; Goering, "Honey and Wormwood: Taste and the Embodiment of Wisdom in the Book of Proverbs," *Hebrew Bible and Ancient Israel* 5 (2016): 23–41.

7. Sun Myung Lyu, *Righteousness in the Book of Proverbs*, Forschungen zum Alten Testament II/55 (Tübingen: Mohr Siebeck, 2012), 62.

8. Nicole L. Tilford, *Sensing World, Sensing Wisdom: The Cognitive Foundation of Biblical Metaphors*, Ancient Israel and Its Literature 31 (Atlanta: SBL Press, 2017); Ryan P. O'Dowd, "Pain and Danger: Unpleasant Sayings and the Structure of Proverbs," *Catholic Biblical Quarterly* 80 (2019): 619–35.

9. Carol A. Newsom, "Models of the Moral Self: Hebrew Bible and Second Temple Judaism," *Journal of Biblical Literature* 131 (2012): 12.

10. Gerhard von Rad, *Wisdom in Israel*, trans. James D. Martin (Harrisburg, PA: Trinity Press International, 1972), 190–95; Suzanna R. Millar, *Genre and Openness in Proverbs 10:1–22:16*, Ancient Israel and Its Literature 39 (Atlanta: SBL Press, 2020), 196–219.

11. See J. N. Aletti, "Seduction et parole en Proverbes I–IX," *Vetus Testamentum* 27 (1977): 129–44.

12. See Michael Polanyi, *Personal Knowledge: Towards a Post-Critical Philosophy* (Chicago: University of Chicago Press, 1962), 53; Meek, *Loving to Know*, 395–468; Johnson, *Biblical Knowing*, 1–21.

13. Norman C. Habel, "The Symbolism of Wisdom in Proverbs 1–9," *Interpretation* 26 (1972): 133–34.

14. Michael V. Fox, *Proverbs 1–9: A New Translation with Introduction and Commentary*, Anchor Bible 18A (New York: Doubleday, 2000), 128–29. Fox's ground metaphor for Proverbs 1–9 is BEHAVIOR IS A PATH.

15. See Christopher B. Ansberry, "What Does Jerusalem Have to Do with Athens? The Moral Vision of the Book of Proverbs and Aristotle's *Nicomachean Ethics*," *Hebrew Studies* 51 (2010): 157–73; Arthur Jan Keefer, *The Book of Proverbs and Virtue Ethics: Integrating the Biblical and Philosophical Traditions* (Cambridge: Cambridge University Press, 2021), 201–22.

16. Stuart Weeks, *Instruction and Imagery in Proverbs 1–9* (Oxford: Oxford University Press, 2007), 75.

17. Habel, "Symbolism of Wisdom," 133–34.

18. William P. Brown, *Wisdom's Wonder: Character, Creation, and Crisis in the Bible's Wisdom Literature* (Grand Rapids: Eerdmans, 2014), 46–49.

19. The material in this section has been adapted from Ansberry, "Proverbs," in *The Cambridge Companion to Biblical Wisdom Literature*, ed. Katharine J. Dell, Suzanna R. Millar, and Arthur Jan Keefer (Cambridge: Cambridge University Press, 2022), 155–56. © Cambridge University Press 2022. Reproduced by permission of Cambridge University through PLSclear.

20. Weeks, *Instruction and Imagery*, 118.

21. Weeks, *Instruction and Imagery*, 117–18; Zoltán Schwáb, "Is Fear of the Lord the Source of Wisdom or Vice Versa?," *Vetus Testamentum* 63 (2013): 652–62.

22. Job Y. Jindo, "On the Biblical Notion of Human Dignity: 'Fear of God' as a Condition for Authentic Existence," *Biblical Interpretation* 19 (2011): 433–53.

23. Jindo, "Notion of Human Dignity," 435, 449.

24. Jindo, "Notion of Human Dignity," 450n33.

25. Jindo, "Notion of Human Dignity," 450.

26. Jindo, "Notion of Human Dignity," 448.

27. Raymond Van Leeuwen, *Context and Meaning in Proverbs 25–27*, Society of Biblical Literature Dissertation Series 96 (Atlanta: Scholars Press, 1988), 105, emphasis added.

28. Jindo, "Notion of Human Dignity," 435.

29. The material in this section has been adapted from Ansberry, "Proverbs," 159–60. © Cambridge University Press 2022. Reproduced by permission of Cambridge University through PLSclear.

30. Klaus Koch, "Gibt es ein Vergeltungsdogma im Alten Testament?," *Zeitschrift für Theologie und Kirche* 52 (1955): 1–42.

31. Lennart Boström, *The God of the Sages: The Portrayal of God in the Book of Proverbs*, Coniectanea Biblica: Old Testament Series 29 (Stockholm: Almqvist & Wiksell, 1990), 134–40.

32. Von Rad, *Wisdom in Israel*, 101.

33. Peter T. H. Hatton, *Contradiction in the Book of Proverbs: The Deep Waters of Counsel* (Burlington, VT: Ashgate, 2008), 115–16.

34. Fox, "Epistemology," 684.

35. Raymond C. Van Leeuwen, "Theology: Creation, Wisdom, and Covenant," in *The Oxford Handbook of Wisdom and the Bible*, ed. Will Kynes (Oxford: Oxford University Press, 2021), 73.

a. Martin Buber, *I and Thou*, trans. Ronald Gregor Smith (London: Bloomsbury Academic, 2013), 43–44.

b. John Calvin, *Institutes of the Christian Religion*, ed. John T. McNeill, trans. Ford Lewis Battles, 2 vols. (Louisville: Westminster John Knox, 1960), 1.1.1.

c. Plato, *Theaetetus* 149a–151d.

d. Matthew B. Crawford, *Shop Class as Soulcraft: An Inquiry into the Value of Work* (New York: Penguin Books, 2010); Crawford, *The World beyond Your Head: How to Flourish in an Age of Distraction* (New York: Penguin Books, 2016).

e. Hilary of Poitiers, *De Trinitate* 10.1, in *Nicene and Post-Nicene Fathers*, second series, ed. Philip Schaff, 13 vols. (Peabody, MA: Hendrickson, 1995), 9:182.

f. Michael V. Fox, "The Epistemology of the Book of Proverbs," *Journal of Biblical Literature* 126 (2007): 669–84.

g. George Lakoff and Mark Johnson, *Metaphors We Live By* (Chicago: University of Chicago Press, 2004), esp. 61–68.

Chapter 4 Theological Themes in Proverbs (2)

1. The following discussion of Lady Wisdom is adapted from Christopher B. Ansberry, *Proverbs*, Zondervan Exegetical Commentary on the Old Testament (Grand Rapids: Zondervan Academic, forthcoming). Copyright© 2024 by Christopher Ansberry. Used by permission of HarperCollins Christian Publishing. http://www.harpercollinschristian.com.

2. Stuart Weeks, "The Context and Meaning of Proverbs 8:30a," *Journal of Biblical Literature* 125 (2006): 437–38; cf. Victor A. Hurowitz, "Nursling, Advisor, Architect? אמון and the Role of Wisdom in Proverbs 8.22–31," *Biblica* 80 (1999): 392–94.

3. Raymond C. Van Leeuwen, "The Book of Proverbs," in *The New Interpreter's Bible*, ed. Leander E. Keck, 12 vols. (Nashville: Abingdon, 1994–99), 5:93–94.

4. William P. Brown, *The Ethos of the Cosmos: The Genesis of Moral Imagination in the Bible* (Grand Rapids: Eerdmans, 1999), 278.

5. T. P. McCreesh, "Wisdom as Wife: Proverbs 31:10–31," *Revue biblique* 92 (1985): 25–46; Claudia V. Camp, *Wisdom and the Feminine in the Book of Proverbs*, Bible and Literature Series 11 (Sheffield: Almond, 1985), 186–208.

6. McCreesh, "Wisdom as Wife," 25–46.

7. Joseph Blenkinsopp, *Sage, Priest, Prophet: Religious and Intellectual Leadership in Ancient Israel*, Library of Ancient Israel (Louisville: Westminster John Knox, 1995), 35.

8. Brian L. Webster, "The Perfect Verb and the Perfect Woman in Proverbs," in *Windows to the Ancient World of the Hebrew Bible: Essays in Honor of Samuel Greengus*, ed. Bill T. Arnold, Nancy L. Erickson, and John H. Walton (Winona Lake, IN: Eisenbrauns, 2014), 263–74. See also Max Rogland, *Alleged Non-Past Uses of Qatal in Classical Hebrew* (Assen, NL: Van Gorcum, 2003), 15–51.

9. Webster, "Perfect Verb," 274.

10. M. Gilbert, "Le discours de la sagesse en Proverbes 8," in *La Sagesse de l'Ancien Testament*, ed. M. Gilbert (Leuven: Leuven University, 1979), 205; G. Baumann, *Die Weisheitsgestalt in Proverbien 1–9*, Forschungen zum Alten Testament 16 (Tübingen: Mohr, 1996), 78–79; Zoltán S. Schwáb, *Toward an Interpretation of the Book of Proverbs: Selfishness and Secularity Reconsidered*, Journal of Theological Interpretation Supplement 7 (Winona Lake, IN: Eisenbrauns, 2013), 179.

11. Baumann, *Weisheitsgestalt in Proverbien 1–9*, 156–57; Schwáb, *Toward an Interpretation*, 178.

12. Van Leeuwen, "Book of Proverbs," 96.

13. Camp, *Wisdom and the Feminine*, 215–17; Alice M. Sinnott, *The Personification of Wisdom*, Society for Old Testament Studies Monograph Series (Burlington, VT: Ashgate, 2005), 18–20.

14. For a summary and discussion of these proposals, along with others, see Baumann, *Weisheitsgestalt in Proverbien 1–9*, 4–25; Michael V. Fox, *Proverbs 1–9: A New Translation with Introduction and Commentary*, Anchor Bible 18A (New York: Doubleday, 2000), 333–45; Sinnott, *Personification of Wisdom*, 34–51.

15. Gerlinde Baumann, "A Figure of Many Facets: The Literary and Theological Functions of Personified Wisdom in Proverbs 1–9," in *Wisdom and Psalms: A Feminist Companion to the Bible*, ed. Athalya Brenner and Carole R. Fontaine (Sheffield: Sheffield Academic, 1998), 52–56.

16. Donald Collett, "A Place to Stand: Proverbs 8 and the Construction of Ecclesial Space," *Scottish Journal of Theology* 70 (2017): 176–81.

17. Schwáb, *Toward an Interpretation*, 184–85.

18. Christopher Seitz, "The Trinity in the Old Testament," in *The Oxford Handbook of the Trinity*, ed. Gilles Emery and Matthew Levering (Oxford: Oxford University Press, 2011), 30.

19. Richard Bauckham, *God Crucified: Monotheism and Christology in the New Testament* (Carlisle, UK: Paternoster, 1998), 22.

20. Larry W. Hurtado, *One God, One Lord: Early Christian Devotion and Ancient Jewish Monotheism* (London: T&T Clark, 1998), 44.

21. Van Leeuwen, "Book of Proverbs," 99.

22. See Hans Boersma, "The Sacramental Reading of Nicene Theology: Athanasius and Gregory of Nyssa on Proverbs 8," *Journal of Theological Interpretation* 10 (2016): 1–30.

23. Van Leeuwen, "Book of Proverbs," 97–98.

24. Raymond C. Van Leeuwen, "Cosmos, Temple, House: Building and Wisdom in Mesopotamia and Israel," in *Wisdom Literature in Mesopotamia and Israel*, ed. Richard J. Clifford, Symposium Series 36 (Atlanta: Society of Biblical Literature, 2007), 81.

25. Van Leeuwen, "Cosmos, Temple, House," 81.

26. Van Leeuwen, "Cosmos, Temple, House," 89.

27. T. Stordalen, *Echoes of Eden: Genesis 2–3 and Symbolism of the Eden Garden in Biblical Hebrew Literature*, Contributions to Biblical Exegesis and Theology 25 (Leuven: Peeters, 2000), 375.

28. See Christine Roy Yoder, "Wisdom Is the Tree of Life: A Study of Proverbs 3:13–20 and Genesis 2–3," in *Reading Proverbs Intertextually*, ed. Katharine J. Dell and Will Kynes, Library of Hebrew Bible / Old Testament Studies 629 (London: Bloomsbury T&T Clark, 2019), 11–19.

29. William P. Brown, *Wisdom's Wonder: Character, Creation, and Crisis in the Bible's Wisdom Literature* (Grand Rapids: Eerdmans, 2014), 24.

30. Esther Lightcap Meek, *Loving to Know: Introducing Covenant Epistemology* (Eugene, OR: Cascade Books, 2011), 79–80.

31. Dru Johnson, *Biblical Knowing: A Scriptural Epistemology of Error* (Eugene, OR: Cascade Books, 2013), 65–96.

32. For this interpretive sketch of Gen. 3, see Johnson, *Biblical Knowing*, 45–64.

33. Johnson, *Biblical Knowing*, 2–3.

34. Ellen F. Davis, *Proverbs, Ecclesiastes, and the Song of Songs* (Louisville: Westminster John Knox, 2000), 138.

35. Sun Myung Lyu, *Righteousness in the Book of Proverbs*, Forschungen zum Alten Testament II/55 (Tübingen: Mohr Siebeck, 2012), 61.

36. Craig G. Bartholomew and Ryan P. O'Dowd, *Old Testament Wisdom Literature: A Theological Introduction* (Downers Grove, IL: IVP Academic, 2011), 250–51.

37. See Michael V. Fox, "The Rhetoric of Disjointed Proverbs," *Journal for the Study of the Old Testament* 29 (2004): 165–77.

Chapter 4 Sidebar Notes

a. For an excellent discussion of Athanasius's readings of Proverbs 8, see Hans Boersma, "The Sacramental Reading of Nicene Theology: Athanasius and Gregory of Nyssa on Proverbs 8," *Journal of Theological Interpretation* 10 (2016): 1–30.

b. Christine Roy Yoder, *Wisdom as a Woman of Substance: A Socioeconomic Reading of Proverbs 1–9 and 31:10–31*, Beihefte zur Zeitschrift für die alttestamentliche Wissenschaft 304 (Berlin: de Gruyter, 2001), esp. 41–72; Claudia V. Camp, *Wisdom and the Feminine in the Book of Proverbs*, Bible and Literature Series 11 (Sheffield: Almond, 1985), 69–147.

c. Carole R. Fontaine, "The Social Roles of Women in the World of Wisdom," in *A Feminist Companion to Wisdom Literature*, ed. Athalya Brenner (Sheffield: Sheffield Academic, 1995), 24–49; Silvia Schroer, "Wise and Counseling Women in Ancient Israel: Literary and Historical Ideals of the Personified ḥokmâ," in Brenner, *Feminist Companion to Wisdom Literature*, 67–84.

d. Michael V. Fox, *Proverbs 1–9: A New Translation with Introduction and Commentary*, Anchor Bible 18A (New York: Doubleday, 2000), 334.

e. Raymond C. Van Leeuwen, "The Book of Proverbs," in *The New Interpreter's Bible*, ed. Leander E. Keck (Nashville: Abingdon, 1999), 5:96.

f. For an excellent discussion of Proverbs 8 and Colossians 1:15–20, see Christopher A. Beetham, *Echoes of Scripture in the Letter of Paul to the Colossians*, Biblical Interpretation Series 96 (Atlanta: Society of Biblical Literature, 2008), 111–41.

g. Richard B. Hays, "Wisdom according to Paul," in *Where Shall Wisdom Be Found? Wisdom in the Bible, the Church and the Contemporary World*, ed. Stephen C. Barton (Edinburgh: T&T Clark, 1999), 111–23.

h. For an excellent discussion of the false lead, see Suzanna R. Millar, "When a Straight Road Becomes a Garden Path: The 'False Lead' as a Pedagogical Strategy in the Book of Proverbs," *Journal for the Study of the Old Testament* 43 (2018): 67–82.

Chapter 5 Job

1. For an excellent discussion of חנם in Job 1:9 and 2:3, see Tod Linafelt and Andrew R. Davis, "Translating חנם in Job 1:9 and 2:3: On the Relationship between Job's Piety and His Interiority," *Vetus Testamentum* 63 (2013): 627–39.

2. John H. Walton, *Job*, NIV Application Commentary (Grand Rapids: Zondervan, 2012), 21.

3. Walton, *Job*, 20–23.

4. Walton, *Job*, 22.

5. Kathryn Schifferdecker, *Out of the Whirlwind: Creation Theology in the Book of Job* (Cambridge, MA: Harvard University Press, 2008), 125.

6. For discussion of the subtlety of the prologue, see David J. A. Clines, "False Naivety in the Prologue of Job," *Hebrew Annual Review* 9 (1985): 127–36; Alan Cooper, "Reading and Misreading the Prologue of Job," *Journal for the Study of the Old Testament* 46 (1990): 67–79.

7. Edward L. Greenstein, "'On My Skin and in My Flesh': Personal Experience as a Source of Knowledge in the Book of Job," in *Bringing the Hidden to Light: Studies in Honor of Stephen A. Geller*, ed. Kathryn F. Kravitz and Diane M. Sharon (Winona Lake, IN: Eisenbrauns, 2007), 63–77.

8. For a brilliant discussion of the social-ideational-symbolic structure of the friends' "iconic narratives" concerning the fate of the righteous and the wicked, see Carol A. Newsom, *The Book of Job: A Contest of Moral Imaginations* (Oxford: Oxford University Press, 2003), 115–25.

9. Norman C. Habel, *The Book of Job: A Commentary*, Old Testament Library (Philadelphia: Westminster, 1985), 392.

Chapter 5 Sidebar Notes

a. Tod Linafelt and Andrew R. Davis, "Translating חנם in Job 1:9 and 2:3: On the Relationship between Job's Piety and His Interiority," *Vetus Testamentum* 63 (2013): 627–39.

b. Tod Linafelt, "Why Is There Poetry in the Book of Job?," *Journal of Biblical Literature* 140 (2021): 683–701.

c. Robert Frost, *A Masque of Reason*, in *Robert Frost: Collected Poems, Prose, and Plays* (New York: Library of America, 1995), 372–88, with quotes on 380–83.

d. Tod Linafelt, "The Undecidability of ברך in the Prologue of Job and Beyond," *Biblical Interpretation* 4 (1996): 154–72.

Chapter 6 Theological Themes in Job (1)

1. Carol A. Newsom, "Woman and the Discourse of Patriarchal Wisdom: A Study of Proverbs 1–9," in *Gender and Difference in Ancient Israel*, ed. Peggy L. Day (Minneapolis: Fortress, 1989), 151.

2. Norman C. Habel, *The Book of Job: A Commentary*, Old Testament Library (Philadelphia: Westminster, 1985), 393–95.

3. For a stimulating discussion of the gaps in these relationships, see Davis Hankins, "Wisdom as an Immanent Event in Job 28, Not a Transcendent Ideal," *Vetus Testamentum* 63 (2013): 210–35, esp. 220–25.

4. Scott C. Jones, "Job 28 and Modern Theories of Knowledge," *Theology Today* 69 (2013): 494.

5. For an excellent discussion of the way in which this distinction maps onto different models of epistemology, see Jones, "Job 28 and Modern Theories," 486–96.

6. "Man and His God," trans. Jacob Klein, in *The Context of Scripture*, ed. William W. Hallo, 3 vols. (Leiden: Brill, 1997–2002), 1:574 (1.179).

7. "Against Congenital Guilt," in *Before the Muses: An Anthology of Akkadian Literature*, ed. Benjamin R. Foster, 3rd ed. (Bethesda, MD: CDL Press, 2005), 645.

8. "Who Has Not Sinned?," in Foster, *Before the Muses*, 724.

9. See Samuel Noah Kramer, *The Sumerians: Their History, Culture, and Character* (Chicago: University of Chicago Press, 1971), 125–26.

10. Peter L. Berger, *The Sacred Canopy: Elements of a Sociological Theory of Religion* (Garden City, NY: Anchor, 1969), 74; James L. Crenshaw, "Introduction: The Shift from Theodicy to Anthropodicy," in *Theodicy in the Old Testament*, ed. James L. Crenshaw, Issues in Religion and Theology 4 (Philadelphia: Fortress, 1983), 1–16.

11. Norman C. Habel, "'Naked I Came': Humanness in the Book of Job," in *Die Botschaft und die Boten: Festschrift für Hans Walter Wolff zum 70. Geburtstag*, ed. Jörg Jeremias and Lothar Perlitt (Neukirchen–Vluyn: Neukirchener Verlag, 1981), 381–82. For a brilliant discussion of the function of Psalm 8:5–6 in Job's argument against God (cf. Job 19:9), see Christian Frevel, *Im Lesen verstehen: Studien zu Theologie und Exegese*, Beihefte zur Zeitschrift für die alttestamentliche Wissenschaft 482 (Berlin: de Gruyter, 2017), 277–304.

12. For further discussion of Job's reconfiguration of metaphors pertaining to anthropology, see Leo G. Perdue, "Metaphorical Theology in the Book of Job: Theological Anthropology in the First Cycle of Job's Speeches (3; 6–7; 9–10)," in *The Book of Job*, ed. W. A. M. Beuken, Bibliotheca Ephemeridum Theologicarum Lovaniensium 114 (Leuven: Leuven University Press, 1994), 142–56.

13. E. W. Nicholson, "The Limits of Theodicy as a Theme of the Book of Job," in *Wisdom in Ancient Israel: Essays in Honour of J. A. Emerton*, ed. John Day, Robert P. Gordon, and H. G. M. Williamson (Cambridge: Cambridge University Press, 1995), 77.

14. Kelly M. Kapic, *You're Only Human: How Your Limits Reflect God's Design and Why That's Good News* (Grand Rapids: Brazos, 2022), 12–15.

15. A. LaCocque, "Sin and Guilt," in *Encyclopedia of Religion*, ed. L. Jones, 2nd ed., 15 vols. (New York: MacMillan, 2005), 12:8403.

16. Frances Young, *God's Presence: A Contemporary Recapitulation of Early Christianity*, Current Issues in Theology (Cambridge: Cambridge University Press, 2013), 136.

17. Slavoj Žižek, *For They Know Not What They Do: Enjoyment as a Political Factor*, 2nd ed. (London: Verso, 2002), lii.

18. Kathryn Schifferdecker, *Out of the Whirlwind: Creation Theology in the Book of Job* (Cambridge, MA: Harvard University Press, 2008), 125. Cf. Davis Hankins, *The Book of Job and the Immanent Genesis of Transcendence*, Diaeresis (Evanston, IL: Northwestern University Press, 2015), 180–83. Hankins offers a stimulating reading of the divine speeches that moves beyond Schifferdecker's ordered but safe world to a world marked by independence and disconnection.

19. Michael V. Fox, "Job the Pious," *Zeitschrift für die alttestamentliche Wissenschaft* 117 (2005): 335.

20. Fox, "Job the Pious," 353.

21. Brian R. Doak, *Consider Leviathan: Narratives of Nature and the Self in Job* (Minneapolis: Fortress, 2014), 191–98.

22. The following account of the types of questions and their rhetorical function is dependent on Michael V. Fox, "Job 38 and God's Rhetoric," *Semeia* 19 (1981): 53–61, esp. 58–60; Craig G. Bartholomew and Ryan P. O'Dowd, *Old Testament Wisdom Literature: A Theological Introduction* (Downers Grove, IL: IVP Academic, 2011), 146.

23. Fox, "Job the Pious," 354.

24. Kathleen M. O'Connor, "Wild, Raging Creativity: The Scene in the Whirlwind (Job 38–41)," in *A God So Near: Essays on Old Testament Theology in Honor of Patrick D. Miller*, ed. Brent A. Strawn and Nancy R. Bowen (Winona Lake, IN: Eisenbrauns, 2003), 175.

25. Carol A. Newsom, *The Book of Job: A Contest of Moral Imaginations* (Oxford: Oxford University Press, 2003), 249.

26. Newsom, *Book of Job*, 248.

27. David J. A. Clines, "On the Poetic Achievement of the Book of Job," in *Palabra, prodigio, poesía: In memoriam P. Luis Alonso Schökel, SJ*, ed. Vicente Collado Bertomeu, Analecta Biblica 151 (Rome: Pontifical Biblical Institute, 2003), 250.

28. Doak, *Consider Leviathan*, 231.

Chapter 6 Sidebar Notes

a. Carol A. Newsom, *The Book of Job: A Contest of Moral Imaginations* (Oxford: Oxford University Press, 2003), 179.

b. For discussion, see C. L. Seow, *Job 1–21: Interpretation and Commentary*, Illuminations (Grand Rapids: Eerdmans, 2013), 624.

c. For further discussion of the motif, see Raymond C. Van Leeuwen, "Proverbs 30:21–23 and the Biblical World Upside Down," *Journal of Biblical Literature* 105 (1986): 599–610.

d. Newsom, *Book of Job*, 180.

e. See "Inanna and Enki," trans. Gertrud Farber, in *The Context of Scripture*, ed. William W. Hallo, 3 vols. (Leiden: Brill, 1997–2002), 1:523 (1.161).

f. "The Babylonian Theodicy," in *Before the Muses: An Anthology of Akkadian Literature*, ed. Benjamin R. Foster, 3rd ed. (Bethesda, MD: CDL Press, 2005), 921.

g. For further discussion of these interpretive issues, see Norman C. Habel, *The Book of Job: A Commentary*, Old Testament Library (Philadelphia: Westminster, 1985), 582–83; John H. Walton, *Job*, NIV Application Commentary (Grand Rapids: Zondervan, 2012), 431–32.

h. For a brilliant discussion of the nodes and trajectories of Behemoth and Leviathan in the history of reception, see Mark R. Sneed, *Taming the Beast: A Reception History of Behemoth and Leviathan*, Studies of the Bible and Its Reception 12 (Berlin: de Gruyter, 2022).

Chapter 7 Theological Themes in Job (2)

1. Michael C. Legaspi, *Wisdom in Classical and Biblical Tradition* (Oxford: Oxford University Press, 2018), 96–97.

2. Davis Hankins, *Job and the Immanent Genesis of Transcendence*, Diaeresis (Evanston, IL: Northwestern University Press, 2015), 42. Hankins takes the expression "bare life" from

Samuel R. Driver and George Buchanan Gray, *A Critical and Exegetical Commentary on the Book of Job* (Edinburgh: T&T Clark, 1921), lii–liii.

3. Christine McKinnon, *Character, Virtue Theories, and the Vices* (Peterborough, ON: Broadview, 1999), 38.

4. McKinnon, *Character, Virtue Theories*, 198.

5. Damian Cox, Marguerite La Caze, and Michael Levine, "Integrity," in *The Handbook of Virtue Ethics*, ed. Stan Van Hooft (Durham, UK: Acumen, 2014), 208.

6. Cox, La Caze, and Levine, "Integrity," 208.

7. Susannah Ticciati, *Job and the Disruption of Identity: Reading beyond Barth* (London: T&T Clark, 2005), 170.

8. Legaspi, *Wisdom*, 102.

9. Lindsay Wilson, "The Book of Job and the Fear of God," *Tyndale Bulletin* 46 (1995): 68.

10. Samuel E. Balentine, "Let Love Clasp Grief lest Both Be Drowned," *Perspectives in Religious Studies* 30 (2003): 390–91.

11. C. L. Seow, *Job 1–21: Interpretation and Commentary*, Illuminations (Grand Rapids: Eerdmans, 2013), 91.

12. Wilson, "Book of Job," 74–78.

13. Francis I. Andersen, *Job*, Tyndale Old Testament Commentary (Downers Grove, IL: InterVarsity, 1976), 98.

14. Lindsay Wilson, *Job*, Two Horizons Old Testament Commentary (Grand Rapids: Eerdmans, 2015), 230.

15. For a brilliant discussion of prayer through the typology of orientation, disorientation, and reorientation, see Walter Brueggemann, "Psalms and the Life of Faith: A Suggested Typology of Function," in *The Psalms and the Life of Faith*, ed. Patrick D. Miller (Minneapolis: Fortress, 1995), 3–32.

16. Carol A. Newsom, *The Book of Job: A Contest of Moral Imaginations* (Oxford: Oxford University Press, 2003), 136.

17. Scott C. Jones, "Corporeal Discourse in the Book of Job," *Journal of Biblical Literature* 132 (2013): 850.

18. John E. Hartley, "From Lament to Oath: A Study of Progression in the Speeches of Job," in *The Book of Job*, ed. W. A. M. Beuken, Bibliotheca Ephemeridum Theologicarum Lovaniensium 114 (Leuven: Leuven University Press, 1994), 89–91.

19. Will Kynes, *My Psalm Has Turned into Weeping: Job's Dialogue with the Psalms*, Beihefte zur Zeitschrift für die alttestamentliche Wissenschaft 437 (Berlin: de Gruyter, 2012), 184–85.

20. Wilson, *Job*, 250–51.

21. For a trial across the entire book, see F. Rachel Magdalene, *On the Scales of Righteousness: Neo-Babylonian Trial Law and the Book of Job*, Brown Judaic Studies 48 (Providence: Brown Judaic Studies, 2007). For the structural significance of the legal metaphor in the book, see Norman C. Habel, *The Book of Job: A Commentary*, Old Testament Library (Philadelphia: Westminster, 1985), 54.

22. Habel, *Book of Job*, 54–55.

23. Newsom, *Book of Job*, 150, 157; Magdalene, *Scales of Righteousness*, 165.

24. Newsom, *Book of Job*, 155.

25. Habel, *Book of Job*, 56.

26. M. B. Dick, "The Legal Metaphor in Job 31," *Catholic Biblical Quarterly* 41 (1979): 37–50.

27. Habel, *Book of Job*, 56.

28. John H. Walton, *Job*, NIV Application Commentary (Grand Rapids: Zondervan, 2012), 22.

29. Daniel J. Estes, "Communicating the Book of Job in the Twenty-First Century," *Themelios* 40 (2015): 251.

30. John Webster, "Providence," in *Mapping Modern Theology: A Thematic and Historical Introduction*, ed. Kelly M. Kapic and Bruce L. McCormack (Grand Rapids: Baker Academic, 2012), 203.

31. Herman Bavinck, *Reformed Dogmatics*, ed. John Bolt, trans. John Vriend, 4 vols. (Grand Rapids: Baker Academic, 2004), 2:596.

32. Mary Midgley, *Beast and Man: The Roots of Human Nature*, rev. ed., Routledge Classics (New York: Routledge, 2002), 349.

33. Webster, "Providence," 207.

34. Balentine, "Let Love Clasp Grief," 381.

35. Balentine, "Let Love Clasp Grief," 381; Patricia Vesely, *Friendship and Virtue Ethics in the Book of Job* (Cambridge: Cambridge University Press, 2019), 4.

Chapter 7 Sidebar Notes

a. For discussion of these proposals, see C. L. Seow, *Job 1–21: Interpretation and Commentary*, Illuminations (Grand Rapids: Eerdmans, 2013), 91–92; Tremper Longman III, *Job*, Baker Commentary on the Old Testament Wisdom and Psalms (Grand Rapids: Baker Academic, 2012), 459; John H. Walton, *Job*, NIV Application Commentary (Grand Rapids: Zondervan, 2012), 433; David J. A. Clines, *Job 38–42*, Word Biblical Commentary 18B (Nashville: Thomas Nelson, 2011), 1231.

b. For a full discussion, see Will Kynes, "Beat Your Parodies into Swords, and Your Parodied Books into Spears: A New Paradigm for Parody in the Hebrew Bible," *Biblical Interpretation* 19 (2011): 276–310; cf. Katharine J. Dell, *The Book of Job as Sceptical Literature*, Beihefte zur Zeitschrift für die alttestamentliche Wissenschaft 197 (Berlin: de Gruyter, 1991).

c. Edmund Burke, *A Philosophical Enquiry into the Origin of Our Ideas of the Sublime and Beautiful with an Introductory Discourse concerning Taste and Several Other Additions* (London, 1812), 237–38.

d. Immanuel Kant, *Critique of the Power of Judgment*, ed. Paul Guyer, trans. Paul Guyer and Eric Matthews, The Cambridge Edition of the Works of Immanuel Kant (Cambridge: Cambridge University Press, 2000), 130–59. For representative biblical scholars who employ the concept of the sublime in their reading of the divine speeches, see Carol A. Newsom, *The Book of Job: A Contest of Moral Imaginations* (Oxford: Oxford University Press, 2003), 234–58; Tod Linafelt, "The Wizard of Uz: Job, Dorothy, and the Limits of the Sublime," *Biblical Interpretation* 14 (2006): 94–109; Hankins, *Job and the Immanent Genesis*, 183–204.

e. Aristotle, *The Nicomachean Ethics*, trans. J. A. K. Thomson (New York: Penguin Books, 2004), 1158b33–1159a2.

Chapter 8 Ecclesiastes

1. Ryan P. O'Dowd, "Epistemology in Ecclesiastes: Remembering What It Means to Be Human," in *The Words of the Wise Are Like Goads: Engaging Qohelet in the 21st Century*, ed. Mark J. Boda, Tremper Longman III, and Cristian G. Rata (Winona Lake, IN: Eisenbrauns, 2013), 195–96.

2. Martin Heidegger, *Being and Time*, trans. Joan Stambaugh (Albany: State University of New York Press, 1996), 283 (§62).

3. Immanuel Kant, "An Answer to the Question: 'What Is Enlightenment?,'" in *Kant: Political Writings*, ed. Hans Reiss, trans. H. B. Nisbet (Cambridge: Cambridge University Press, 1991), 54.

4. Raymond C. Van Leeuwen, "Creation and Contingency in Qoheleth," in *The Identity of Israel's God in Christian Scripture*, ed. Don Collett, Mark Elliott, Mark Gignilliat, and Ephraim Radner, Resources for Biblical Study 96 (Atlanta: SBL Press, 2020), 143–59.

5. Davis Hankins, "The Internal Infinite: Deleuze, Subjectivity, and Moral Agency in Ecclesiastes," *Journal for the Study of the Old Testament* 40 (2015): 43–59, esp. 45, 48–49.

6. Choon-Leong Seow, *Ecclesiastes: A New Translation with Introduction and Commentary*, Anchor Bible 18C (New Haven: Yale University Press, 1997), 59–60.

7. For Qoheleth's epistemological concern, see Michael V. Fox, "Qohelet's Epistemology," *Hebrew Union College Annual* 58 (1987): 137–55; Annette Schellenberg, *Erkenntnis als Problem: Qohelet und die alttestamentliche Diskussion um das menschliche Erkennen*, Orbis Biblicus et Orientalis 188 (Göttingen: Vandenhoeck & Ruprecht, 2002); O'Dowd, "Epistemology in Ecclesiastes," 195–217; Arthur Keefer, "The Meaning of Life in Ecclesiastes: Coherence, Purpose, and Significance from a Psychological Perspective," *Harvard Theological Review* 112 (2019): 447–66.

8. Mark Sneed, "הבל as 'Worthless' in Qoheleth: A Critique of Michael V. Fox's 'Absurd' Thesis," *Journal of Biblical Literature* 136 (2017): 879–94, esp. 891.

9. I am grateful to the late Rev. Dr. Michael J. Ovey, who helped me see the inseparable relationship among the members of this philosophical trinity. As Ovey notes on one of the handouts of our cotaught class on hermeneutics, epistemology, and knowledge of God, what something is (i.e., ontology) determines how one should know it (i.e., epistemology), as well as what it owes the knower and what the knower owes it (i.e., ethics).

10. Eric S. Christianson, *Ecclesiastes through the Centuries*, Blackwell Bible Commentaries (Malden, MA: Wiley-Blackwell, 2007), 89–98; James L. Kugel, "Qohelet and Money," *Catholic Biblical Quarterly* 51 (1989): 32–49, esp. 46; Stuart Weeks, *Ecclesiastes and Scepticism*, Library of Hebrew Bible / Old Testament Studies 541 (London: T&T Clark, 2012), 12–43; Thomas M. Bolin, *Ecclesiastes and the Riddle of Authorship* (New York: Routledge, 2017).

11. Michael V. Fox, "Frame-Narrative and Composition in the Book of Qohelet," *Hebrew Union College Annual* 48 (1977): 83–106.

12. Michael V. Fox, *Qohelet and His Contradictions*, Journal for the Study of the Old Testament Supplement Series 71 (Sheffield: Almond, 1989), 159.

13. R. N. Whybray, "Qoheleth, Preacher of Joy," *Journal for the Study of the Old Testament* 23 (1982): 87–98.

14. Michael V. Fox, *A Time to Tear Down and a Time to Build Up: A Rereading of Ecclesiastes* (1999; repr., Eugene, OR: Wipf & Stock, 2010), 3; Doug Ingram, *Ambiguity in Ecclesiastes*, Library of Hebrew Bible / Old Testament Studies 431 (London: T&T Clark, 2006), 44–74.

15. Jacques Ellul, *Reason for Being: A Meditation on Ecclesiastes* (Grand Rapids: Eerdmans, 1990), 40.

16. For a crisp summary and critique of these approaches, see Fox, *Time to Tear Down*, 14–26.

17. George A. Barton, *The Book of Ecclesiastes*, International Critical Commentary (Edinburgh: T&T Clark, 1908), 44–45.

18. Craig G. Bartholomew, *Ecclesiastes*, Baker Commentary on the Old Testament Wisdom and Psalms (Grand Rapids: Baker Academic, 2009), 59.

19. Robert Gordis, *Koheleth: The Man and His World* (New York: Bloch, 1955), 73–74.

20. For *hebel* as an evaluative term or, better, a term of "devaluation," see Klaus Seybold, "הֶבֶל hebhel," in *Theological Dictionary of the Old Testament*, ed. G. Johannes Botterweck, et al., trans. John T. Willis et al. (Grand Rapids: Eerdmans, 1974–2021), 3:319. For discussion of the interrelationships among Qoheleth's contradictions, ambiguities, and *hebel*, see Samuel T. S. Goh, "The *Hebel* World, Its Ambiguities and Contradictions," *Journal for the Study of the Old Testament* 45 (2020): 198–216.

21. Weeks, *Ecclesiastes and Scepticism*, 108.

22. Douglas B. Miller, *Symbol and Rhetoric in Ecclesiastes: The Place of Hebel in Qohelet's Work*, Society of Biblical Literature Academia Biblica 2 (Leiden: Brill, 2002), 15.

23. For an excellent survey of the renderings of *hebel* in Ecclesiastes, see Russell L. Meek, "Twentieth- and Twenty-First-Century Readings of *Hebel* (הֶבֶל) in Ecclesiastes," *Currents in Biblical Research* 14 (2016): 279–97.

24. Seow, *Ecclesiastes*, 103; Fox, *Time to Tear Down*, 40–41.

25. Seow, *Ecclesiastes*, 102; Mark R. Sneed, *The Politics of Pessimism in Ecclesiastes: A Social-Science Perspective*, Ancient Israel and Its Literature 12 (Atlanta: Society of Biblical Literature, 2012), 165.

26. Weeks, *Ecclesiastes and Scepticism*, 119; Sneed, *Politics of Pessimism*, 162–66.

a. Thomas Bolin, "Rivalry and Resignation: Girard and Qoheleth on the Divine-Human Relationship," *Biblica* 86 (2005): 245–59.

b. For representative treatments of these compositional contexts, see Choon-Leong Seow, *Ecclesiastes: A New Translation with Introduction and Commentary*, Anchor Bible 18C (New Haven: Yale University Press, 1997), 11–36; Thomas Krüger, *Qoheleth*, Hermeneia (Minneapolis: Fortress, 2004), 19–27.

c. Daniel C. Fredericks, *Qoheleth's Language: Re-evaluating Its Nature and Date*, Ancient Near Eastern Texts and Studies 3 (Lewiston, NY: Edwin Mellen, 1988).

d. For an excellent discussion of these Christian readings of Ecclesiastes, see Jennie Grillo, "Is Patristic Exegesis Good for Biblical Scholarship? Jerome and Gregory of Nyssa on Qohelet," in *Perspectives on Israelite Wisdom: Proceedings of the Oxford Old Testament Seminar*, ed. John Jarick, Library of Hebrew Bible / Old Testament Studies 618 (London: Bloomsbury T&T Clark, 2016), 232–53.

e. John Jarick, "The Rhetorical Structure of Ecclesiastes," in Jarick, *Perspectives on Israelite Wisdom*, 208–31.

f. For discussion, see David J. H. Beldman, "Framed! Structure in Ecclesiastes," in *The Words of the Wise Are Like Goads: Engaging Qohelet in the 21st Century*, ed. Mark J. Boda, Tremper Longman III, and Cristian G. Rata (Winona Lake, IN: Eisenbrauns, 2013), 137–61.

Chapter 9 Theological Themes in Ecclesiastes

1. Roland E. Murphy, *The Tree of Life: An Exploration of Biblical Wisdom Literature*, 3rd ed. (Grand Rapids: Eerdmans, 2002), 58.

2. Michael V. Fox, *A Time to Tear Down and a Time to Build Up: A Rereading of Ecclesiastes* (1999; repr., Eugene, OR: Wipf & Stock, 2010), 137.

3. Mark R. Sneed, *The Politics of Pessimism in Ecclesiastes: A Social-Science Perspective*, Ancient Israel and Its Literature 12 (Atlanta: Society of Biblical Literature, 2012), 166.

4. Ephraim Radner, *A Time to Keep: Theology, Mortality, and the Shape of a Human Life* (Waco: Baylor University Press, 2016), 152.

5. Fox, *Time to Tear Down*, 138.

6. Sneed, *Politics of Pessimism*, 164.

7. For an excellent discussion of this tension in Ecclesiastes, see Thomas Bolin, "Rivalry and Resignation: Girard and Qoheleth on the Divine-Human Relationship," *Biblica* 86 (2005): 245–59.

8. John Webster, "Life in and of Himself," in *God without Measure: Working Papers in Christian Theology*, 2 vols. (London: Bloomsbury T&T Clark, 2016), 1:13–28, esp. 19.

9. Steven D. Boyer and Christopher A. Hall, *The Mystery of God: Theology for Knowing the Unknowable* (Grand Rapids: Baker Academic, 2012), 11, 13.

10. Fox, *Time to Tear Down*, 166; Choon-Leong Seow, *Ecclesiastes: A New Translation with Introduction and Commentary*, Anchor Bible 18C (New Haven: Yale University Press, 1997), 106. Cf. Graham Ogden, "The Interpretation of דור in Ecclesiastes 1:4," *Journal for the Study of the Old Testament* 34 (1986): 91–92.

11. Peter Enns, *Ecclesiastes*, Two Horizons Old Testament Commentary (Grand Rapids: Eerdmans, 2011), 33.

12. Roland E. Murphy, *Ecclesiastes*, Word Biblical Commentary 23A (Dallas: Word, 1992), 6; Thomas Krüger, *Qoheleth*, Hermeneia (Minneapolis: Fortress, 2004), 49–50; Craig G. Bartholomew, *Ecclesiastes*, Baker Commentary on the Old Testament Wisdom and Psalms (Grand Rapids: Baker Academic, 2009), 111; Katharine J. Dell, "The Cycle of Life in Ecclesiastes," *Vetus Testamentum* 29 (2009): 183–84; Raymond C. Van Leeuwen, "Creation and Contingency in Qoheleth," in *The Identity of Israel's God in Christian Scripture*, ed. Don Collett, Mark Elliott, Mark Gignilliat, and Ephraim Radner, Resources for Biblical Study 96 (Atlanta: SBL Press, 2020), 144–45.

13. Van Leeuwen, "Creation and Contingency," 144.

14. Stuart Weeks, *Ecclesiastes and Scepticism*, Library of Hebrew Bible / Old Testament Studies 541 (London: T&T Clark, 2012), 47–54.

15. Van Leeuwen, "Creation and Contingency," 150.

16. Christopher R. Seitz, *The Elder Testament: Canon, Theology, Trinity* (Waco: Baylor University Press, 2018), 228.

17. Contra Fox, *Time to Tear Down*, 166, who argues that "the permanence of the physical earth has no relevance to the individual life."

18. Van Leeuwen, "Creation and Contingency," 150.

19. Seitz, *Elder Testament*, 240.

20. Mette Bundvad, "Ecclesiastes," in *The Cambridge Companion to Biblical Wisdom Literature*, ed. Katharine J. Dell, Suzanna R. Millar, and Arthur Jan Keefer (Cambridge: Cambridge University Press, 2022), 194–95.

21. Rolf P. Knierim, *The Task of Old Testament Theology: Substance, Method, and Cases* (Grand Rapids: Eerdmans, 1995), 192.

22. Knierim, *Task of Old Testament Theology*, 192.

23. Knierim, *Task of Old Testament Theology*, 195.

24. Knierim, *Task of Old Testament Theology*, 195.

25. For an excellent exploration of how to live as a temporal creature, see James K. A. Smith, *How to Inhabit Time: Understanding the Past, Facing the Future, Living Faithfully Now* (Grand Rapids: Brazos, 2022).

26. Davis Hankins, "The Internal Infinite: Deleuze, Subjectivity, and Moral Agency in Ecclesiastes," *Journal for the Study of the Old Testament* 40 (2015): 48–49.

27. Kelly M. Kapic, *You're Only Human: How Your Limits Reflect God's Design and Why That's Good News* (Grand Rapids: Brazos, 2022), 201.

28. David H. Kelsey, *Eccentric Existence: A Theological Anthropology*, 2 vols. (Louisville: Westminster John Knox, 2009), 1:309.

29. For an excellent discussion of archetypal and ectypal knowledge, see Herman Bavinck, *Reformed Dogmatics*, ed. John Bolt, trans. John Vriend, 4 vols. (Grand Rapids: Baker Academic, 2004), 2:107–10. Archetypal knowledge is knowledge appropriate to God; it denotes that God knows all things, all at once, absolutely—that is, as they are in themselves. Ectypal knowledge, by contrast, is knowledge appropriate to humans; it is limited and provisional yet true and sufficient.

30. Michael V. Fox, "Qohelet's Epistemology," *Hebrew Union College Annual* 58 (1987): 152.

31. Fox, "Qohelet's Epistemology," 142.

32. Weeks, *Ecclesiastes and Scepticism*, 129.

33. Fox, *Time to Tear Down*, 76.

34. Robert D. Holmstedt, "אֲנִי וְלִבִּי: The Syntactic Encoding of the Collaborative Nature of Qohelet's Experiment," *Journal of Hellenic Studies* 9 (2009): 2–27, esp. 14. Holmstedt's careful analysis of Qoheleth's pronominal syntax underwrites the observations in this paragraph. Cf. Fox, *Time to Tear Down*, 78.

35. Holmstedt, "Syntactic Encoding," 20.

36. Holmstedt, "Syntactic Encoding," 20.

37. Fox, *Time to Tear Down*, 86.

38. Esther Lightcap Meek, *Loving to Know: Introducing Covenant Epistemology* (Eugene, OR: Cascade Books, 2011), 410. Also, see Bartholomew, *Ecclesiastes*, 277.

39. Meek, *Loving to Know*, 410. For a brilliant discussion of these aspects of creaturehood and their implications for interpretation, see Hans-Georg Gadamer, *Truth and Method*, trans. Joel Weinsheimer and Donald G. Marshall, 2nd ed. (London: Continuum, 2004), 268–321.

40. While Fox argues that Qoheleth's epistemology is "essentially empirical," many of his assertions operate under basic assumptions, axiomatic beliefs, or value judgments (e.g.,

Eccles. 3:12, 14; 7:2; 8:12–13). This suggests that Qoheleth's epistemology is better characterized as "autonomous." For discussion, see Fox, "Qohelet's Epistemology," 137–54; Bartholomew, *Ecclesiastes*, 269–77; Ryan P. O'Dowd, "Epistemology in Ecclesiastes: Remembering What It Means to Be Human," in *The Words of the Wise Are Like Goads: Engaging Qohelet in the 21st Century*, ed. Mark J. Boda, Tremper Longman III, and Cristian G. Rata (Winona Lake, IN: Eisenbrauns, 2013), 195–217.

41. Weeks, *Ecclesiastes and Scepticism*, 127.

42. Fox, *Time to Tear Down*, 71.

43. William P. Brown, *Wisdom's Wonder: Character, Creation, and Crisis in the Bible's Wisdom Literature* (Grand Rapids: Eerdmans, 2014), 158.

44. Van Leeuwen, "Creation and Contingency," 148.

45. Sneed, *Politics of Pessimism*, 162, 168.

46. O'Dowd, "Epistemology in Ecclesiastes," 208, 215–17.

47. Murphy, *Tree of Life*, 58.

48. Sneed, *Politics of Pessimism*, 168; Hankins, "Internal Infinite," 55–56.

49. Norman Wirzba, *Food and Faith: A Theology of Eating*, 2nd ed. (Cambridge: Cambridge University Press, 2019), 41.

50. Leon R. Kass, *The Hungry Soul: Eating and the Perfecting of Our Nature* (Chicago: University of Chicago Press, 1999), 196.

51. Krüger, *Qoheleth*, 206.

52. Jacques Ellul, *Reason for Being: A Meditation on Ecclesiastes* (Grand Rapids: Eerdmans, 1990), 31.

53. Job Y. Jindo, "On the Biblical Notion of Human Dignity: 'Fear of God' as a Condition for Authentic Existence," *Biblical Interpretation* 19 (2011): 433–53.

54. Michael C. Legaspi, *Wisdom in Classical and Biblical Tradition* (Oxford: Oxford University Press, 2018), 74.

55. James L. Crenshaw, *Ecclesiastes: A Commentary*, Old Testament Library (Philadelphia: Westminster, 1987), 100; Tremper Longman III, *The Book of Ecclesiastes*, New International Commentary on the Old Testament (Grand Rapids: Eerdmans, 1998), 36, 123–24.

56. Jindo, "Notion of Human Dignity," 435, 449.

57. Krüger, *Qoheleth*, 24–25.

58. C. L. Seow, "'Beyond Them, My Son, Be Warned': The Epilogue of Qohelet Revisited," in *Wisdom, You Are My Sister: Studies in Honor of Roland E. Murphy, O. Carm., on the Occasion of His Eightieth Birthday*, ed. Michael L. Barré, Catholic Biblical Quarterly Monograph Series 29 (Washington, DC: Catholic Biblical Association of America, 1997), 139.

59. Seow, "'Beyond Them, My Son,'" 139–41; Fox, *Time to Tear Down*, 144–45, 359; Stuart Weeks, "'Fear God and Keep His Commandments': Could Qohelet Have Said This?," in *Wisdom and Torah: The Reception of "Torah" in the Wisdom Literature of the Second Temple Period*, ed. Bernd U. Schipper and D. Andrew Teeter, Supplements to the Journal for the Study of Judaism 163 (Leiden: Brill, 2013), 115–17.

60. Gerald T. Sheppard, "The Epilogue to Qoheleth as Theological Commentary," *Catholic Biblical Quarterly* 39 (1977): 182–89.

61. Brent A. Strawn, "What Does Ecclesiastes Have to Say to Our Moment? Qoheleth Meets COVID-19," *Christian Century*, January 13, 2021, 28.

62. For examples of these evangelistic readings of Ecclesiastes, see Michael A. Eaton, *Ecclesiastes: An Introduction and Commentary*, Tyndale Old Testament Commentary (Leicester, UK: Inter-Varsity, 1983), 42–46.

63. Hannah Arendt, "The Eggs Speak Up," in *Essays in Understanding, 1930–1954*, ed. Jerome Kohn (New York: Harcourt, 1994), 270–84, esp. 283.

64. Iain Provan, "Fresh Perspectives on Ecclesiastes: 'Qohelet for Today,'" in *The Words of the Wise Are Like Goads: Engaging Qohelet in the 21st Century*, ed. Mark J. Boda, Tremper Longman III, and Cristian G. Rata (Winona Lake, IN: Eisenbrauns, 2013), 412.

65. Jennie Grillo, "Is Patristic Exegesis Good for Biblical Scholarship? Jerome and Gregory of Nyssa on Qohelet," in *Perspectives on Israelite Wisdom*, 232–53, esp. 237–49.

Chapter 9 Sidebar Notes

a. Nili Samet, "Qohelet 1,4 and the Structure of the Book's Prologue," *Zeitschrift für die alttestamentliche Wissenschaft* 126 (2014): 92–100, esp. 97–98.

b. Tremper Longman III, *The Book of Ecclesiastes*, New International Commentary on the Old Testament (Grand Rapids: Eerdmans, 1998), 34–36, esp. 35.

c. Peter Enns, *Ecclesiastes*, Two Horizons Old Testament Commentary (Grand Rapids: Eerdmans, 2011), 69.

d. Longman, *Book of Ecclesiastes*, 284.

e. Stuart Weeks, "'Fear God and Keep His Commandments': Could Qohelet Have Said This?," in *Wisdom and Torah: The Reception of "Torah" in the Wisdom Literature of the Second Temple Period*, ed. Bernd U. Schipper and D. Andrew Teeter, Supplements to the Journal for the Study of Judaism 163 (Leiden: Brill, 2013), 103.

f. Thomas Krüger, *Qoheleth*, Hermeneia (Minneapolis: Fortress, 2004), 25.

g. Daniel J. Treier, "The Gift of Finitude: Wisdom from Ecclesiastes for a Theology of Education," *Christian Scholar's Review* 48 (2019): 371–90, with quote on 389.

Chapter 10 Song of Songs

1. Leon R. Kass, *The Hungry Soul: Eating and the Perfecting of Our Nature* (Chicago: University of Chicago Press, 1999), 48.

2. David J. A. Clines, "Why Is There a Song of Songs, and What Does It Do to You If You Read It?," in *Interested Parties: The Ideology of Writers and Readers of the Hebrew Bible*, ed. David J. A. Clines, Journal for the Study of the Old Testament Supplement Series 205 (Sheffield: Sheffield Academic, 1995), 94–121.

3. Michael V. Fox, *The Song of Songs and the Ancient Egyptian Love Songs* (Madison: University of Wisconsin Press, 1985), 227–52; Martti Nissinen, "Song of Songs and Sacred Marriage," in *Sacred Marriages: The Divine-Human Sexual Metaphor from Sumer to Early Christianity*, ed. Martti Nissinen and Risto Uro (Winona Lake, IN: Eisenbrauns, 2008), 173–218.

4. Ellen F. Davis, *Proverbs, Ecclesiastes, and the Song of Songs*, Westminster Bible Companion (Louisville: Westminster John Knox, 2000), 232–33.

5. Mark S. Gignilliat, *Reading Scripture Canonically: Theological Instincts for Old Testament Interpretation* (Grands Rapids: Baker Academic, 2019), 92.

6. Don C. Collett, *Figural Reading and the Old Testament: Theology and Practice* (Grand Rapids: Baker Academic, 2020), 30.

7. Aren M. Wilson-Wright, "Love Conquers All: Song of Songs 8:6b–7a as a Reflex of the Northwest Semitic Combat Myth," *Journal of Biblical Literature* 134 (2015): 339–43.

8. Jonathan Kaplan and Aren M. Wilson-Wright, "How Song of Songs Became a Divine Love Song," *Biblical Interpretation* 26 (2018): 334–51, with quote on 339.

9. For a nuanced discussion of the echoes to the Song of Songs in Revelation, see Jonathan Kaplan, "The Song of Songs from the Bible to the Mishnah," *Hebrew Union College Annual* 81 (2010): 43–66, esp. 57–66.

10. For this sentiment and a defense of allegorical forms of reading, see Andrew Louth, *Discerning the Mystery: An Essay on the Nature of Theology* (1983; repr., Oxford: Oxford University Press, 2003), 96–131.

11. Fox, *Song of Songs*, 253–66.

12. P. Harris 500, Group A, Nos. 3–4. The translation is taken from Fox, *Song of Songs*, 9–10 (parenthetical question marks omitted).

13. Fox, *Song of Songs*, 267–331.

14. Fox, *Song of Songs*, 315–22.

15. Fox, *Song of Songs*, 280–81, 326.

16. This conclusion is affirmed by many commentators. Among them, see J. Cheryl Exum, *Song of Songs: A Commentary*, Old Testament Library (Louisville: Westminster John Knox, 2005), 42–45, 78; Richard S. Hess, *Song of Songs*, Baker Commentary on the Old Testament Wisdom and Psalms (Grand Rapids: Baker Academic, 2005), 24. Dramatic readings of the Song perceive a coherent plot across the poems, involving either two or three characters. For this form of reading, see Franz Delitzsch, *Commentary on the Song of Songs and Ecclesiastes*, trans. M. G. Easton (Edinburgh, 1877); Christian D. Ginsberg, *The Song of Songs: Translated from the Original Hebrew, with a Commentary Historical and Critical* (London, 1857); Iain Provan, *Ecclesiastes, Song of Songs*, NIV Application Commentary (Grand Rapids: Zondervan, 2001).

17. Brian P. Gault, *Body as Landscape, Love as Intoxication: Conceptual Metaphors in the Songs of Songs*, Ancient Israel and Its Literature 36 (Atlanta: SBL Press, 2019).

18. Danilo Verde, *Conquered Conquerors: Love and War in the Song of Songs*, Ancient Israel and Its Literature 41 (Atlanta: SBL Press, 2020).

19. Jill M. Munro, *Spikenard and Saffron: A Study of the Poetic Language of the Song of Songs*, Journal for the Study of the Old Testament Supplement Series 203 (Sheffield: Sheffield Academic, 1995), esp. 143.

20. F. W. Dobbs-Allsopp, *On Biblical Poetry* (Oxford: Oxford University Press, 2015), 215.

21. This unity is the product of "an artistic vision" or "a conscious artistic design." For discussion, see Gault, *Body as Landscape*, 224; Exum, *Song of Songs*, 34–37. Also, for the relationship between the Song of Songs and "wisdom literature," see Jennifer L. Andruska, *Wise and Foolish Love in the Song of Songs*, Oudtestamentische Studiën 75 (Leiden: Brill, 2019); Katharine J. Dell, *The Solomonic Corpus of 'Wisdom' and Its Influence* (Oxford: Oxford University Press, 2020), 43–60.

22. For this reading, see Othmar Keel, *The Song of Songs: A Continental Commentary*, trans. Frederick J. Gaiser (Minneapolis: Fortress, 1994), 128–29; Duane Garrett and Paul R. House, *Song of Songs/Lamentations*, Word Biblical Commentary 23B (Nashville: Thomas Nelson, 2004), 177; Hess, *Song of Songs*, 118; Daniel C. Fredericks and Daniel J. Estes, *Ecclesiastes and Song of Songs*, Apollos Old Testament Commentary 16 (Downers Grove, IL: InterVarsity, 2010), 339.

23. Exum, *Song of Songs*, 143.

24. For the former proposal, see Annette Schellenberg, "The Description of Solomon's Wedding: Song 3:6–11 as a Key to the Overall Understanding of the Song of Songs," *Vetus Testamentum* 70 (2020): 177–92. For the latter proposal, see Roland E. Murphy, *The Song of Songs*, Hermeneia (Minneapolis: Fortress, 1990), 151; Tremper Longman III, *Song of Songs*, New International Commentary on the Old Testament (Grand Rapids: Eerdmans, 2001), 133, 135–36; and Exum, *Song of Songs*, 141–43.

25. Exum, *Song of Songs*, 259–61.

26. Hess, *Song of Songs*, 246–47.

27. Cf. Fredericks and Estes, *Ecclesiastes and Song of Songs*, 414–15.

28. For the different uses of לְ, see Bruce K. Waltke and M. O'Connor, *An Introduction to Biblical Hebrew Syntax* (Winona Lake, IN: Eisenbrauns, 1990), 205–12 (§11.2.10).

29. Douglas Sean O'Donnell, *The Song of Solomon: An Invitation to Intimacy*, Preaching the Word (Wheaton: Crossway, 2012), 23. O'Donnell follows a medieval reading popularized by the Jewish scholar Rashi.

30. Rosalind Clarke, "Seeking Wisdom in the Song of Songs," in *Exploring Old Testament Wisdom: Literature and Themes*, ed. David G. Firth and Lindsay Wilson (London: Apollos, 2016), 112. In contrast to Solomon's portrayal in Kings, Chronicles omits any material that would tarnish Solomon's image in its paradigmatic sketch of the kingdom of God. Chronicles excludes the construction of Solomon's palace, the organization of his administration, and his idolatry, focusing on Solomon's construction and dedication of the temple.

31. J. Cheryl Exum, "How Does the Song of Songs Mean? On Reading the Poetry of Desire," *Svensk exegetisk årsbok* 64 (1999): 48.

a. Marvin H. Pope, *Song of Songs: A New Translation with Introduction and Commentary*, Anchor Bible 7C (Garden City, NY: Doubleday, 1977), 89.

b. For an excellent discussion of lyric poetry, see F. W. Dobbs-Allsopp, *On Biblical Poetry* (Oxford: Oxford University Press, 2015), 178–232.

c. Saint Augustine, *On Christian Teaching*, trans. R. P. H. Green (Oxford: Oxford University Press, 2008), 8–9. For a superb discussion of reference in biblical interpretation, see Frances M. Young, *Biblical Exegesis and the Formation of Christian Culture* (1997; repr., Peabody, MA: Hendrickson, 2002), 17–39.

d. Spinoza's approach is given specific expression in chaps. 7 and 15 of his *Theological-Political Treatise*, ed. Jonathan Israel, trans. Michael Silverthorne and Jonathan Israel, Cambridge Texts in History and Philosophy (Cambridge: Cambridge University Press, 2007). For an excellent account of Spinoza's approach and the ways in which he redefined classic theological and interpretive concepts (e.g., *sola scriptura* and *scriptura sui interpres*), see J. Samuel Preus, *Spinoza and the Irrelevance of Biblical Authority* (Cambridge: Cambridge University Press, 2001).

e. For a discussion and illustration of Scripture's pressure, see Brevard Childs, "Toward Recovering Theological Exegesis," *Pro Ecclesia* 6 (1997): 16–26, and C. Kavin Rowe, "Biblical Pressure and Trinitarian Hermeneutics," *Pro Ecclesia* 11 (2002): 295–312, respectively.

f. Aren M. Wilson-Wright, "Love Conquers All: Song of Songs 8:6b–7a as a Reflex of the Northwest Semitic Combat Myth," *Journal of Biblical Literature* 134 (2015): 333–45.

g. For the myth, see "The Baʿlu Myth," trans. Dennis Pardee, in *The Context of Scripture*, ed. William W. Hallo, 3 vols. (Leiden: Brill, 1997–2002), 1:241–74 (1.86).

h. Origen, *The Song of Songs: Commentary and Homilies*, trans. and ed. R. P. Lawson, Ancient Christian Writers 26 (New York: Newman, 1956), 218.

i. Ellen Davis, "Reading the Song Iconographically," in *Scrolls of Love: Ruth and Song of Songs*, ed. Peter S. Hawkins and Lesleigh Cushing Stahlberg (New York: Fordham University Press, 2006), 172–84.

j. Chloe T. Sun, *Conspicuous in His Absence: Studies in the Song of Songs and Esther* (Downers Grove, IL: IVP Academic, 2021), 90–96.

k. For this dramatic reading, see Franz Delitzsch, *Commentary on the Song of Songs and Ecclesiastes*, trans. M. G. Easton (Edinburgh, 1877).

l. For this dramatic reading, see Iain Provan, *Ecclesiastes, Song of Songs*, NIV Application Commentary (Grand Rapids: Zondervan, 2001).

Chapter 11 Theological Themes in Song of Songs

1. Ellen F. Davis, *Opening Israel's Scriptures* (Oxford: Oxford University Press, 2019), 366.

2. J. Cheryl Exum, *Song of Songs: A Commentary*, Old Testament Library (Louisville: Westminster John Knox, 2005), 15.

3. Francis Landy, *Paradoxes of Paradise: Identity and Difference in the Song of Songs*, Bible and Literature Series 7 (Sheffield: Almond, 1983), 61–133.

4. Exum, *Song of Songs*, 167–68.

5. Danilo Verde, *Conquered Conquerors: Love and War in the Song of Songs*, Ancient Israel and Its Literature 41 (Atlanta: SBL Press, 2020), 203–5.

6. For this reading of Song 8:8–10, see Elaine T. James, "A City Who Surrenders: Song 8:8–10," *Vetus Testamentum* 67 (2017): 448–57.

7. Exum, *Song of Songs*, 203.

8. Francis Landy, by contrast, interprets this depiction of the man as "coldly metallic and disjointed." *Paradoxes of Paradise*, 80.

9. Exum, *Song of Songs*, 203.

10. Michael V. Fox, "Love, Passion, and Perception in Israelite and Egyptian Love Poetry," *Journal of Biblical Literature* 102 (1983): 219–28, with quote on 227.

11. Exum, *Song of Songs*, 93.

12. Daniel Grossberg, "Two Kinds of Sexual Relationships in the Hebrew Bible," *Hebrew Studies* 35 (1994): 7–25.

13. Michael V. Fox, *The Song of Songs and the Ancient Egyptian Love Songs* (Madison: University of Wisconsin Press, 1985), 138–39.

14. See Othmar Keel, *The Song of Songs: A Continental Commentary*, trans. Frederick J. Gaiser (Minneapolis: Fortress, 1994), 252; Richard S. Hess, *Song of Songs*, Baker Commentary on the Old Testament Wisdom and Psalms (Grand Rapids: Baker Academic, 2005), 224.

15. Phyllis Trible, *God and the Rhetoric of Sexuality*, Overtures to Biblical Theology (Philadelphia: Fortress, 1978), 160.

16. Davis, *Opening Israel's Scriptures*, 371.

17. Hess, *Song of Songs*, 224.

18. Karl Barth, *Church Dogmatics*, vol. III/2, *The Doctrine of Creation*, ed. G. W. Bromiley and T. F. Torrance, trans. H. Knight, G. W. Bromiley, J. K. S. Reid, and R. H. Fuller (Edinburgh: T&T Clark, 1960), 294.

19. Barth, *Church Dogmatics* III/2, 294.

20. Havilah Dharamraj, *Altogether Lovely: A Thematic and Intertextual Reading of the Song of Songs* (Minneapolis: Fortress, 2018), 82.

21. Chloe T. Sun, *Conspicuous in His Absence: Studies in the Song of Songs and Esther* (Downers Grove, IL: IVP Academic, 2021), 243.

22. Harold Fisch, *Poetry with a Purpose: Biblical Poetics and Interpretation* (Bloomington: Indiana University Press, 1988), 141.

23. Fox, *Song of Songs*, 237.

24. Davis, *Opening Israel's Scriptures*, 371.

25. Davis, *Opening Israel's Scriptures*, 373.

26. Anselm C. Hagedorn, "Place and Space in the Song of Songs," *Zeitschrift für die alttestamentliche Wissenschaft* 127 (2015): 207–23, with quote on 210.

27. Elaine James, "Battle of the Sexes: Gender and the City in the Song of Songs," *Journal for the Study of the Old Testament* 42 (2017): 93–116, esp. 102–4.

28. James, "Battle of the Sexes," 106–7.

29. Ellen F. Davis, *Scripture, Culture, and Agriculture: An Agrarian Reading of the Bible* (Cambridge: Cambridge University Press, 2009), 171. Cf. Fox, *Song of Songs*, 157–58.

30. Davis, *Scripture, Culture, and Agriculture*, 171.

31. Davis, *Scripture, Culture, and Agriculture*, 170–73.

32. Hagedorn, "Place and Space," 219.

33. Jill M. Munro, *Spikenard and Saffron: A Study of the Poetic Language of the Song of Songs*, Journal for the Study of the Old Testament Supplement Series 203 (Sheffield: Sheffield Academic, 1995), 144.

34. Athalya Brenner, "The Food of Love: Gendered Food and Food Imagery in the Song of Songs," *Semeia* 86 (1999): 101–12.

35. Sun, *Conspicuous in His Absence*, 244–47.

36. Davis, *Opening Israel's Scriptures*, 372.

37. Katharine J. Dell, *The Solomonic Corpus of 'Wisdom' and Its Influence* (Oxford: Oxford University Press, 2020), 195–204.

38. Trible, *God and the Rhetoric*, 154–55.

39. Trible, *God and the Rhetoric*, 155–57.

40. Trible, *God and the Rhetoric*, 145.

41. Trible, *God and the Rhetoric*, 144.

42. Trible, *God and the Rhetoric*, 159.

43. Marcia Falk, *Love Lyrics from the Bible: The Song of Songs* (New York: Harper, 1990), 140.

44. Trible, *God and the Rhetoric*, 161. Cf. Francis Landy, "The Song of Songs and the Garden of Eden," *Journal of Biblical Literature* 98 (1979): 513–28.

45. J. Cheryl Exum, "How Does the Song of Songs Mean? On Reading the Poetry of Desire," *Svensk exegetisk årsbok* 64 (1999): 48.

46. Tod Linafelt, "The Arithmetic of Eros," *Interpretation* 59 (2005): 244–58, esp. 257.

47. Exum, *Song of Songs*, 263.

48. For an excellent discussion of this reading, see Brian P. Gault, "An Admonition against 'Rousing Love': The Meaning of the Enigmatic Refrain in Song of Songs," *Bulletin for Biblical Research* 20 (2010): 161–84.

49. Roland E. Murphy, *The Song of Songs*, Hermeneia (Minneapolis: Fortress, 1990), 137; Tremper Longman III, *Song of Songs*, New International Commentary on the Old Testament (Grand Rapids: Eerdmans, 2001), 115–16; Exum, *Song of Songs*, 117–18.

50. Carey Ellen Walsh, *Exquisite Desire: Religion, the Erotic, and the Song of Songs* (Minneapolis: Fortress, 2000), 161.

51. Walsh, *Exquisite Desire*, 162.

52. Walsh, *Exquisite Desire*, 167.

53. Jonathan Kaplan and Aren M. Wilson-Wright, "How Song of Songs Became a Divine Love Song," *Biblical Interpretation* 26 (2018): 339.

54. For an excellent discussion of the traditional view of divine impassibility, see Thomas G. Weinandy, *Does God Suffer?* (Edinburgh: T&T Clark, 2000). For a discussion of the meaning of divine impassibility in the Christian tradition, which exposes the category errors in modern theological treatments of the attribute, see Paul L. Gavrilyuk, *The Suffering of the Impassible God: The Dialectics of Patristic Thought* (Oxford: Oxford University Press, 2004).

55. David Bentley Hart, "No Shadow of Turning: On Divine Impassibility," *Pro Ecclesia* 11 (2002): 184–206, with quote on 185.

56. Hart, "No Shadow of Turning," 193.

57. John Chrysostom, *On Providence* 6:1; quoted in Steven D. Boyer and Christopher A. Hall, *The Mystery of God: Theology for Knowing the Unknowable* (Grand Rapids: Baker Academic, 2012), 189.

58. Ellen F. Davis, *Proverbs, Ecclesiastes, and the Song of Songs*, Westminster Bible Companion (Louisville: Westminster John Knox, 2000), 232–33.

59. "What's Love Got to Do with It," written by Terry Britten and Graham Lyle, performed by Tina Turner, 1984.

60. Davis, *Song of Songs*, 232.

61. Sarah Coakley, *God, Sexuality, and the Self: An Essay "On the Trinity"* (Cambridge: Cambridge University Press, 2013), 309.

62. Coakley, *God, Sexuality, and the Self*, 316.

63. Hans Boersma, "Nuptial Reading: Hippolytus, Origen, and Ambrose on the Bridal Couple of the Song of Songs," *Calvin Theological Journal* 51 (2016): 227–58, with quote on 258.

64. Davis, *Song of Songs*, 259.

Chapter 11 Sidebar Notes

a. Fiona C. Black, "Beauty or the Beast? The Grotesque Body in the Song of Songs," *Biblical Interpretation* 8 (2000): 302–23, with quotes on 311–12.

b. For an excellent discussion of honor, shame, and guilt, see Jerry Hwang, *Contextualization and the Old Testament: Between Asian and Western Perspectives* (Carlisle, UK: Langham Global Library, 2022), 117–40.

c. David Carr, "Gender and the Shaping of Desire in the Song of Songs and Its Interpretation," *Journal of Biblical Literature* 119 (2000): 233–48, with quotes on 245, 247.

d. Ellen F. Davis, *Proverbs, Ecclesiastes, and the Song of Songs*, Westminster Bible Companion (Louisville: Westminster John Knox, 2000), 255.

Chapter 12 Psalms

1. Elie Wiesel, *Night*, trans. Marion Wiesel (New York: Penguin Books, 2008).

2. Elie Wiesel, *Macht Gebete aus meinen Geschichten: Essays eines Betroffenen* (Freiberg: Herder, 1986).

3. Wiesel, *Macht Gebete*, 33; quotation and translation taken from Bernd Janowski, *Arguing with God: A Theological Anthropology of the Psalms*, trans. Armin Siedlecki (Louisville: Westminster John Know, 2013), 347.

4. George Steiner, *Grammars of Creation* (London: Faber & Faber, 2001), 16.

5. This expression is taken from Jason Byassee, *Praise Seeking Understanding: Reading the Psalms with Augustine* (Grand Rapids: Eerdmans, 2007).

6. William P. Brown, "Happiness and Its Discontents in the Psalms," in *The Bible and the Pursuit of Happiness: What the Old and New Testaments Teach Us about the Good Life*, ed. Brent A. Strawn (Oxford: Oxford University Press, 2012), 95–115, with quote on 97.

7. John Calvin, *Institutes of the Christian Religion*, ed. John T. McNeill, trans. Ford Lewis Battles, 2 vols. (Louisville: Westminster John Knox, 1960), 1.1.1.

8. William P. Brown, *Seeing the Psalms: A Theology of Metaphor* (Louisville: Westminster John Knox, 2002), 1.

9. Hermann Gunkel, *An Introduction to the Psalms: The Genres of the Religious Lyric of Israel*, with Joachim Begrich, trans. James D. Nogalski (Macon, GA: Mercer University Press, 1998); the German original is *Einleitung in die Psalmen: Die Gattungen der religiösen Lyrik Israels* (Göttingen: Vandenhoeck & Ruprecht, 1933).

10. Kenton L. Sparks, *Ancient Texts for the Study of the Hebrew Bible: A Guide to the Background Literature* (Peabody, MA: Hendrickson, 2005), 6.

11. Sigmund Mowinckel, *The Psalms in Israel's Worship*, trans. D. R. Ap-Thomas, Biblical Resource Series (Grand Rapids: Eerdmans, 2004), 31–33.

12. Mowinckel, *Psalms in Israel's Worship*, 35.

13. Mowinckel, *Psalms in Israel's Worship*, 30.

14. Mowinckel, *Psalms in Israel's Worship*, 129–30.

15. Erhard S. Gerstenberger, *Psalms: Part 1, with an Introduction to Cultic Poetry*, Forms of the Old Testament Literature 14 (Grand Rapids: Eerdmans, 1988), 21.

16. Claus Westermann, *Praise and Lament in the Psalms*, trans. Keith R. Crim and Richard N. Soulen (Atlanta: John Knox, 1981), esp. 15–35, 152–62.

17. Walter Brueggemann, "Psalms and the Life of Faith: A Suggested Typology of Function," *Journal for the Study of the Old Testament* 17 (1980): 3–32.

18. For a distillation of Brueggemann's typology, see Walter Brueggemann, *The Message of the Psalms: A Theological Commentary* (Minneapolis: Augsburg, 1984), 19–22.

19. Brown, *Seeing the Psalms*.

20. For example, see Alison Ruth Gray, *Reading Psalm 18 in Words and Pictures: A Reading through Metaphor*, Biblical Interpretation 127 (Leiden: Brill, 2014).

21. Gerald Henry Wilson, *The Editing of the Hebrew Psalter*, Society of Biblical Literature Dissertation Series 76 (Chico: Scholars Press, 1985).

22. Wilson, *Editing of the Hebrew Psalter*, 185–86.

23. Wilson, *Editing of the Hebrew Psalter*, 143, 205.

24. Wilson, *Editing of the Hebrew Psalter*, 209–28.

25. Wilson, *Editing of the Hebrew Psalter*, 215.

26. Wilson, *Editing of the Hebrew Psalter*, 215.

27. Wilson, *Editing of the Hebrew Psalter*, 227.

28. Wilson, *Editing of the Hebrew Psalter*, 228.

29. Gerald H. Wilson, "The Shape of the Book of Psalms," *Interpretation* 46 (1992): 129–42; Wilson, "Shaping the Psalter: A Consideration of Editorial Linkage in the Book of Psalms," in *The Shape and Shaping of the Psalter*, ed. J. Clinton McCann, Journal for the Study of the Old Testament Supplement Series 159 (Sheffield: JSOT Press, 1993), 72–82; Wilson, "The Structure of the Psalter," in *Interpreting the Psalms: Issues and Approaches*, ed. David Firth and Philip S. Johnston (Downers Grove, IL: IVP Academic, 2005), 229–46.

30. J. Clinton McCann, ed., *The Shape and Shaping of the Psalter*, Journal for the Study of the Old Testament Supplement Series 159 (Sheffield: JSOT Press, 1993); Nancy L.

deClaisse-Walford, *Reading from the Beginning: The Shaping of the Hebrew Palter* (Macon, GA: Mercer University Press, 1997).

31. Walter Brueggemann, "Bounded by Obedience and Praise: The Psalms as Canon," *Journal for the Study of the Old Testament* 50 (1991): 63–92, esp. 81.

32. Brueggemann, "Bounded by Obedience and Praise," 80–83.

33. Brueggemann, "Bounded by Obedience and Praise," 72, 79.

34. David C. Mitchell, *The Message of the Psalter: An Eschatological Programme in the Book of Psalms*, Journal for the Study of the Old Testament Supplement Series 252 (Sheffield: Sheffield Academic, 1997).

35. James Luther Mays, "The Place of the Torah-Psalms in the Psalter," *Journal of Biblical Literature* 106 (1987): 3–12. Also, see Jamie A. Grant, *King as Exemplar: The Function of Deuteronomy's Kingship Law in the Shaping of the Book of Psalms*, Society of Biblical Literature Academia Biblica 17 (Atlanta: Society of Biblical Literature, 2004), which offers a brilliant analysis of the interplay between the torah psalms, the royal psalms, and the law of the king in Deut. 17.

36. Robert L. Cole, *The Shape and Message of Book III (Psalms 73–89)*, Journal for the Study of the Old Testament Supplement Series 307 (Sheffield: Sheffield Academic, 2000); David M. Howard Jr., *The Structure of Psalms 93–100*, Biblical and Judaic Studies from the University of California, San Diego 5 (Winona Lake, IN: Eisenbrauns, 1997); W. Dennis Tucker Jr., *Constructing and Deconstructing Power in Psalms 107–150*, Ancient Israel and Its Literature 19 (Atlanta: Society of Biblical Literature, 2014).

37. Jerome F. D. Creach, *Yahweh as Refuge and the Editing of the Hebrew Psalter*, Journal for the Study of the Old Testament Supplement Series 217 (Sheffield: Sheffield Academic, 1996); Rolf A. Jacobson, "'The Faithfulness of the Lord Endures Forever': The Theological Witness of the Psalter," in *Soundings in the Theology of the Psalms: Perspectives and Methods in Contemporary Scholarship*, ed. Rolf A. Jacobson (Minneapolis: Fortress, 2011), 111–38; James L. Mays, *The Lord Reigns: A Theological Handbook to the Psalms* (Louisville: Westminster John Knox, 1994).

38. For an excellent discussion of the reception history of the Psalms among Jews and Christians, see William L. Holladay, *The Psalms through Three Thousand Years: Prayerbook of a Cloud of Witnesses* (Minneapolis: Fortress, 1993). Among the texts recovered from Qumran, thirty-six fragments bear witness to Psalms. For a sophisticated analysis of these manuscripts, see Peter W. Flint, *The Dead Sea Psalms Scrolls and the Book of Psalms*, Studies on the Texts of the Desert of Judah 17 (Leiden: Brill, 1997).

39. For discussion of these matters, see Brevard S. Childs, "Psalm Titles and Midrashic Exegesis," *Journal of Semitic Studies* 16 (1971): 137–50; Bruce K. Waltke, *An Old Testament Theology: An Exegetical, Canonical, and Thematic Approach*, with Charles Yu (Grand Rapids: Zondervan, 2007), 871–74.

40. Brian E. Daley, "Finding the Right Key: The Aims and Strategies of Early Christian Interpretation of the Psalms," in *The Harp of Prophecy: Early Christian Interpretation of the Psalms*, ed. Brian E. Daley and Paul R. Kolbet, Christianity and Judaism in Antiquity 20 (Notre Dame, IN: University of Notre Dame Press, 2015), 19.

41. Byassee, *Praise Seeking Understanding*, 92.

42. Athanasius, *Letter to Marcellinus* §§14–23, in *The Life of Antony and the Letter to Marcellinus*, trans. Robert C. Gregg, Classics of Western Spirituality (New York: Paulist Press, 1980).

43. For an excellent discussion of Scripture's usefulness among early interpreters, see Michael Graves, *The Inspiration and Interpretation of Scripture: What the Early Church Can Teach Us* (Grand Rapids: Eerdmans, 2014), 17–41.

44. Paul R. Kolbet, "Athanasius, the Psalms, and the Reformation of the Self," in Daley and Kolbet, *Harp of Prophecy*, 78.

45. Daley, "Finding the Right Key," 20.

46. Athanasius, *Letter to Marcellinus* §12.

47. Kolbet, "Athanasius, the Psalms," 82–83.

48. Byassee, *Praise Seeking Understanding*, 110.

49. Athanasius, *Letter to Marcellinus* §14.

50. Athanasius, *Letter to Marcellinus* §28.

51. Gregory of Nyssa, *Gregory of Nyssa's Treatise on the Inscriptions of the Psalms: Introduction, Translation, Notes*, trans. and ed. Ronald E. Heine (Oxford: Clarendon, 1995), 121–22 (1.67–68).

52. Gregory of Nyssa, *Treatise on the Inscriptions of the Psalms*, 96, 122 (1.39, 1.68).

53. Gregory of Nyssa, *Treatise on the Inscriptions of the Psalms*, 96–98 (1.39–40).

54. Gregory of Nyssa, *Treatise on the Inscriptions of the Psalms*, 98–100 (1.41–43).

55. Gregory of Nyssa, *Treatise on the Inscriptions of the Psalms*, 101–3 (1.43–45).

56. Gregory of Nyssa, *Treatise on the Inscriptions of the Psalms*, 108–9 (1.52).

57. Michael Cameron, "The Emergence of *Totus Christus* as Hermeneutical Center in Augustine's *Enarrationes in Psalmos*," in Daley and Kolbet, *Harp of Prophecy*, 214.

58. Maria Boulding, notes to *Expositions of the Psalms 1–32*, by Augustine, intro. Michael Fiedrowicz, trans. and annot. Maria Boulding, ed. John E. Rotelle, Works of Saint Augustine III/15 (Hyde Park, NY: New City, 2000), 77–84.

59. Boulding, notes to *Expositions of the Psalms 1–32*, 323–26.

60. Augustine, *Expositions of the Psalms 33–50*, trans. and annot. Maria Boulding, ed. John E. Rotelle, Works of Saint Augustine III/16 (Hyde Park, NY: New City, 2000), 232.

61. Augustine, *Expositions of the Psalms 121–150*, trans. and annot. Maria Boulding, ed. Boniface Ramsey, Works of Saint Augustine III/20 (Hyde Park, NY: New City, 2004), 304–5.

62. Rowan Williams, "Augustine and the Psalms," *Interpretation* 58 (2004): 17–27, esp. 20.

63. Basil the Great, *Homilia in psalmum I*, vol. 29 of *Patrologiae cursus completes, series graeca*, ed. J. P. Migne (Paris: 1857), 209–21; translation provided in James McKinnon, ed., *Music in Early Christian Literature*, Cambridge Readings in the Literature of Music (New York: Cambridge University Press, 1987), 65.

64. Ambrose, *Explanatio psalmi I*, 9, vol. 14 of *Patrologiae cursus completes, series Latina*, ed. J. P. Migne (Paris, 1845), 924–25; translation provided in McKinnon, *Music in Early Christian Literature*, 126.

65. John Chrysostom, *In psalmum xli*, 1–2, vol. 55 of *Patrologiae cursus completes, series graeca*, ed. J. P. Migne (Paris: 1862), 157; translation provided in McKinnon, *Music in Early Christian Literature*, 80.

66. Martin Luther, 1528 Preface to the Psalms, in *Martin Luther: Selections from His Writings*, ed. John Dillenberger (New York: Anchor, 1961), 37.

67. John Calvin, *Commentary on the Book of Psalms*, 5 vols. (Grand Rapids: Eerdmans, 1948–49), 1:xxxvii.

68. Gerhard von Rad, *Old Testament Theology*, vol. 1, *The Theology of Israel's Historical Traditions*, trans. D. M. G. Stalker, Old Testament Library (Louisville: Westminster John Knox, 2001), 355.

69. John D. Witvliet, *The Biblical Psalms in Christian Worship: A Brief Introduction and Guide to Resources* (Grand Rapids: Eerdmans, 2007), 15.

70. Rolf A. Jacobson and Karl N. Jacobson, *Invitation to the Psalms: A Reader's Guide for Discovery and Engagement* (Grand Rapids: Baker Academic, 2013), 174.

71. Jamie A. Grant, "The Psalter, Worship, and Worldview," in *The Identity of Israel's God in Christian Scripture*, ed. Don Collett, Mark Elliott, Mark Gignilliat, and Ephraim Radner, Resources for Biblical Study 96 (Atlanta: SBL Press, 2020), 131–42.

Chapter 12 Sidebar Notes

a. For discussion of the moral self in the Old Testament, see Jacqueline E. Lapsley, *Can These Bones Live? The Problem of the Moral Self in the Book of Ezekiel*, Beihefte zur Zeitschrift für die alttestamentliche Wissenschaft 301 (Berlin: de Gruyter, 2000); Carol A.

Newsom, "Models of the Moral Self: Hebrew Bible and Second Temple Judaism," *Journal of Biblical Literature* 131 (2012): 5–25.

b. Paul Ricoeur, "The Hermeneutical Function of Distanciation," in *Hermeneutics and the Social Sciences: Essays on Language, Action and Interpretation*, ed. and trans. John B. Thompson, Cambridge Philosophy Classics (Cambridge: Cambridge University Press, 2016), 105–6.

c. For further discussion, see Paul Ricoeur, "Biblical Hermeneutics," *Semi* 4 (1975): 29–148; Ricoeur, *Interpretation Theory: Discourse and the Surplus of Meaning* (Fort Worth: Texas Christian University Press, 1976); Ricoeur, *Oneself as Another*, trans. Kathleen Blamey (Chicago: University of Chicago Press, 1992).

d. For further discussion of this image and representative iconography with reference to Psalms, see Joel M. LeMon, *Yahweh's Winged Form in the Psalms: Exploring Congruent Iconography and Texts*, Orbis Biblicus et Orientalis 242 (Göttingen: Vandenhoeck & Ruprecht, 2010).

e. For discussion of the psalms at Qumran, see Peter W. Flint, *The Dead Sea Psalms Scrolls and the Book of Psalms*, Studies on the Texts of the Desert of Judah 17 (Leiden: Brill, 1997); William L. Holladay, *The Psalms through Three Thousand Years: Prayerbook of a Cloud of Witnesses* (Minneapolis: Fortress, 1993), 95–112.

f. Athanasius, *Letter to Marcellinus* §10, in *The Life of Antony and the Letter to Marcellinus*, trans. Robert C. Gregg, Classics of Western Spirituality (New York: Paulist Press, 1980).

g. For discussion of Hellenistic music theory and its use by Augustine, see Carol Harrison, "Augustine and the Art of Music," in *Resonant Witness: Conversations between Music and Theology*, ed. Jeremy Begbie and Steven R. Guthrie, Calvin Institute of Christian Worship Liturgical Studies (Grand Rapids: Eerdmans, 2011), 27–45.

h. Gregory of Nyssa, *Gregory of Nyssa's Treatise on the Inscriptions of the Psalms: Introduction, Translation, Notes*, trans. and ed. Ronald E. Heine (Oxford: Clarendon, 1995), 84 (1.26).

i. Augustine, *Expositions of the Psalms 1–32*, intro. Michael Fiedrowicz, trans. and annot. Maria Boulding, ed. John E. Rotelle, Works of Saint Augustine III/15 (Hyde Park, NY: New City, 2000), 44–45.

j. For discussion of prosopological exegesis and its presence in the New Testament, see Boulding's notes in Augustine, *Expositions of the Psalms 1–32*, 57–60; Matthew W. Bates, *The Hermeneutics of the Apostolic Proclamation: The Center of Paul's Method of Scriptural Interpretation* (Waco: Baylor University Press, 2012), 183–221, respectively.

k. Jeffrey Bilbro, *Virtues of Renewal: Wendell Berry's Sustainable Forms* (Lexington: University Press of Kentucky, 2019), 138.

l. Wendell Berry, "The Responsibility of the Poet," in *What Are People For? Essays* (Berkeley: Counterpoint, 2010), 89.

Chapter 13 Theological Themes in Psalms

1. See Herman Bavinck, *Reformed Dogmatics*, ed. John Bolt, trans. John Vriend, 4 vols. (Grand Rapids: Baker Academic, 2004), 2:99.

2. James L. Mays, *The Lord Reigns: A Theological Handbook to the Psalms* (Louisville: Westminster John Knox, 1994), 22.

3. William P. Brown, *Seeing the Psalms: A Theology of Metaphor* (Louisville: Westminster John Knox, 2002), 7–8.

4. Rolf Jacobson, "Christian Theology of the Psalms," in *The Oxford Handbook of the Psalms*, ed. William P. Brown (Oxford: Oxford University Press, 2014), 499–512, esp. 509–10.

5. For a crisp discussion of the ways in which the different types of psalms bear witness to God's loving faithfulness, see Jacobson, "Christian Theology of the Psalms," 507–10.

6. Gerhard von Rad, *Old Testament Theology*, vol. 1, *The Theology of Israel's Historical Traditions*, trans. D. M. G. Stalker, Old Testament Library (Louisville: Westminster John Knox, 2001), 369–70.

7. Philip S. Johnston, "The Psalms and Distress," in *Interpreting the Psalms: Issues and Approaches*, ed. David Firth and Philip S. Johnston (Downers Grove, IL: IVP Academic, 2005), 63–84.

8. Ellen F. Davis, *Opening Israel's Scriptures* (Oxford: Oxford University Press, 2019), 326.

9. The difficulty of this movement from lament to praise is explored by Federico G. Villanueva and captured by the title of his monograph *The 'Uncertainty of a Hearing': A Study of the Sudden Change of Mood in the Psalms of Lament*, Supplements to Vetus Testamentum 121 (Leiden: Brill, 2008).

10. Rolf A. Jacobson and Karl N. Jacobson, *Invitation to the Psalms: A Reader's Guide for Discovery and Engagement* (Grand Rapids: Baker Academic, 2013), 158–61.

11. For an excellent analysis of Psalm 119, see David Noel Freedman, *Psalm 119: The Exaltation of Torah*, Biblical and Judaic Studies from the University of California, San Diego 6 (Winona Lake, IN: Eisenbrauns, 1999).

12. This reading of Psalms is developed in J. Clinton McCann Jr., *A Theological Introduction to the Book of Psalms: The Psalms as Torah* (Nashville: Abingdon, 1993).

13. Gordon J. Wenham, *Psalms as Torah: Reading Biblical Song Ethically*, Studies in Theological Interpretation (Grand Rapids: Baker Academic, 2012), 57.

14. Wenham, *Psalms as Torah*, 57.

15. The seminal work on speech-act theory is J. L. Austin's William James lectures at Harvard University. These lectures are published in J. L. Austin, *How to Do Things with Words*, ed. J. O. Urmson and Marina Sbisà, 2nd ed. (Oxford: Oxford University Press, 1975).

16. Austin, *How to Do Things with Words*.

17. Wenham, *Psalms as Torah*, 59.

18. Wenham, *Psalms as Torah*, 75.

19. Walter Brueggemann, *Praying the Psalms: Engaging Scripture and the Life of the Spirit*, 2nd ed. (Eugene, OR: Cascade Books, 2007), 63–81.

20. David G. Firth, *Surrendering Retribution in the Psalms: Responses to Violence in the Individual Complaints*, Paternoster Biblical Monographs (Milton Keynes, UK: Paternoster, 2005).

21. Athanasius, *Letter to Marcellinus* §10, in *The Life of Antony and the Letter to Marcellinus*, trans. Robert C. Gregg, Classics of Western Spirituality (New York: Paulist Press, 1980).

22. Athanasius, *Letter to Marcellinus* §30, emphasis added.

23. J. Todd Billings, *The Word of God for the People of God: An Entryway to the Theological Interpretation of Scripture* (Grand Rapids: Eerdmans, 2010), 13–16.

24. Erich Zenger, *A God of Vengeance? Understanding the Psalms of Divine Wrath*, trans. Linda M. Maloney (Louisville: Westminster John Knox, 1996), 66.

25. Joel M. LeMon, "Saying Amen to Violent Psalms: Patterns of Prayer, Belief, and Action in the Psalter," in *Soundings in the Theology of the Psalms: Perspectives and Methods in Contemporary Scholarship*, ed. Rolf A. Jacobson (Minneapolis: Fortress, 2011), 93–109, esp. 93. LeMon extends this maxim to consider the relationship between *lex orandi* (the pattern of prayer) and *lex agendi* (the pattern of behavior).

26. Christian Smith, *Soul Searching: The Religious and Spiritual Lives of American Teenagers*, with Melinda Lundquist Denton (Oxford: Oxford University Press, 2005), 162–63.

27. For these statistics, see Jean M. Twenge, *iGen: Why Today's Super-Connected Kids Are Growing Up Less Rebellious, More Tolerant, Less Happy—and Completely Unprepared for Adulthood—and What That Means for the Rest of Us* (New York: Atria, 2017), 121–23.

28. Twenge, *iGen*, 126.

29. Twenge, *iGen*, 128.

30. For a crisp and beautiful account of Christian lament and hope, see Jamie A. Grant, "Hope in Lament," *Big Picture*, July 2022, https://kirbylaingcentre.co.uk/the-big-picture/online-magazine/issue-04/hope-in-lament/.

a. For further discussion, see Michael Allen, "Exodus 3 after the Hellenization Thesis," *Journal of Theological Interpretation* 3 (2009): 179–96; Craig A. Carter, *Reading Scripture with the Great Tradition: Recovering the Genius of Premodern Exegesis* (Grand Rapids: Baker Academic, 2018); Carter, *Contemplating God with the Great Tradition: Recovering Trinitarian Classical Theism* (Grand Rapids: Baker Academic, 2021).

b. John R. Searle, *Expression and Meaning: Studies in the Theory of Speech Acts* (Cambridge: Cambridge University Press, 1979).

c. Brent A. Strawn, "Sanctified and Commercially Successful Curses: On Gangsta Rap and the Canonization of the Imprecatory Psalms," *Theology Today* 69 (2013): 403–17.

Index

christological debates, 35
Christology, 38, 40, 41
Chrysostom, John, 171
church
  in Psalms, 169
  sexuality concerns in, 156
city, in Song of Songs, 148–49
Clines, David J. A., 53, 76
Coakley, Sarah, 155–56
Codex Alexandrinus, 165
contingency, 51, 190
convocation, 169
coram deo, 91, 116, 122, 157, 190. *See also* face of God
cosmic time, 111–12
covenant, 7, 158, 190
covenant infidelity, 146–47
Crawford, Matthew B., 21
creation
  constancy, 110
  goodness, 18, 126
  Qoheleth on, 109–12
  and Wisdom, 41–44
Creator-creature distinction, 29–30, 106–7, 116, 154
creaturehood, 51, 71, 96, 125
cult-functional approach to Psalms, 159–60

Davidic covenant, 160, 163
Davidic king, 163
Davis, Andrew, 52
Davis, Ellen, 132, 153, 156
Dead Sea Scrolls, 164
death
  comes to all, 96
  path of, 26–27
  Qoheleth on, 107, 109
"Death is strong" motif, 131
deception, 27
demonology, 52
dependence on God, 47, 71, 122, 124, 126–27
Descartes, René, 21
desire, 22–23, 48, 128, 143–45
  in Proverbs, 143–44
  in Song of Songs, 143–44
desire seeking understanding, 2, 129, 155
Dharamraj, Havilah, 147
disinterested contemplation, 3
disinterested piety, 52–53
divine aseity, 108, 173, 190
divine council, 81, 190
divine-human love song, Song of Songs as, 130–32
divine immutability, 173, 174, 190
divine impassibility, 154, 173, 190
divine simplicity, 173, 190

divine warrior, 87, 131
Doak, Brian R., 78
doubt, 116
doxologies in Psalms, 162, 167
dramatic irony, 54, 190
dust to dust, 112

Ecclesiastes
  contradictions in, 101–2
  date, 99
  language, 100
  as public speech, 102
  structural markers in, 102
  structure, 100–101
  and Torah, 125
  as wisdom literature, 5
economic Trinity, 154, 190
ectypal knowledge, 113, 116, 190
Eden, 44, 145, 152
  "east of Eden," 7, 43, 44
Egyptian love songs, 132–34
elementary wisdom, 15, 16
Elihu, 53, 54, 59, 84–85, 89
Eliphaz, 53, 57–58, 67–68, 84–86, 88, 93
elliptical expressions, 10–11
Elohim, 72, 105
embodied wisdom, 19
empiricism, 24, 190
encomia, 13, 190
enjoyment, as resignation, 122, 123
Enlightenment, 95
enthronement festival, 160
Enuma Elish, 81
epic journeys, 63
epigrams, 13, 191
epistemology, 29, 30, 97–98, 103, 104, 113–18, 191
eschatology, 52, 191
eternal generation of the Son, 35, 36, 163, 191
ethics, 82, 98–99, 104, 105, 188, 182, 183, 191
expressive individualism, 158
external authority, submission to, 25

face of God, 8, 91, 117, 188. See also *coram Deo*
faith, 1–2, 7, 50, 51–52, 86, 90–91, 157, 172, 178–81, 185, 188, 191
faith seeking understanding, 1–2, 3, 4, 7, 44, 48
false leads, 48
fear
  in life of faith, 180
  as terror, 123
fear of Yahweh, 17, 18, 29, 44, 83–86, 122–23
  without benefit, 52–53
  embodied by valiant woman, 16

encompasses whole of life, 83
  as firstfruit of wisdom, 29, 83, 122
  as first principle of wisdom, 29, 83, 122
  and friendship of God, 93–94
  through laments, complaints, and protests, 85
  recognizes human finitude, 122
fear seeking understanding, 2, 17, 18, 44
Feast of Tabernacles. *See* Sukkoth (Feast of Tabernacles)
Fiedrowicz, Michael, 170
finite knowledge, 116
finite wisdom, 66
finitude, 70, 95, 103, 126, 127, 191
finitude seeking understanding, 2, 104, 125
first Solomonic collection (Proverbs), 14
flourishing, 16, 17, 44, 51, 177
folly, 27, 114. *See also* Woman Folly
fool, 11, 26–27, 30–31
form criticism, 158–59, 191
fortified city language and imagery, 141
Fox, Michael C., 24, 39, 116, 133, 143
Fredericks, Daniel, 100
friendship, 15, 93–94
Frost, Robert, 55
functional theology, 186–87

garden, in Song of Songs, 151–52
generative transmission, 67, 68
gifts of God, rejoicing in, 118, 119–21
Gilgamesh, 63
God
  and creation, 41–44, 69
  as Creator, 175–76
  distinct from all other reality, 39
  gives life, 108
  justice, 51, 53, 61, 72, 74–79, 185
  as King, 176–77
  love stronger than death, 154
  loving faithfulness, 164, 177–80, 186
  metaphors in Psalms, 176–77
  names in Job, 83
  names in Psalms, 173–74
  Qoheleth's depiction of, 105–9
  as shepherd, 176, 177, 180
  sight, 65
  sovereignty, 72, 106
  strength manifest in human weakness, 126
  transcendence and immanence, 106–7, 174
  uniqueness, 172–74
  wisdom, 73–75, 79
golden calf, 177
good life, 12, 14, 18, 45, 46, 47
Greek philosophy, 173. *See also* Hellenism
Gregory of Nyssa, 100, 165, 166–67

grotesque, 142
ground metaphors, 26
Gunkel, Hermann, 159–60, 164, 165

Hallelujah, 162
Hays, Richard B., 40
heart/mind. See *leb* (heart/mind)
heavenly adversaries, 52
hebel (vanity), 97, 98, 102–4, 110, 115, 119–20, 126, 127
Hebrew Bible, 162, 191
hedonism, 121
Hellenism, 99, 166, 171, 191
hesed (loving faithfulness), 177–78
Hilary of Poitiers, 22
hinnam (suffering for nothing), 52
historical time, 111–12
Holocaust, 154, 157
hope, 188
human love song, Song of Songs as, 132–34
human memory, 117–19
humans
  as contingent creatures, 110–12, 113, 116, 125
  as dependent, 108, 112, 118, 126
  desire to transcend mortal existence, 96
  as finite, 16, 61, 66, 96, 113, 125, 127
  fragility, 67, 122
  infidelity to the divine, 147
  limitations, 61–66, 71
  mortality, 68–70, 109, 127, 176
  status and dignity bestowed on, 176
human wisdom, 102
  limitations, 16, 58, 74, 98, 117
  sources, 114–15
humility, 16, 47
hymns, in Psalms, 178–79, 180
hypostasis, 39, 191

illocutions, 182–83
image of God, 35
imagination, 4, 48
immanent Trinity, 154, 191
imprecatory psalms, 183–86
Inanna and Enki, 67
inclusio, 58, 191
innate wisdom, 21
innocent suffering, 53
Instruction of Amenemope, 12
instructions
  in Proverbs, 13
  in Psalms, 181–82
integrity, 80
intellect, 21–22, 48
intermediate wisdom, 15, 16

interpersonal instruction, 25
intertextuality, 7, 191
iron smithing, 10
Israel
    adultery of, 146
    dual conceptions of time, 111–12
    harlotry of, 146

Jerome, 100
Jerusalem, 141, 149
Jesus Christ
    as authoritative guide, 46
    as Davidic king, 163
    parables of, 49
    and Psalms, 165
    speaking in Psalms, 169
    transfiguration, 45–46
    union with the church, 130
    as Wisdom of God, 40
Jindo, Job, 29–30
Job (book)
    divine speeches in, 59, 73–75, 76–79, 80
    epilogue, 54, 56
    poetry of, 53
    as wisdom literature, 5
Job (patriarch)
    as blameless, 80–87
    confession of, 71
    curses the day of his birth, 7, 57
    friendship with Yahweh, 94
    integrity, 80–83
    lament, 86–88
    lawsuit against God, 88–90
    model of perseverance, 91
    self-examination of, 82–83
    suffering, 50–51, 87, 89, 90
justice, 24, 27, 34, 87–88, 89, 91, 96. *See also* God:
    justice

Kant, Immanuel, 3, 92, 95
keeping God's commandments, 123–25
kinsman redeemer, 88, 89
Knierim, Rolf, 111–12
knowledge, 19, 20, 29
    of God, 186
    of self, 186
Krüger, Thomas, 125
Kynes, Will, 5–6, 7

labor in the Lord, not in vain, 126
Lady Wisdom, 14, 22, 25, 27, 28, 34–41, 63, 143, 144
    as divine hypostasis, 39
    emerges before creation, 35

and life of flourishing, 44
    possesses all that is desirable, 34–35
lament, 86–88
    failure to, 188
    and fear of Yahweh, 122
    in Psalms, 159, 179–80, 183, 188
leadership, 16
leb (heart/mind), 22, 115–16
Legaspi, Michael C., 122–23
Lemuel's mother, 16
Leviathan, 77–78, 92
lex orandi, lex credendi, 187
lex talionis, 184, 191
life and death (as satellite images), 27, 28
Linafelt, Tod, 52, 53
lived theology, 171
locutions, 182–83
Logos, 166
love
    between God and his people, 155
    sensory exposition in Song of Songs, 153
Lundquist, Melinda, 187
Luther, Martin, 171
lyric poetry, 128, 129, 192

male violence, 146
marital sex, 144, 145
marriage metaphor, in the prophets, 130–31, 146–47
Mays, James Luther, 164
McKinnon, Christine, 82
meaningfulness of life, 105
Meek, Esther Lightcap, 45, 116
memento mori, 95, 192
merism, 44, 192
Mesopotamian worldview, 67–68
metallurgical imagery, 142–43
metaphysics, 96, 173, 192
military imagery, 141–42
Miller, Douglas B., 102
mind. See *leb* (heart/mind)
Mitchell, David C., 164
moral aesthetics, 24
Moralistic Therapeutic Deism, 187
Mot, 131
Mowinckel, Sigmund, 160

new heavens and new earth, 7
Newsom, Carol, 62, 66
Northwest Semitic combat myth, 131, 154
nuclear symbol, 26, 27, 28

O'Connor, Flannery, 4
ontology, 29, 30, 96–97, 103–13, 192

Song of Songs
  allegorical reading, 129
  as drama, 134
  historical reading, 130, 132–34
  iconographic reading, 132
  language of desire, 143–44
  and marriage metaphor, 147
  theological reading, 130–32
  as wisdom literature, 5
speech-act theory, 182–83
Spinoza, Baruch, 130
stated theology, 186–87
stormwind, 72–73
strange woman, 27, 37, 143
Strawn, Brent, 184
sublime, 92
suffering, 50–51, 66
suffering seeking understanding, 2, 50, 60, 90
Sukkoth (Feast of Tabernacles), 127, 160, 193
Sumerian Man and His God, 66
Sun, Chloe T., 134
synecdoche, 109, 193

tabernacle/temple, 44, 45
text criticism, 193
texts, and the human self, 161
thanksgiving, in Psalms, 180–81
theological anthropology, 66–71
theology
  and personal experience, 90
  and relational commitment, 93
time, in Song of Songs, 134
Tirzah, 141
Torah, 124, 125, 193
torah psalms, 159, 164, 180
total depravity, 70
totus Christus, 168–70
tradition, 62
tree of life, 7, 43, 44
tree of the knowledge of good and evil, 46
Treier, Daniel J., 126
Trible, Phyllis, 145
Trinity, 169, 193
trust, 47, 180–81
truthful imagination, 4
"twice-told" proverbs, 11

unauthorized guide, 45–46
union with Christ, 156, 167–70
Unitarianism, 39, 193

valiant woman, 16, 21, 36–37
vineyard, in Song of Songs, 150–51

Van Leeuwen, Raymond, 39
virtue ethics, 82
vocational wisdom, 15, 16
von Rad, Gerhard, 171

way (as nuclear metaphor), 26–28
way of life, 27–28
way of wisdom, 25–27
Webster, John, 91
Weeks, Stuart, 124
Wenham, Gordon, J., 182, 183
Westermann, Claus, 160
Who Has Not Sinned? (Akkadian prayer), 67–68
wicked, flourishing of, 51
Wiesel, Elie, 157
wild animals, 75, 76
Wilson, Gerald, 161–64, 167
Wilson-Wright, Aren, 131
Wirzba, Norman, 120–21
wisdom
  aesthetic dimensions, 22, 33
  cognitive dimensions, 22, 33
  and creation, 34, 38, 40, 41–44, 62–65
  as deeply ironic, 66
  differs from knowledge, 19
  as elusive, 114
  as embodied skill, 19, 20, 21, 33
  emotional dimensions, 22, 33
  as gift, 23–25, 45–47, 66
  growth in, 47
  inaccessibility, 61–66
  as interpersonal, 19, 25
  and justice, 61
  in New Testament, 40
  not innate, 20, 24, 47
  personification, 33, 38–39
  pursuit, 14
  tactile dimensions, 22
wisdom literature
  beginning of, 7
  as category, 5–6, 7
  as Christian Scripture, 1–2
wisdom psalms, 159, 180
Wisdom of Solomon, 5, 39–40
wise women, in ancient Israel, 37
Witvliet, John D., 171
Woman Folly, 14, 25, 27, 28
Word, and Wisdom, 40
"words of the wise," 15–16
work, 119–20
world
  chaotic in Job, 72
  orderly in Proverbs, 72

world-projection, through poetry, 3–4
"world upside down" motif, 63

Yahweh
   "answer" to Job, 71–72
   as covenant name, 72
   in Job, 62
   kingship, 160

relationship with his people as a marriage, 146
speeches in Job, 59, 73–75, 76–79, 80
   See also God
"Yahweh of hosts," 81
Yoder, Christine Roy, 37

Žižek, Slavoj, 71–72
Zophar, 53, 57–58, 62, 93